LABOR AND EMPLOYMENT

RELATIONS ASSOCIATION SERIES

Employee Pensions: Policies, Problems, and Possibilities

EDITED BY

Teresa Ghilarducci and Christian E. Weller

First Edition

ISBN 978-0913447-95-6

Price: $29.95

LABOR AND EMPLOYMENT RELATIONS ASSOCIATION SERIES
Proceedings of the Annual Meeting
Annual Research Volume
LERA 2006 Membership Directory (published every four years)
LERA Newsletter (published quarterly)
Perspectives on Work (published biannually)

Information regarding membership, subscriptions, meetings, publications, and general affairs of the LERA can be found at the Association website: www.lera.uiuc.edu. Members can make changes to their member records, including address changes, by accessing the online directory at the website or by contacting the LERA national office.

LABOR AND EMPLOYMENT RELATIONS ASSOCIATION
University of Illinois at Urbana-Champaign
121 Labor & Industrial Relations Bldg.
504 East Armory Ave.
Champaign, IL 61820
Telephone: 217/333-0072   Fax: 217/265-5130
Internet: www.lera.uiuc.edu   E-mail: leraoffice@uiuc.edu

CONTENTS

CHAPTER 1

Issues Still Facing Employer-Based Pensions: Introduction to the Volume

TERESA GHILARDUCCI
University of Notre Dame

CHRISTIAN E. WELLER
Center for American Progress

The U.S. stands apart from developed market economies in relying heavily on individual employers to achieve the common goal of securing retirement income for American workers. Employer plans include traditional pensions (defined benefit [DB] plans) and 401(k)-type plans (defined contribution [DC] plans).[1]

To induce employers to provide a pension plan or a retirement savings vehicle, the U.S. government grants tax-favored treatment to all retirement accounts' contributions and earnings. Money is taxed as income only at withdrawal. In 2006, the federal government's tax break, referred to as tax expenditures, was worth more than $113 billion.

The existence and sheer size of this subsidy to employer plans mean policy makers are always looking for ways to regulate pensions or offer more finely honed tax incentives to elicit voluntary employer plans that meet social goals.

High on the list of unmet social goals is getting coverage for the more than half of the workforce without pension coverage—most likely middle class and lower income workers. Only one in five full-time workers in the bottom third of the earnings distribution, those earning under approximately $30,000 per year in 2005, worked for an employer who offered a retirement savings plan at work. For those in the middle third, about half were offered pensions, and a full 76% of those in the top third, earning over $60,000, worked for employers who sponsored a pension.[2]

These estimated pension sponsorship rates are liberally calculated and are at the high range of those reported. If we used sponsorship rates for all workers, not full-time workers, the rates would be lower, because part-time workers are less likely to be working for employers with pension plans. If we measured how many people actually participate in an employer's plan, those rates are lower than sponsorship rates. No matter how the situation is reported, uneven and incomplete sponsorship rates represent a devastating failure of the American system of retirement saving.

Moreover, the use of tax deductions—rather than, for instance, refundable tax credits—to entice people to participate in retirement saving plans can result in greater inequality. Because the incentives are in the form of a tax deduction, the more than one third of earners who pay no federal income tax because they earn too little—over 93% of them earn less than $30,000 per year (Hodge 2005)—receive no subsidy for retirement saving. Their tax liability cannot be reduced with a deduction because they already pay no federal income taxes. In contrast, those with the highest earnings receive a subsidy equivalent to 38% of their contributions, because their contributions reduce their taxable income. Research has generally found that these tax deductions, with their largest effect on high-income tax payers, have little or no positive effect on personal saving. Instead, those earners, who stand to gain the most from the deductions, are likely to swap tax-advantaged saving for non-tax-advantaged saving, instead of increasing the overall amount saved. An example helps show how this happens: two 50-year-olds save 20% in a retirement account. The worker earning too little to file income taxes receives no tax subsidy, while the worker earning average wages will receive about $600— and a family earning over $400,000 could be receiving over $7,000 in tax subsidies. When it is all totaled, 70% of tax expenditures for contributions to DC plans go to the top 20% of tax filers. Tax policy for retirement savings thus contributes to a rising retirement wealth inequality, especially as DC plans become more important as retirement saving vehicles (Burman et al. 2004).

Lastly, employees can face sometimes growing risks with their retirement saving, which can reduce their chance of accumulating adequate funds. For DB plans, the primary risk is the chance of employer default. Under DC plans, there are several risks: the risk of making unlucky or unwise investment decisions, the risk of financial assets underperforming, market risk, and longevity risk (the risk of outliving one's savings). Because the risk exposure is often greater under DC plans than under DB plans, the rise of DC plans and the decline of DB plans imply on average a greater risk exposure than in the past for workers saving for retirement.

In their desire to design efficient public policy that can help workers overcome these problems in saving for retirement, policy makers are continually seeking to improve existing laws and regulations. The most recent example is the Pension Protection Act of 2006 (PPA). While this new law was a massive undertaking that restructured many parts of the retirement saving landscape, it also left large swaths of the problems unaddressed or only partially addressed. The problems include high degrees of inequality in retirement saving accumulations by income and race, high costs of DC plan administration, lack of support for innovative DB pension design, and corporate disincentives to sponsor pensions, among others. As a result, it is unclear if the PPA will meet its intended goal to increase pension coverage and reduce retirement saving inequality and employees' risk exposure.

One of the biggest shortcomings of the PPA is its effect on employer contributions to single-employer DB plans. The law was aimed at improving the funding status of these plans, and though the PPA does nothing to kill DB plans outright, the new rules do much to discourage firms from continuing DB plans. While the old law did give firms the opportunity to avoid some or all of their funding responsibilities for some time, the PPA goes overboard in the opposite direction by making perfectly sound companies speed up funding for any pension debt, thereby raising the unpredictability of pension contributions. In our conclusion, we describe a way to alter funding rules that can address employers' needs for stable contributions and employees' needs for secure pension plans.

Since firms freezing or eliminating their DB plans are not required to make up for their workers' losses of expected future benefits, converting to a DC plan is a way companies can reduce their labor costs, and it is a way to reduce the volatility of contributions to employee pensions. Many employers that sponsor DB plans opposed the single-employer DB pension provisions of the PPA, arguing that the provisions would make funding of their DB plans more erratic, likely contributing to more and more DB plan sponsors freezing their existing pension plans. Often employees lose out when employers freeze their DB pensions. Benefit economist Jack VanDerhei (2006) estimates that employers would have to contribute about 16% of payroll to a replacement DC plan to recover what most workers would lose when their plans were frozen. Instead, most employers will contribute less than 6% of payroll to a 401(k) pension. The challenge thus is to design not only policies that make it easier for employers to keep their existing DB plans but also rules and regulations for DC plans to become much improved retirement saving vehicles.

Whereas the 907-page PPA does quite a bit to discourage DB plans, the legislation packs in a list of "goodies" for 401(k) plan managers and sponsors, without fully addressing the existing shortcomings of DC plans. First, the PPA introduced some regulatory relief for employers who sponsor DC plans that make it easier for employees to save. It is unclear what effect this will have on the share of private sector workers with a DC plan. While as a result of these changes more employees may participate, it is also possible that fewer employers will sponsor plans or contribute to their employees' DC plans to keep their costs at their current levels. Second, the bill exempts, under some circumstances, investment firms that manage DC plan assets from conflict-of-interest protections, so they can advise employees to buy the products they sell. Third, Congress ignored pleas to force employers to disclose 401(k) administrative fees that can erode a large share, 20% to 30%, of the value of an account. Hence, the law ensures less scrutiny, accountability, and competition from and among investment management firms. Fourth, the PPA permits workers to shelter up to $20,000 per year in a tax-free account. Most economists agree this encourages the highest earners to shelter their wealth from taxes and does little to increase the amount saved, while depleting federal government revenues and stimulating the financial industry. Fifth, though supporters of the PPA intended to encourage employers to include middle- and low-income workers in their 401(k) plans, Congress should have gone all the way and implemented universal employer coverage for everyone.

By focusing on pension plans from the point of view of the employer and employee, this volume outlines a fresh view. In addition to federal pension reforms, employers, employees, and unions can better structure pension plans to meet retirement income security goals.

The book's first part of four, "Justification for the Employer-Based System," examines the benefits to employers from sponsoring a DB plan. In chapter 2, "The Labor Supply Effects of Employer-Provided Pensions: Theory, Evidence, and Implications for the Future," University of Georgia economists Jeff Wenger and Laura D'Arcy not only examine how employer pensions affect savings behavior and elderly labor supply but go further to identify these micro effects on the macro economy. Importantly, employers use pensions as personnel tools, usually intending to boost profits and productivity. Specifically, DB plans are used to directly influence the labor supply of workers—mostly they are used either to induce workers to work longer, by offering high returns for longer service, or to ease layoffs or downsizing by offering subsidies for early retirement. With the shift toward DC plans, employers have fewer opportunities to influence the labor supply of their workers.

Next, economist and economic historian William Lazonick of the University of Massachusetts Lowell and INSEAD addresses, in chapter 3, "Economic Institutional Change and Employer Pensions," the argument that pension changes are driven by American employers' no longer needing long-term employment contracts because technology is changing.

He emphasizes that a production system that switches from relying on long-term labor contracts to one that thrives on short-term ones is due in large part to the pressure corporations face to eliminate long-term contracts, including DB pensions, because of changes in finance markets. Lazonick challenges the commonly held view that the change from DB to DC plans arose from fundamental changes in the labor market. Some analysts concentrate on technological changes and changes in consumer demand for services over American-made manufactured goods as the main reasons for the shift in employer pensions from DB to DC plans. Lazonick contrasts this with other analysts who concentrate on the shifting power balances between workers and certain types of employers, employers who influence the compensation and labor relations of many other employers.

In chapter 4, "Partial Retirement: Widespread Desire Among Workers, But Limited Demand by Employers," Government Accountability Office economist Sharon Hermes explores, based on surveys, whether workers are acting on their expressed wish to phase into retirement and whether firms accommodate productive and experienced workers who want to phase their retirement by working fewer hours. She uses data from the Health and Retirement Survey to show that phased retirement rarely happens, although there is support for it from both employers and employees.

The second section, "Getting Defined Benefit Plans Ready for the Future," focuses on ways to stabilize DB plan coverage.

Syl Schieber, director of research of the employee benefits firm Watson Wyatt Worldwide, provides in chapter 5 the metaphor of a lovely creature, the Dodo bird, killed by plunderers to describe the plight of the DB plan. Schieber argues in "Tales of the Dodo Bird and the Yellowstone Wolf: Lessons for DB Pensions and the Retirement Ecosystem" that widespread use of cash balance plan design would save DB plans and may be the only way to prevent their extinction. In particular, Schieber provides a productivity reason for why employers would rather sponsor a cash balance plan than a 401(k) and why cash balance plans meet employers' and workers' needs.

In chapter 6, Beth Almeida, associate director of strategic resources for the International Association of Machinists and Aerospace Workers, examines in "Multi-employer Plans: Plan Design for the Future" another variant of the single-employer DB plan—the multi-employer plan that meets employers' and employees' needs by creating an efficient, diversified way to provide DB pensions. She focuses on the recent plan terminations in the airline industry and the solutions that well-funded multi-employer plans could offer to struggling single-employer plans. Importantly,

Almeida argues that multi-employer plans are a high-performing but overlooked area of pension plan design that offers important lessons for future plan design due to a stand-alone corporate structure, regular employer contributions, joint trusteeship, and benefit portability.

The third section, "Ways to Improve Defined Contribution Plans," addresses the need for changes in regulations governing DC plans and offers a number of innovative policy solutions.

The chronic lack of pension coverage among workers who are lifelong low- and moderate-income earners, rising pension and income inequality, and the increasing and changing risks facing workers in retirement readiness are addressed in chapter 7, "How Can Defined Contribution Plans Meet Workers' Needs?" by Eric Rodriguez, director of the National Council of La Raza Policy Analysis Center, and Luisa Grillo-Chope, economic security policy analyst at the National Council of La Raza. Importantly, Grillo-Chope and Rodriguez offer a number of policy options in addition to existing legislative changes to improve DC plans.

Pamela Perun, policy director of the Initiative on Financial Security of the Aspen Institute, argues in chapter 8, "Putting Annuities Back into Savings Plans," that DC plans and other individual accounts used for retirement saving face two issues. First is the issue of sufficient wealth accumulation, and second is the question of whether workers will buy annuities to insure against longevity risk. Considerable evidence supports the commonsense notion that retirees greatly value a source of income that is secure, especially if it is indexed to inflation, to address the fear of running out of money before dying. Research and historical precedent support humans' desire to protect against certain risks in old age—longevity, inflation, financial uncertainty, and the risk of a surviving spouse's indigence—but the individual account setup is terrible at providing such protection. What institutional setup helps individuals withdraw from their retirement wealth in such a way as to protect against longevity risks? Perun argues that employers who sponsor DC plans shy away from offering their employees an annuity option due to fiduciary liability concerns. She proposes an optional national life insurance charter in an effort to reduce the costs of annuities to employees and the liability risks to employers.

The final section, "Understanding the Political Dimensions of Pension Reform," provides some insights into the political and institutional constraints that may impede the creation of new pension legislation that could help strengthen DB plans and improve DC plans.

Michelle Varnhagen, senior staff counsel for the U.S. House of Representatives' Committee on Education and Labor, offers in "U.S. Federal Pension Policy: Its Potential and Pitfalls," chapter 9, a description of the legislative process surrounding pension reform. One fear is that in the early 1990s federal legislation inhibited the formation of DB plans. Another fear is that public policy tools are uncreative. Varnhagen argues that it is precisely employers' reactions, as well as other stakeholders' concerns, that drive federal pension policy in this environment. She examines how federal pension policy has evolved to poorly balance the need for a reliable pension supplement to Social Security, while respecting the voluntary nature of employer pension plans.

In chapter 10, "The Politics of Pension Cuts," David Madland, graduate student in political science at Georgetown University, uses surveys of workers to assess worker reaction to pension defaults. Though now a small part of the workforce, unions have had a very large influence on pension policy and design. Currently union members are twice as likely as nonunion members to be covered by pensions. In addition, unions have engaged the public debate when companies like United Airlines and Polaroid terminated or froze their plans. However, given that the losses were substantial there was less protest than would have been expected. Madland examines the conditions necessary for protest to happen in the pension crises context and explains why protests were subdued.

In chapter 11, "Pension Policy Options: Meeting in the Middle," we summarize and interpret the major findings in each chapter. We particularly emphasize the importance of blending the best aspects of DB plans with the best of DC plans. We describe the possibilities in American labor relations and in Congress to meet employers' needs to compete and to fulfill the enduring desire of workers to plan for a financially secure period of leisure at the end of their working lives.

Endnotes

[1] Under a DB plan, the employee is guaranteed a benefit upon retirement, usually based on years of service, age, and final earnings, and employees usually accrue most of their benefits during their last years of service. Employees are typically vested in five years, and in private sector plans these benefits are insured by the Pension Benefit Guaranty Corporation (PBGC). Cash balance plans are DB plans that accrue evenly over a career, and the benefit is determined by the accumulations in the plan that earned an employer-guaranteed rate. Under the most common DC plan, the 401(k)-type plan, private sector employees can but are not required to contribute a share of their earnings to individual accounts after deciding to have some of their pay deducted for contributions. The investment choices, vendors, and fees are controlled by the employer, and the employer also chooses whether or not to set up the administrative apparatus to sponsor a DC plan.

[2] Authors' calculation from CPS data for all workers over age 18 working more than 20 hours (the data for 2005 is slightly inflated because of the 20 hours restriction).

References

Burman, Leonard E., William G. Gale, Matthew Hall, and Peter R. Orszag. 2004. "Distributional Effects of Defined Contribution Plans and Individual Retirement Arrangements." *National Tax Journal*, Vol. 57, no. 3 (September), 671–701.

Hodge, Scott A. 2005. "Number of Americans Outside the Income Tax System Continues to Grow." *Fiscal Facts*, June 9. Washington, DC: Tax Foundation. http://www.taxfoundation.org/publications/printer/542.html>. [January 29, 2007].

VanDerhei, Jack. 2006. "Defined Benefit Plan Freezes: Who's Affected, How Much, and Replacing Lost Accruals." *EBRI Issue Brief*, No. 291 (March). Washington, DC: Employee Benefit Research Institute.

CHAPTER 2

The Labor Supply Effects of Employer-Provided Pensions: Theory, Evidence, and Implications for the Future

JEFFREY B. WENGER
University of Georgia

LAURA P. D'ARCY
University of North Carolina

Individual decisions about when to work and how many hours to work are very complex. For most workers, the difficulty of these decisions is compounded by family formation, childrearing, and, ultimately, retirement. Yet research about the role of pensions in workers' labor supply decisions has been isolated to how retirement savings impact labor force withdrawal (retirement) for older workers. An important and underresearched issue is the labor supply effects of the shift from defined benefit (DB) to defined contribution (DC) pension plans. Will this historically large shift in pension types have a sizable impact on individual labor supply decisions?

This research gap seems particularly important because the effects of pension type and pension generosity are likely to be different for workers based on age cohorts and income levels. Older workers are much more likely than their younger counterparts to receive pension benefits from their employers in the form of more traditional DB packages. Younger workers' pension benefits are more likely to be delivered through DC plans. Consequently, changes in labor supply resulting from changes in pension generosity are likely to differ among older and younger workers and among workers at different income levels.

The participation decision is only one level of the complexity faced by younger workers planning for retirement. Today's retirement landscape is even more daunting than in the past. Planning is more difficult due to the advent and expansion of 401(k) DC programs in lieu of traditional DB programs, such as company pensions. Workers who save for retirement through DC programs not only must choose to participate, they must also choose a savings amount and manage their asset allocation so as to balance a host of risks, including employment risk, market timing risk, longevity risk, and inflation risk (Burtless 2000; Brown 2001; Samwick and Skinner 2004).

Consider that many young workers have only small DC pensions or no pension savings at all. With a sufficiently high discount rate, many of these younger workers perceive a change in pension generosity as inconsequential. However, it is clear that even for workers with high discount rates, retirement decisions later in life will be predicated on decisions that they made early in their careers. For most workers, yesterday's employment decisions become tomorrow's budget constraints. Consequently, workers who decide to forgo saving in favor of current consumption may not have saved adequately for retirement when the time comes. One consequence of this is that the shift from DB pensions (which once provided nearly universal coverage and were often mandatory) to DC pensions (which are voluntary) may result in a significant reduction of retirement savings for younger workers.

Firms that offer DB plans face a variety of risks, such as investment risk and longevity risk, and they are additionally subject to regulatory risk. The Pension Protection Act of 2006 requires firms to increase their minimum funding for pension plans and may also increase the funding volatility of DB plans, factors that may make DB pensions unattractive to employers. From the employee's perspective, DB plans require only an enrollment decision, and even this decision is often automatic. Once enrolled, the worker is guaranteed a benefit amount based on years of service and a predetermined benefit factor. For example, a typical employer may guarantee 1.5% of final pay for each year of job tenure. Final pay is calculated as the average of the three highest years of earnings. Benefits are guaranteed until death, and in rare cases they may even be adjusted for inflation. Workers who opted for this DB plan and remained employed for 25 years would be guaranteed 37.5% of their highest pay.

During the most recent economic downturn, which lasted from March to November 2001, many employers decided to reduce their 401(k) pension plan contributions (Munnell and Sunden 2004). Such a reduction leaves workers in a quandary: how should they alter their labor supply to reflect this pay cut? Their options are to work more hours, work more years, or save more. Workers in both DB and DC plans face the same options, but workers with DC plans may have more opportunities to increase or reduce savings in light of changes to retirement benefit generosity. More importantly, changes in retirement benefit generosity raise questions about a worker's ability to alter current labor supply, the willingness of younger workers to participate in 401(k)-type plans, and ultimately the timing of retirement decisions.

Standard Theory of Pensions and Labor Supply

The microeconomic theory underlying the labor supply effects of pensions is based on a framework of maximizing individual utility. If leisure is a normal good, then increases in compensation (including pension generosity) have theoretically ambiguous effects on labor supply. Increases in pension generosity simultaneously raise the opportunity cost of leisure, consequently reducing leisure consumption (substitution effect), and raise income overall, resulting in an increase in leisure consumption (income effect). These effects work in opposite directions, making the predicted net effect of an increase in compensation unclear. If the income effect dominates, workers reduce their labor supply; conversely, if the substitution effect dominates, workers increase their labor supply.

Since pensions are just another form of compensation, the effects of their generosity (or lack thereof) can be analyzed in the framework just outlined. There are, however, a number of factors that complicate matters. For example, tax policies may treat future income preferentially, by allowing workers to realize labor income after retirement when marginal tax rates are lower. Employers may alter their compensation strategies in concert with tax policy; for instance, they may raise the matching contribution to a pension plan in the face of government-established pension funding requirements.

The kinds of decisions workers make about their labor supply (assuming they can adjust their hours or time off over the life cycle) are difficult to determine *ex ante*. At minimum, they would have to consider at least two factors: the expected net present value of working (conditional on the choice of hours), and the expected net present value of consuming leisure. That both of these factors involve considerable risk only makes the decision more difficult.

One way of modeling the decision is seen in the standard one-period analysis of labor–leisure choice. These original single-period models argued that labor–leisure decisions can be made separately over each period in an individual's life; that is, each period can be considered in isolation. Clearly this is not the case, and these strong separability assumptions compromise the soundness of this approach. Nevertheless, many researchers have used this model to evaluate the effect of Social Security on retirement (Feldstein 1974; Munnell 1974; Boskin 1977; Boskin and Hurd 1978). In general, this line of research has found that increases in retirement generosity result in earlier retirement and lower individual retirement savings. Treating each period in isolation is problematic, primarily because isolating the periods does not allow information from prior periods and future periods to influence current decisions. For example, in a single-period model, information about the future wage profile and value of leisure cannot be explicitly modeled. As Lazear (1987) points out, the optimization problem for the worker becomes problematic if there exist multiple times in a worker's life where expected compensation is equal to the expected future value of leisure. This means that multiperiod models are necessary to understand the effects of changes in pensions but that evaluating (and certainly optimizing) within this framework is much more difficult. Yet these models present the most realistic evaluation of how factors influence workers' retirement and savings decisions. Aaron and Burtless (1984) provide a collection of papers using multiperiod analysis. For further treatment of the dynamics of retirement see Mitchell and Fields (1984), Stock and Wise (1990), and Berkovec and Stern (1991).

Labor Supply and the Change from Defined Benefit to Defined Contribution Plans

Since the decision to retire is made over multiple periods and is usually the result of a complex set of circumstances, it is not surprising that the models developed to analyze retirement decisions are complex. With DB plans, workers have traditionally made a complex decision about when to retire against a relatively stable backdrop of pension benefits. However, this "stable" backdrop has become less so as firms have shifted from DB to DC pensions. Over the last 25 years, the shift has been considerable: in 1985 among full-time employees in medium to large private establishments, 41% reported participating in a DC plan, while 80% of similarly situated workers reported participating in a DB plan. By 2003, DC participation had increased to 51%, and DB participation had fallen to 33% (Employee Benefit Research Institute 2005). While the overall reduction in retirement savings participation is interesting, the effect that the changes in institutional structure will have on individual labor supply decisions have largely been ignored in the literature.

In theory, the primary effect of a shift from DB to DC plans will be to increase the size of the income effect discussed earlier. For workers with a DB plan, the change in work hours resulting from an increase in pension generosity implies that workers would like to work more hours (substitution effect), yet for most workers with DB pensions, there is no direct relationship between additional hours of work and pension contributions. As a consequence, the full effect of the change in benefits falls on the income effect (to reduce work hours). Conversely, workers with a DC plan can make additional contributions to their pension and experience both a substitution and an income effect. For workers with DB plans there isn't much purpose to increasing work hours, because the firm's contribution to the plan is unrelated to work hours, so the income effect is more important. The income effect implies that workers will increase their hours of leisure when faced with an increase in retirement benefits.

Prior to the large-scale declines in DB plans, only workers nearing retirement ages were able to alter their labor supply in response to the change in retirement benefits. Lazear (1979) argues that firms structured retirement generosity to encourage labor force exit and retirement. Consequently, employers could alter their retirement plans to achieve an age–skill mix that was optimal for the firm. This optimizing could most easily be accomplished on the extensive margin (i.e., retirement decision) with older workers. Younger workers were unaffected because their ability to alter their labor supply was considerably more limited. Younger workers could not retire due to age requirements set by the firm (limited extensive margin), and they could change their hours only if the change was approved by the firm (limited intensive margin). Since many workers have no alternative source of retirement savings (no personal savings), they have no ability to adjust retirement savings downward since they cannot borrow against their employer pension. Workers with personal retirement savings could choose to reduce their savings or otherwise alter their consumption.

In contrast to the limited reductions in work hours expected for workers with DB plans, the size of the aggregate income effect for younger workers could be quite large under DC plans. Workers have more access to their retirement savings under DC plans than under DB plans; consequently, the income effect no longer affects only those workers who are nearing retirement. With a DB plan, an increase in benefit generosity results in the income effect falling fully on leisure in retirement. Workers in this situation have no choice other than to take a higher portion of their compensation as retirement. Conversely, the voluntary nature of the DC programs allows workers who are given increases in retirement generosity the option of offsetting the firm's increase by reducing their own contribution. Reducing employee contributions raises the current income of employees; the additional current income may be used to purchase leisure in the form of replacing home production with leisure. Workers with high discount rates and those who are less risk-averse (weak tastes for retirement security) may opt to lower their voluntary contribution to offset the increase in employer contributions. For example, given an increase in retirement benefit generosity, some workers may choose to purchase home services such as cleaning or home repair and consume a concomitant portion of leisure. This implies that workers are increasing their leisure time today and forgoing leisure consumption in the future, effectively postponing retirement (or reducing retirement savings). This differs from the structure of retirement benefits in DB plans, in which leisure was the only good that could be consumed. Essentially, under the DB structure the firm's decision to increase retirement benefits encouraged early retirement. With DC plans, the overall effect on retirement may be considerably larger than with DB plans, because workers have more flexibility in hours and savings. Conversely, the DC effects on retirement could be much smaller, because the shift to this type of plan eliminates much of the incentive for early retirement (Munnell, Triest, and Jivan 2004). In the end, the income effect is spread among all normal goods in a person's consumption bundle—leisure is only one of many choices. This means that while the effect is widespread, it may not be large.

The transition from DB to DC plans can also be thought of as altering the liquidity constraints on workers. Workers cannot borrow against their future DB plan wealth, and many lack access to other forms of credit. As a result, they wait until their DB plan allows them to retire, even though they would prefer to retire earlier and borrow to finance their consumption. Should a change from DB to DC plans take place, workers would suddenly have access to their retirement wealth. This means that they may borrow against their wealth by taking out loans from their 401(k) savings. It seems that the effect of "showing workers the money" is that they tend to access it (Burman, Coe, and Gale 1999). Consequently, the current retirement conditions may not hold 20 years from now. If many workers have accessed their money earlier as a result of changing voluntary withholding, cashing out benefits prior to retirement, or borrowing against retirement savings, fewer workers will have adequate savings in retirement and may extend their labor supply well into their late 60s.

Here we have an empirical dilemma. Under the DB plan structure, workers had few options when firms increased retirement benefit generosity. With DC plans, many more workers are likely to change their behavior (because all are affected and needn't restrict their consumption to future leisure), but by altering their retirement savings decisions in tandem with the firm's decisions, these workers may choose to spend their income on a wide array of goods, reducing the income effect on retirement. The interesting issue is the gulf that separates younger and older workers. Older workers are much more likely to have DB plans than younger workers. Consequently, the labor market effects that we are observing today are not likely to hold for the future. To see how wide the gulf is between older and younger workers, we turn to the empirical literature on retirement savings.[1]

Evidence of Retirement Savings by Age

Evidence from the Survey of Consumer Finances (SCF) documents an increase in recent years in the percentage of families with retirement accounts across all age groups (Federal Reserve Board 2006). In 1989, approximately 27% of families headed by a person under age 35 had a retirement account; in 2004, the share was 40%. The proportion of families headed by a 35-to-44-year-old, a 45-to-54-year-old, or a 55-to-64-year-old saw similar changes during the 15-year period. Approximately 50% of families in the three groups had a retirement account in 1989; on average, the number increased by 10 percentage points between 1989 and 2004.

In addition to broad documentation of the change in savings in recent decades, much has been written about the specific vehicles used for retirement savings. Wolff (2005) calculates that from 1983 to 2001, the share of households with a DC plan increased by 41.3 percentage points, while the share with a DB plan decreased by 18.2 points. This is consistent with Ghilarducci (2006), who found that although participation in DB plans has fallen, a large proportion of DC plans exist as supplements to a traditional pension plan. As a result, pension participation is not correlated with DC coverage (Ghilarducci 2006). Although DC plans have become much more prevalent in recent years, changes in pension plan types were not uniform across age groups. The percentage of households headed by a person younger than 47 with a DC account increased by a factor of four. In contrast, the share of families headed by a 47-to-64-year-old and by an individual 65 or older with a DC account increased by factors of 5.2 and 16.7, respectively. In 1983, only 2.1% of households headed by someone 65 or older had a DC plan; the figure in 2001 was 35.0%.

Examining participation rates in 401(k) plans conditional on eligibility may be more useful than looking simply at participation rates. Poterba, Venti, and Wise (2005) found that participation given eligibility rose between 1984 and 2003 for all age groups. Younger workers increased participation more in terms of both percentage and percentage points. For example, approximately 47% of those aged 35 to 39 participated in 1984; in 2003, the share was 75%. In contrast, the increase for those aged 55 to 59 was approximately 5 percentage points, from 74 to 79%.

For the remainder of the chapter, we offer a discussion of the differences by comparing workers both across age groups and within age groups over time. There has been little empirical research on the effect of the transition from DB to DC plans for younger workers as compared with older workers. However, by using multiple data sets we can begin to examine the effects of retirement savings by age. The SCF is a triennial survey of the finances of American families. The survey contains data on equity holdings, bond holdings, mutual fund holdings and other assets, pension wealth, income, and debt as well as other demographic characteristics (including age, education, and occupation of household head). The SCF interviews are conducted between May and December of each survey year and comprise a nationally representative cross-section of housing units as well as an oversample designed to disproportionately select relatively wealthy families. Sample weights are used to make the estimates representative of the total U.S. population. We use data from the 1995 and 2004 surveys to compare workers in different age groups. In our discussion, we decompose the age groups into 10-year increments, with the youngest group being less than 35 years old.

Table 1 presents our results on the changes in family income, retirement savings,[2] and debt for workers in 1995 and 2004.[3] In 1995 median income for workers less than 35 years old was $31,500; by 2004, it had grown by 4.4% to $32,900. For workers between 35 and 44 years old, the comparable figures were $47,200 and $49,800, a 5.5% increase. Older workers fared much better: in 1995 the median family with a 45-year-old as head had a family income of $49,600. By 2004 a similarly situated family would have $61,100 in income, a 23% percent change. While incomes for younger cohorts of workers do not appear to have changed much (4.4% and 5.5%), the share of families with retirement accounts actually declined by half a percentage point for the youngest families (those whose head of household was under 35 years old). What is particularly interesting is the effect that this decline in pension participation had on the mean and median retirement savings. Again, average retirement accounts for the youngest workers were worth 8.6% more in 2004 compared to 1995. When we couple this small change in the mean with the large change in the median (a 48.7% increase), we conclude that households with smaller retirement accounts were the ones who dropped out. The exit from participation of families with small retirement account values will not have much effect on the mean, but it will push the median upward. This reduction in participation for those with little retirement savings means that these workers may either postpone retirement and increase labor supply or curtail their consumption.

The rest of Table 1 provides further evidence that this youngest group of workers is opting out of retirement savings relative to cohorts before them and using the money to alter their debt profile. While we can only surmise the relationship given the data, the association between

TABLE 1
Retirement Wealth, 1995 and 2004 (in Thousands; 2004 Dollars)

	Mean		Median		Participation rate (%)		Percentage change		
	1995	2004	1995	2004	1995	2004	Mean	Median	%
Family income (before tax)									
Under 35 years	38.4	45.1	31.5	32.9	—	—	17.4	4.4	—
35–44 years	60	73.8	47.2	49.8	—	—	23.0	5.5	—
45–54 years	81.4	94.4	49.6	61.1	—	—	16.0	23.2	—
55–64 years	66.4	100.3	41.6	54.4	—	—	51.1	30.8	—
Value of retirement accounts									
Under 35 years	23.2	25.2	7.4	11.0	40.7	40.2	8.6	48.6	-0.5
35–44 years	43.9	66.7	18.1	27.9	54.3	55.9	51.9	54.1	1.6
45–54 years	106.2	141.1	34.5	55.5	57.4	57.7	32.9	60.9	0.3
55–64 years	113.4	210.9	38.9	83.0	50.9	62.9	86.0	113.4	12.0
Debt									
Under 35 years	46.0	52.8	18.5	33.6	83.5	79.8	14.8	81.6	-3.7
35–44 years	71.2	86.9	45.6	87.2	87.0	88.6	22.1	91.2	1.6
45–54 years	81.7	90.2	48.2	83.2	86.3	88.4	10.4	72.6	2.1
55–64 years	62.4	79.7	25.9	48.0	73.7	76.3	27.7	85.3	2.6
Credit card debt									
Under 35 years	3.5	3.7	1.6	1.5	54.7	47.5	5.7	-6.3	-7.2
35–44 years	4.0	5.2	2.3	2.5	55.9	58.8	30.0	8.7	2.9
45–54 years	4.5	6.2	2.5	2.9	56.4	54.0	37.8	16.0	-2.4
55–64 years	3.5	5.7	1.6	2.2	43.2	42.1	62.9	37.5	-1.1

17

reduced participation and reductions in debt is interesting. For example, the under-35 group was the only group to see the percentage of families with debt decline. All other families saw an increase in the percentage with debt. In the subcategory of credit card debt, the under-35 group had the largest decline of all. It appears that workers who were under 35 years of age in 2004 were more likely than others to forgo retirement savings and instead pay for current (and past) consumption.

Why would this group of families headed by someone under the age of 35 act so differently from their counterparts only a decade ago? The answer may lie in the advent and widespread adoption of 401(k)-type programs in the 1990s. The earlier cohort of young families (those who were less than 35 in 1995) began working in the early to mid-1980s, when 401(k) programs were just beginning to gain popularity. As we discussed earlier, in 1985 nearly 80% of workers at medium or large firms in the United States had a DB pension plan.[4] In the intervening years, there have been significant changes in the type of pension wealth held by all workers, and in particular, young families. Wolff (2005) calculated that among households headed by someone under 47 years old, 32.6% had a DB account in 1983, compared to 22.8% in 2001. In contrast, only 13.7% had a DC account in 1983. Almost 20 years later, the share had jumped to 53.8%. The difference in retirement plans is likely to be even larger for families with a head under 35 years old. A major reason for the change in the dominant type of retirement savings is that unlike their older counterparts, younger workers entered the labor force at a time when DC plans were more common than DB plans.

Table 2 provides some additional evidence of the reduction of retirement savings for young workers. After adjusting for wages, we find that in households with a worker under the age of 35, the ratio of average retirement savings to income was 0.6 in 1995 and fell to 0.54 in 2004. For all other age groups this ratio increased dramatically. Using the median measure, we find that the under-35 groups saw a modest increase in median retirement savings relative to earnings, but all other groups witnessed significantly higher increases. Overall, adjusting for income does not change our main finding that younger workers, who were more likely to have only a DC pension available to them, were saving less than the cohort that immediately preceded them. More importantly, they were the only age group that saw their total retirement income decline. All of the retirement savings figures presented thus far are conditional on having a pension.[5] As a result, families without retirement savings are not included in our results.

Just as participation in pension programs is a necessary precondition for retirement savings, so too is employment. Yet on this measure,

TABLE 2
Retirement Savings as a Proportion of Income, 1995 and 2004

	Mean		Median		Percentage change	
	1995	2004	1995	2004	Mean	Median
Ratio of total retirement savings to annual income						
Under 35 years	0.60	0.56	0.23	0.33	−4.5	9.9
35–44 years	0.73	0.90	0.38	0.56	17.2	17.7
45–54 years	1.30	1.49	0.70	0.91	19.0	21.3
55–64 years	1.71	2.10	0.94	1.53	39.5	59.1

younger workers do not look like past generations. Figure 1 represents the employment-to-population ratios for workers 25 to 34 years old and 35 to 44 years old, separately for men and women, from 1967 to 2005. The figure illustrates the decline in employment rates of younger men. Women's employment rates increased through the 1980s but leveled off in the 1990s and have recently started to decline.

The employment story for younger cohorts, in particular for males, is discouraging from a retirement savings perspective. Juhn, Murphy, and Topel (2002) examined the labor force participation, nonemployment rates, and unemployment rates of prime-age males (25 to 54 years old) from 1967 to 2000. In general, they found that while the unemployment rate declined considerably from its labor market peak to trough (9% in 1982–83 to 3% in 1999–2000), the percentage of prime-age men who were not participating in the labor market increased throughout the period. As the authors argued, there are a number of men "missing" from the U.S. labor force: some are incarcerated, some are disabled, and others are unaccounted for.

This shift away from retirement savings for the younger cohort coupled with the reduction in employment rates for young workers does not bode well for retirement savings in 25 to 30 years, when these workers will be seriously thinking about retirement. Unfortunately for them, many of their later retirement decisions will be predicated on earlier labor supply and savings decisions. Since the early evidence seems to indicate that young workers are unlikely to save as much as were their similarly aged predecessors and that they have postponed employment, we can only conclude that these workers will consume less in the future relative to the previous cohort, plan on working more (either hours or retire later), or will retire with less wealth.

FIGURE 1

Male and Female Employment-to-Population Ratios, 1967–2006, for Workers 25 to 44 Years Old

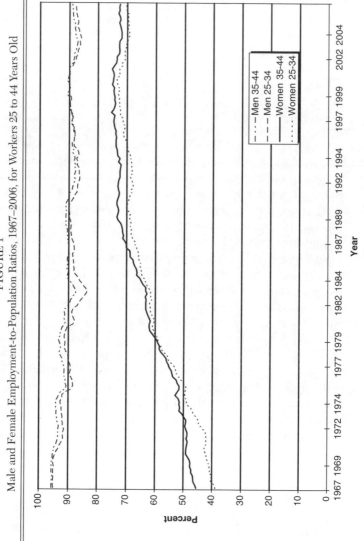

Older Workers

Thus far, most of our discussion has concentrated on the effects of the transition from DB to DC plans. Consequently, we have focused our attention on younger workers. Because most current workers began careers when the majority of pension plans were DB plans, it is important to discuss how changes in these plans alter labor supply decisions. Unfortunately, there is very limited evidence of how changes in employer plans alter labor supply decisions. Nevertheless, it is likely that we can use some of the research from Social Security to examine the effects of changes in private pensions.

Historically, Social Security has altered its benefit generosity considerably. Researchers have focused particular interest on the dramatic benefit increases for birth cohorts from 1906 through 1926. Engelhardt and Gruber (2004) note that "the early cohorts in this range saw enormous exogenous increases in Social Security benefits"(p. 3). Researchers have used this variation to examine how changes in Social Security benefit generosity has altered labor supply decisions. Krueger and Pischke (1992) examined cohort-level data during the period when Social Security benefits initially increased and subsequently fell. This adjustment occurred because benefits were improperly indexed, raising their level too much. Once Congress realized this, they corrected the error, and as a result abruptly adjusted benefits downward. This had the effect of creating "notch babies" who experienced large, unanticipated changes in Social Security benefits. Workers with otherwise identical work histories received different benefit amounts depending on whether they were born before or after 1917.

This abrupt change in benefit generosity created a "natural experiment" that Krueger and Pischke used to determine the labor supply effects for otherwise identical workers who differed only in their Social Security benefit generosity. In general, Krueger and Pischke found that overall male labor force participation trended steadily downward for the notch babies, and that this general trend is unrelated to the changes in Social Security benefit generosity. Krueger and Pischke's finding is at odds with the predicted behavioral response to increases in benefit generosity. Interestingly, their paper is not the only one that finds no systematic relationship between Social Security benefit generosity and labor supply. Krueger and Meyer (2002) summarized the literature in this way: "In our opinion, studies that use a more plausible identification strategy—for example, using variability in benefits due to legislated changes that cause breaks in the steady trend toward more generous benefits—tend to find a very modest impact of Social Security wealth on labor supply in the United States" (p. 48).

If Social Security generosity does not translate into earlier retirement, can we infer that increases in private pension generosity have no discernable effect on retirement? Again, there is limited evidence that increases in private pension generosity substantively reduce the age of retirement. In general, workers with more generous pensions retire earlier; however, this could be due solely to selection effects. Gustman, Mitchell, and Steinmeier (1994) argue that only a few empirical pension studies have the data necessary to answer this question—information on pension offerings and longitudinal data on retirement flows. In general, those studies find that a 10% increase in present value of retirement income at age 60 results in retirement occurring one to two months earlier than it otherwise would. Gustman, Mitchell, and Steinmeier argue that this effect, while statistically significant, is quite small; in fact, it is miniscule. Additionally, research using longitudinal data on employer pensions and retirement has not been able to disentangle the causal story as to whether pensions influence retirement or retirement expectations influence pension generosity. In general, pension benefit generosity does not appear to have a large effect on older workers' labor supply. This probably results from the multitude of factors that influence the retirement decision, including health, spouse's age and work status, and a host of other economic and non-separation-economic factors.

One final mechanism for determining the effect of retirement savings on retirement decisions is to examine changes in the employment rates of older workers. Congressional Research Service (CRS) analysis of labor force participation rates of older workers using the March Current Population Surveys for various years found that there has been a significant reversal in the long downward trend in retirement age (Purcell 2006). According to the CRS, men and women age 62 and older are more likely to be working today than the same group was 10 years ago. From 1996 to 2005, the number of 62-to-64-year-old men employed in March of each year rose from 43% to 51%. During this period, men from 65 to 69 years old increased their employment rate from 27% to 30%. Employment rates for older women increased too. Women from 62 to 64 years old increased their employment rate from 32% in 1996 to 37% in 2005; similarly, 65-to-69-year-old women's employment rates increased from 17% to 23%. It is important to note that over this period the populations of all these groups increased, meaning that the total number of workers in these age categories rose considerably.

This increase in the percentage of older workers in the labor force raises one final issue about the effect of wealth on retirement. The unhistorically large returns on equities in the late 1990s should have reduced the employment rates of older workers. Cheng and French (2000) examined this period and theorized that workers with the largest unexpected increases in wealth would reduce their labor force participation. Cheng and French found that workers over 54 years old had the greatest wealth increases, largely because that group holds the most equities. Yet the authors found that labor force participation rates for those over 54 *increased* between 1994 and 1999. Consequently, it is difficult to argue that large unanticipated changes in retirement wealth had the aggregate effect of reducing labor supply. Of course, it is possible that low overall unemployment and higher wages induced more labor supply, which overcame the retirement incentive due to increases in income. Figure 2 illustrates the labor supply of men and women over 54. Note too that the employment-to-population ratio continued to climb even after the equity bubble burst. Weller, Wenger, and Gould (2004) have argued that the simultaneous decline in retiree health coverage may have offset some of the wealth effect of the increasing stock market.

Conclusion

In this chapter we have argued that numerous facets of pension structure influence labor supply. Of particular importance is the transition from traditional DB pensions to DC pensions. DB plans require workers to take their increased pension benefits solely in the form of additional months or years of retirement. This is the case because participation in DB plans rarely requires workers to make explicit contributions by payroll deduction. Consequently, there is no way for workers to access the benefit; their decision is simply when to retire. Because DC plans require a payroll contribution and collect the money in an account that is accessible to the worker, changes in pension benefits can have an immediate effect on the worker's labor supply.

We presented some empirical evidence that younger workers, particularly workers who started their careers after DB plans were being phased out by many employers, have changed their retirement savings behavior. In particular, they are less likely to have a retirement plan, and they have smaller account balances relative to their pay than the cohort that preceded them. It seems clear to us that workers under 35 years old in 2004 are saving less than the previous cohort, although whether this is purely an employer-driven labor market phenomenon is an open question.

Finally, we investigated the evidence on the effects of Social Security, pension, and wealth on retirement decisions and found that in past decades, changes in benefit generosity have not significantly affected employment rates in the United States. In fact, the general trend is for older workers to remain in the labor force, despite the wealth effects of

FIGURE 2

Male and Female Employment-to-Population Ratios, 1967–2006, for Workers 55 Years and Older

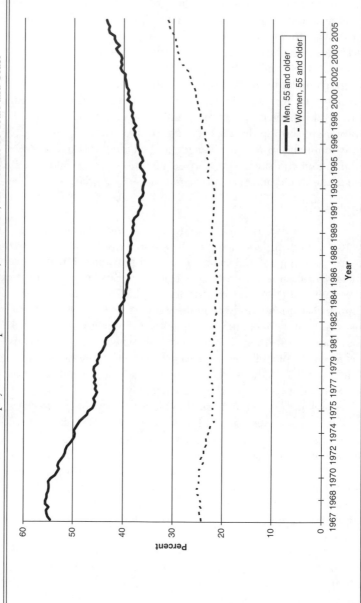

equities or the generosity of public or employer pensions. In light of the evidence suggesting that increased generosity in Social Security does not induce a significant decrease in retirement age, additional research might investigate the magnitudes of the effects of more recent phenomena on retirement age. To what extent will the loss of wealth in equities, removal of money from 401(k) plans, and the extremely low (and in some cases negative) private savings rate in recent years affect the labor supply of older workers and income security in retirement? Interesting too is the issue of how the demand for near-elderly and elderly labor will change as the workforce changes. What will be the direction of the effect between labor demand and labor supply? Although the impact of the pervasive shift to DC plans will be less ripe for investigation once the phenomenon has worked its way through all age cohorts, many questions remain about the specifics of how a lack of retirement savings by the current cohort of younger workers will affect the labor market.

Endnotes

[1] Our discussion focuses on the differential effect between younger and older workers. However, there is also likely to be a differential effect of DB and DC plans between rich and poor workers; see for example Wolff 2005. Particularly for DB plans, the tax incentives are spread out evenly, at least for all workers who are vested. In a DC plan, tax incentives favor high-income workers.

[2] The definition of retirement account includes only those account balances where the family has the ability to take from, or borrow against, the account. Consequently, most traditional DB account balances are not included.

[3] We chose 1995 and 2004 because these years represent similar points in the business cycle. Unemployment in the U.S averaged 5.6 in 1995 and 5.5 in 2004. Additionally, many financial fundamentals, such as price-to-earnings ratios, were similar.

[4] We should note that different surveys use different measures of pension coverage. For example, the Employee Benefits Research Institute and the Department of Labor define coverage as relative to all current workers, whereas the Survey of Consumer Finance measures coverage for families cumulatively (i.e., how many families have accumulated any retirement savings over their lifetime). This latter measure is likely to increase as the workforce ages.

[5] We note that there is some discrepancy in our reporting here. The Survey of Consumer Finance allows us to measure only wealth that families currently have access to; we are measuring both DB and DC plan coverage.

References

Aaron, Henry J., and Gary T. Burtless. 1984. *Retirement and Economic Behavior: Studies in Social Economics*. Washington, DC: Brookings Institution Press.

Berkovec, James, and Steven Stern. 1991. "Job Exit Behavior of Older Men." *Econometrica*, Vol. 59, no. 1, pp. 189–210.

Boskin, Michael J. 1977. "Social Security and Retirement Decisions." *Economic Inquiry*, Vol. 15, no. 1, pp. 1–25.

Boskin, Michael J., and Michael D. Hurd. 1978. "The Effect of Social Security on Early Retirement." *Journal of Public Economics*, Vol. 10, no. 3, pp. 361–77.

Brown, Jeffrey R. 2001. "Private Pensions, Mortality Risk, and the Decision to Annuitize." *Journal of Public Economics*, Vol. 82, no. 1, pp. 29–62.

Burman, Leonard E., Norma B. Coe, and William G. Gale. 1999. *What Happens When You Show Them The Money? Lump-Sum Distributions, Retirement Income Security, and Public Policy*. Washington, DC: Brookings Institution Press.

Burtless, Gary. 2000. *How Would Financial Risk Affect Retirement Income Under Individual Accounts?* Boston, MA: Center for Retirement Research.

Cheng, Ing-Haw, and Eric French. 2000. "The Effect of the Run-up in the Stock Market on Labor Supply." *Economic Perspectives*, Vol. 25, no. 4, pp. 48–65.

Employee Benefit Research Institute. 2005. "Participation in Employee Benefit Programs." In *EBRI Databook on Employee Benefits*. <http://www.ebri.org/publications/books/index.cfm?fa=databook>. [January 28, 2007].

Engelhardt, Gary V., and Jonathan Gruber. 2004. *Social Security and the Evolution of Elderly Poverty*. NBER Working Paper 10466. Cambridge, MA: National Bureau of Economic Research.

Federal Reserve Board. 2006. *2004 Survey of Consumer Finances Chartbook*. <http://www.federalreserve.gov/pubs/oss/oss2/2004/scf2004home.html>. [February 1, 2007].

Feldstein, Martin. 1974. "Social Security, Induced Retirement, and Aggregate Capital Accumulation." *Journal of Political Economy*, Vol. 82, no. 5, pp. 905–27.

Ghilarducci, Teresa. 2006. "Future Retirement Income Security Needs Defined Benefit Pensions." <http://www.americanprogress.org/kf/defined_benefit_layout.pdf>. [January 20, 2007].

Gustman, Alan L., Olivia S. Mitchell, and Thomas L. Steinmeier. 1994. "The Role of Pensions in the Labor Market: A Survey of the Literature." *Industrial and Labor Relations Review*, Vol. 47, no. 3, pp. 417–38.

Juhn, Chinhui, Kevin M. Murphy, and Robert H. Topel. 2002. "Current Unemployment, Historically Contemplated." *Brookings Papers on Economic Activity*, Vol. 20, no. 1, pp. 88–97.

Krueger, Alan, and Bruce Meyer. 2002. "Labor Supply Effects of Social Insurance." In Alan J. Auerbach and Martin Feldstein, eds., *Handbook of Public Economics*. Amsterdam: Elsevier, pp. 2327–92.

Krueger, Alan, and Jörn-Steffen Pischke. (1992.) "The Effect of Social Security on Labor Supply: A Cohort Analysis of the Notch Generation." *Journal of Labor Economics*, Vol. 10, no. 4, pp. 412–37.

Lazear, Edward P. 1979. "Why is there Mandatory Retirement?" *Journal of Political Economy*, Vol. 87, no. 6, pp. 1261–84.

———. 1987. "Retirement from the Labor Force." In Orley Ashenfelter and Richard Layard, eds., *Handbook of Labor Economics*. Amsterdam: Elsevier, pp. 305–55.

Mitchell, Olivia S., and Gary S. Fields. 1984. "The Economics of Retirement Behavior." *Journal of Labor Economics*, Vol. 2, no. 1, pp. 84–105.

Munnell, Alicia H. 1974. *The Effect of Social Security on Personal Saving*. Cambridge, MA: Ballinger Publishing.

Munnell, Alicia H., and Annika E. Sunden. 2004. *Coming Up Short: The Challenge of 401(k) Plans*. Washington, DC: Brookings Institution Press.

Munnell, Alicia H., Robert K. Triest, and Natalia Jivan. 2004. *How Do Pensions Affect Expected and Actual Retirement Ages?* Center for Retirement Research Working Paper 2004-27.

Poterba, James, Steven Venti, and David A. Wise. 2005. *Demographic Change, Retirement Saving, and Financial Market Returns: Part 1.* Papers on Retirement Research Center Projects NB05-01. Cambridge, MA: National Bureau of Economic Research.

Purcell, Patrick. 2006. *Older Workers: Employment and Retirement Trends (Findings from Domestic Social Policy Division).* CRS Report #RL30629. Washington, DC: Congressional Research Service.

Samwick, Andrew A., and Jonathan Skinner. 2004. "How Will 401(k) Pension Plans Affect Retirement Income?" *American Economic Review*, Vol. 94, no. 1, pp. 329–43.

Stock, James H., and David A. Wise. 1990. "Pensions, the Option Value of Work, and Retirement." *Econometrica*, Vol. 58, no. 5, pp. 1151–80.

Weller, Christian, Jeffrey Wenger, and Elise Gould. 2004. *Health Insurance Coverage in Retirement: The Erosion of Retiree Income Security.* Washington, DC: Economic Policy Institute.

Wolff, Edward N. 2005. *Is the Equalizing Effect of Retirement Wealth Wearing Off?* Working Paper No. 420. Blithewood, NY: Levy Economics Institute.

CHAPTER 3

Economic Institutional Change and Employer Pensions[1]

WILLIAM LAZONICK

University of Massachusetts Lowell and INSEAD

The Shift to Defined Contribution Pensions

Since the 1980s, two major trends in employer pension coverage of U.S. workers stand out. First, employer pension plans have covered a steadily declining proportion of business-sector workers. In 1980 35% of business-sector wage and salary workers were active participants in employer pension plans insured by the U.S. Government's Pension Benefit Guaranty Corporation (2006). Since then this proportion has declined steadily, falling to 19% by 2003. Even though the size of the U.S. business-sector labor force increased by 47% from 1980 to 2003, there were 6.2 million fewer workers active in an employer pension plan in 2003 than in 1980.

Second, among those covered there has been a shift from defined benefit (DB) to defined contribution (DC) plans. Between 1985 and 2005 the ratio of assets in DC plans to DB plans rose from 0.54:1 to 1.61:1. Over the past two decades, individual retirement accounts (IRAs)—that is, non-employer pensions—became increasingly important as a form of retirement saving, rising from 20% of combined DB and DC assets in 1985 to 78% in 2005 (see Figure 1).

Those business-sector employees who still are covered by DB plans tend to obtain that benefit by working for very large corporations. Since the 1980s, about 80% of active participants in DB plans have been in single-employer plans; the proportion of those in such plans with 10,000 or more participants rose from 43% in 1985 to 65% in 2005, and the proportion in plans with 5,000 to 9,999 participants stayed steady at about 11% (Pension Benefit Guaranty Corporation 2006). The plans with 10,000 or more participants had a total of 12.7 million participants in 1985 and 22.3 million in 2005; the plans with 5,000 to 9,999 participants had 3.1 million participants in 1985 and 3.6 million in 2005.

FIGURE 1
Total U.S. DB, DC, and IRA Assets, 1985–2005

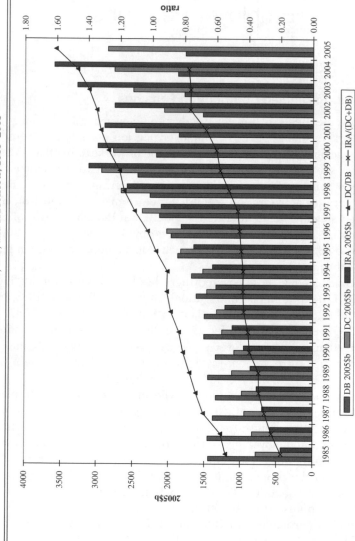

DB 2005$b   DC 2005$b   IRA 2005$b   DC/DB   IRA/(DC+DB)

Source: Federal Reserve Board 2006.

These trends in pension coverage reflect the growing insecurity of employment at major U.S. corporations compared with the post-World War II decades. DB pension coverage became widespread in that era as employment with one company over the course of one's career became the norm at major U.S. companies. Traditional DB plans rewarded years of service with one company and, being generally nonportable, discouraged interfirm labor mobility. It was logical to combine the expectation of "lifelong" employment with one company and a noncontributory, nonportable DB pension plan, and in the postwar decades this combination provided millions of corporate employees with secure incomes at work and in retirement.

In the 1980s and 1990s, however, the restructuring of these "Old Economy" business corporations increasingly put an end to the expectation of employment with one company over the course of one's career (Lazonick 2004). With interfirm labor mobility on the rise, from the 1980s forward DC pensions, typically in the form of 401(k) savings plans as well as individual retirement accounts (IRAs), became widespread. High-growth "New Economy" companies never held out the expectation of lifelong employment and hence had no reason to offer employees a pension plan that rewarded seniority. These trends in pension coverage thus are integral to a more fundamental transformation in the ways business enterprises employ people in the U.S. economy.

Over the past quarter century, leading both the growth of the U.S. economy and the transformation of employment relations have been companies in the information and communication technologies (ICT) industries. In ICT, a "New Economy business model" (NEBM) has replaced the "Old Economy business model" (OEBM) (see Lazonick 2006a, 2006b, and 2007b). As shown in Table 1, OEBM and NEBM can be compared in terms of the strategy, organization, and finance of their constituent business enterprises.

In this chapter, I argue that the change from DB to DC pensions over the past quarter century has been integral to the transition from OEBM to NEBM as the dominant business model in U.S. ICT industries. I first discuss the role of the traditional DB pension as a logical form of deferred compensation for a person with the expectation of a career with one company—what in the mid-1950s William Whyte (1956) called the "organization man"—at the leading Old Economy ICT companies into the 1980s. I then analyze how and why the evolution of employment relations and pension systems at the leading New Economy ICT companies assumed, in sharp contrast to the concept of the "organization man," interfirm labor mobility in the pursuit of a career. Next I document the transitions in the 1990s and first half of the 2000s of the

TABLE 1
Characteristics of Old Economy and New Economy Business Models in the Information and Communication Technology Industries

	Old economy business model	New economy business model
Strategy, product	Growth by building on internal capabilities; expansion into new product markets based on related technologies; geographic expansion to access national product markets	New firm entry into specialized markets; branded components sold to system integrators; new capabilities accumulated by acquiring young technology firms
Strategy, process	Development and patenting of proprietary technologies; vertical integration of the value chain, at home and abroad	Cross-license technology based on industry standards; vertical specialization of value chain; outsourcing/offshoring of routine work
Organization	Secure employment: "organization man" (career with one company); industrial unions; DB pension; employer-funded medical insurance in employment and retirement	Insecure employment: interfirm mobility of labor; broad-based stock options; non-union; DC pension; greater burden of medical insurance borne by employee
Finance	Venture finance from personal savings, family, and business associates; NYSE listing; steady dividends; growth finance from retentions leveraged with bond issues	Organized venture capital; IPO on NASDAQ; low or no dividends; growth finance from retentions plus stock as an acquisition currency; stock repurchases to support stock price

pension systems of major Old Economy ICT companies from traditional, nonportable DB plans to portable "cash balance" DB plans to DC plans, primarily 401(k) savings plans, as key aspects of the transformation from OEBM to NEBM in ICT. In the conclusion, I draw out the implications of the transition from OEBM to NEBM for the future of employee pensions, given both the ongoing globalization of the labor force employed by major U.S. business corporations and the state of the U.S. stock markets on which U.S. pensions have increasingly relied to generate returns.

Employment Relations and Pensions in OEBM

Business Models, Old and New

In 2005 there were 53 ICT companies in the U.S. Fortune 500, with a total of $909 billion in revenues and 2.6 million employees. Of these 53 companies, 26, with $332 billion in revenues and 871,000 employees in 2005, can be defined as "New Economy." Tables 2 and 3 list the top 20 Old Economy and top 20 New Economy ICT companies by revenues in 2005 and the numbers of people employed by these companies over the previous decade. For inclusion as "New Economy" in Table 3, a company had to a) be founded in 1955 or later, b) not have been established by the spinoff of an existing division from an Old Economy company, and c) not have grown through acquisition of, or merger with, an Old Economy company (as was the case for EDS, Comcast, and IAC, which are included as Old Economy companies).

I have chosen 1955 as the earliest date for inclusion in the New Economy list because that was the year that William Shockley, the co-inventor of the transistor, established Shockley Semiconductor Laboratories in Mountain View, California, inadvertently sparking a chain reaction that resulted in the emergence of Silicon Valley as a center for the development of microelectronics. As I outline in the next section, it was first and foremost in Silicon Valley, beginning in the late 1950s, that NEBM emerged as a viable, and ultimately dominant, business model. Note that 14 of the 20 New Economy companies in Table 3 are based in California, with 11 of them (all but Qualcomm, Computer Sciences, and SAIC) in Silicon Valley.

Headed by the giants, International Business Machines (IBM) and Hewlett-Packard (HP), six of the Old Economy companies in Table 2, including Xerox, Electronic Data Systems (EDS), First Data, and NCR, are strictly information technology companies. The two semiconductor companies, Texas Instruments (TI) and Freescale Semiconductor, supply chips to both the information technology and communication technology sectors of ICT. TI's major business is the design and manufacture of digital signal processing chips for the cell phone industry, while Freescale is a recent spinoff of the wireless communications technology company Motorola. Along with TI and Motorola in the communications equipment segment of ICT is Lucent Technologies, which was spun off from AT&T Corp. in 1996 and has recently merged with the French telecommunications equipment company Alcatel to became Alcatel-Lucent.[2]

The remaining 10 companies in Table 2 are communications service providers. Five are direct descendents of the old Bell System, which, until its breakup on January 1, 1984, functioned as a regulated monopoly in providing local and long distance telephone services. Besides the parent company, AT&T, the system included regional Bell operating companies; Western Electric, wholly owned by AT&T, which manufactured equipment for the Bell System; and Bell Labs, the world-famous research organization jointly owned by AT&T and Western Electric. The breakup separated the seven regional companies, also known as the Baby Bells, from AT&T Corp., which now included within its internal organization Western Electric and Bell Labs as its AT&T Technologies division. The seven regional companies were Ameritech, Bell Atlantic,

TABLE 2

Employment, 1996 and 2000–2005, at the Top 20 "Old Economy" Companies by 2005 Sales

Old economy companies (year of founding, state in which headquartered, rank in 2006 Fortune 500 list)	2005 sales ($b)	Number of employees							2005 sales per employee ($)
		1996	2000	2001	2002	2003	2004	2005	
International Business Machines (1911, NY, 10)	91.1	240,615	316,309	319,876	315,889	319,273	329,001	329,373	277,000
Hewlett-Packard (1939, CA, 11)	86.7	112,000	88,500	86,200	141,000	142,000	151,000	150,000	578,000
Verizon Communications (1885, NY, 18)	75.1	62,600	260,000	247,000	229,500	203,100	210,000	217,000	346,000
AT&T Inc.[1] (1885, TX, 39)	43.9	61,540	220,090	193,420	175,400	168,950	162,000	189,950	231,000
Motorola (1928, IL, 54)	36.8	139,000	147,000	111,000	97,000	88,000	68,000	69,000	533,000
Sprint Nextel[2] (1899, KS, 59)	34.7	48,024	84,100	83,700	72,200	66,900	59,900	79,900	434,000
Comcast[3] (1963; PA, 194)	22.3	16,400	35,000	38,000	82,000	68,000	74,000	80,000	279,000
Bellsouth (1885; GA, 106)	20.6	81,241	103,900	87,875	77,000	76,000	62,564	63,066	326,000
Electronic Data Systems[4] (1962, TX, 108)	20.5	100,000	122,000	143,000	137,000	132,000	117,000	117,000	175,000
Xerox (1906, CT, 142)	15.7	86,700	92,500	78,900	67,800	61,100	58,100	55,200	284,000
Qwest Communications (1885, CO, 160)	13.9	720	67,000	61,000	47,000	47,000	41,401	39,348	353,000
Texas Instruments (1930, TX, 167)	13.4	59,927	42,481	34,724	34,589	34,154	35,472	35,207	381,000
Directv Group (1932, CA, 168)	13.2	86,000	9,000	13,700	11,600	12,300	11,800	9,200	1,435,000
First Data (1871, CO, 224)	10.5	40,000	27,000	29,000	29,000	29,000	32,000	33,000	318,000
Alltel (1943, AR, 251)	9.5	16,307	27,257	23,955	25,348	19,986	18,598	21,373	444,000
Lucent Technologies (1869, NJ, 255)	9.4	124,000	126,000	77,000	47,000	34,500	31,800	30,500	308,000

Cox Communications (1898, GA, 273)	9.0	7,200	19 000	20,700	21,600	22,150	22,350	22,530	399,000
IAC/InterActiveCorp[5] (1977, NY, 313)	7.1	4,750	20,780	16,900	23,200	25,700	26,000	28,000	254,000
NCR (1884, OH, 357)	6.0	38,600	32,900	31,400	30,100	29,000	28,500	28,200	213,000
Freescale Semiconductor[6] (1928, TX, 368)	5.8	-	-	-	-	-	-	22,700	256,000
Averages (per firm, except for sales per employee)	27.3	72,808	96,885	89,334	87,621	83,111	81,062	81,027	391,000

Included in the ICT industries are companies that the Fortune 500 2006 list classifies as being in the following industries: a) computer peripherals, b) computer software, c) computers, office equipment, d) financial data services, e) information technology services, f) Internet services and retailing, g) network and other communications equipment, h) semiconductors and other electronic components, and i) telecommunications.

[1] In 2005 SBC Communications, founded in Texas in 1885 and ranked 33rd on the Fortune 500 2005 list, acquired AT&T, founded in 1877 and ranked 56th on the 2005 list. SBC then changed its name to AT&T Inc. Employment figures for 1996 and 2000–2004 are for SBC. AT&T Corp.'s employment figures were 1996, 130,000; 2000, 166,000; 2001, 117,800; 2002, 71,000; 2003, 61,600; 2004, 47,565.

[2] In August 2005 Sprint, 65th on the Fortune 500 2005 list, acquired Nextel, founded in 1987 and 157th on the 2005 list.

[3] Comcast began its transformation into the largest Internet cable company in the United States through its acquisition of subscribers from AT&T Broadband in 2000–2001.

[4] General Motors bought Electronic Data Systems in 1984 and spun it off as an independent company in 1996.

[5] In 1998 HSN (formed out of Home Shopping Network) purchased USA Networks, which had been owned by Paramount and MCA. In the early 2000s the company changed its name, first to USA Interactive and then to IAC/InterActiveCorp.

[6] In late 2004 Motorola spun off its semiconductor division as Freescale Semiconductor.

Sources: "The Fortune 1,000 Ranked Within Industries." 2006; http://www.hoovers.com (subscription database); Compustat subscription database.

TABLE 3

Employment, 1996 and 2000–2005, at the Top 20 "New Economy" Companies by 2005 Sales

New Economy companies (year of founding, state in which headquartered, rank in 2006 Fortune 500 list)	2005 sales ($b)	Number of employees							2005 sales per employee ($)
		1996	2000	2001	2002	2003	2004	2005	
Dell Computer (1984, TX, 25)	55.9	8,400	36,500	40,000	34,600	39,100	55,200	65,200	857,000
Microsoft (1975, WA, 48)	39.8	20,561	39,100	47,600	50,500	55,000	57,000	61,000	652,000
Intel (1968, CA, 49)	38.8	48,500	86,100	83,400	78,700	79,700	85,000	99,900	388,888
Cisco Systems (1984, CA, 83)	24.8	8,782	34,000	38,000	36,000	34,000	34,000	38,413	646,000
Computer Sciences (1959, CA, 141)	15.8	33,850	58,000	68,000	67,000	90,000	90,000	79,000	200,000
Apple Computer (1977, CA, 159)	13.9	10,896	8,568	9,603	10,211	10,912	12,561	15,810	879,000
Oracle (1977, CA, 196)	11.8	23,111	41,320	42,297	42,006	40,650	41,658	49,872	236,000
Sanmina-SCI (1980, CA, 198)	11.7	1,726	24,000	48,774	46,030	45,008	42,115	42,821	273,000
Sun Microsystems (1982, CA, 211)	11.1	17,400	38,900	43,700	39,400	36,100	32,600	31,000	358,000
Solectron (1977, CA, 227)	10.5	10,781	65,273	60,000	73,000	66,000	59,500	47,000	223,000
EMC (1979, MA, 249)	9.7	4,800	24,100	20,100	17,400	20,000	22,700	21,000	462,000
Amazon.com (1994, WA, 272)	8.5	151	9,000	7,800	7,500	7,800	9,000	12,000	708,000
EchoStar Communications (1993, CO, 273)	8.4	1,200	11,000	11,000	15,000	15,000	20,000	21,000	400,000
SAIC (1969, CA, 285)	8.0	20,931	39,078	41,500	40,400	38,700	44,900	43,800	183,000
Jabil Circuit (1966, FL, 303)	7.5	2,649	19,115	17,097	20,000	26,000	34,000	40,000	188,000
Applied Materials (1967, CA, 317)	7.0	11,403	19,220	17,365	16,077	12,050	12,960	12,750	549,000
Google (1998, CA, 353)	6.1					1,628	3,021	5,680	1,074,000
Advanced Micro Devices (1969, CA, 367)	5.8	12,200	14,696	14,415	12,146	14,300	15,900	15,900	365,000
Qualcomm (1985, CA, 381)	5.7	6,000	6,300	6,500	8,100	7,400	7,600	9,300	613,000
Yahoo! (1995, CA, 412)	5.3	155	3,259	3,000	3,600	5,500	7,600	9,800	541,000
Averages (per firm, except for sales per employee)	15.3	12,816	30,396	32,640	32,509	32,242	34,366	36,062	424,000

Included in the ICT industries are companies that the Fortune 500 2006 list classifies as being in the following industries: a) computer peripherals, b) computer software, c) computers, office equipment, d) financial data services, e) information technology services, f) Internet services and retailing, g) network and other communications equipment, h) semiconductors and other electronic components, and i) telecommunications.

Sources: "The Fortune 1,000 Ranked Within Industries." 2006; http://www.hoovers.com (subscription database); Compustat subscription database.

36

BellSouth, NYNEX, Pacific Telesis (PacTel), Southwestern Bell Corp. (SBC), and US West. Subsequently Bell Atlantic and NYNEX were merged into Verizon; Ameritech, Pacific Telesis, and AT&T Corp. into SBC, which in 2005 changed its name to AT&T Inc.; and US West into Qwest. In December 2006 AT&T Inc. acquired BellSouth. In the 13 years since the breakup of the Bell System, therefore, AT&T Corp. and the seven Baby Bells have now been consolidated into three companies: AT&T Inc., Verizon, and Qwest.[3]

In Table 3 only three companies are clearly communications technology companies—Cisco Systems, which makes Internet routers and switches; EchoStar, a major force in satellite television; and Qualcomm, a wireless equipment manufacturer. Cisco's rise to dominance of its industry derives from its development of software that has enabled the convergence of information and communication technology—what is now called the "triple play" of voice, data, and video—using the same infrastructures and equipment. The evolution of those infrastructures and equipment has depended critically on the development of ever more powerful, compact, and affordable computers—in short, the microelectronics revolution. At the center of this revolution were Intel and Microsoft, both of which grew large supplying crucial inputs to the IBM PC and what used to be called its "clones," including Dell Computer, number 1 on the 2005 New Economy list. Advanced Micro Devices (AMD), founded in Silicon Valley a year following Intel, sustained its growth for decades by serving as a "second source" for the supply of Intel chips, although in recent years it has increasingly been competing head to head with Intel with its own chip designs.

Applied Materials is the world's largest maker of semiconductor production equipment, while Solectron, Sanmina-SCI, and Jabil Circuit are among the world's leading electronic manufacturing service providers, supplying printed circuit boards and other components to companies such as IBM, HP, Dell, and Cisco. Apple in innovative computer products, Sun Microsystems in computer workstations, and EMC in information management and storage established distinctive niches in the information technology sector. Oracle is the leader in database management software, while Computer Sciences (CS) and SAIC, both of which count the U.S. federal government, including the Department of Defense, as main clients, line up behind "Old Economy" EDS in providing information technology services. Finally, Amazon.com, Google, and Yahoo! are, along with "Old Economy" IAC, in a newly created Fortune industry classification, Internet services and retailing, and it was the revenues that each generated in 2005 that propelled it onto the top 20 New Economy list for the first time.

Old Economy Employment Relations in the 1980s

In the post–World War II decades, many Americans, both white-collar and blue-collar, the vast majority of whom were white males, enjoyed substantial employment security working for the large-scale corporations that dominated the U.S. economy. From the 1970s, however, this employment security weakened. Corporations that in the conglomerate movement of the 1960s acquired too many companies in too many unrelated lines of business became impossible to manage strategically and overextended financially, and they began to unravel. Also in the 1970s, U.S. corporations faced new competitive challenges from the Japanese in the very industries—cars, consumer electronics, business machines, machine tools, semiconductors, and steel—in which the United States had been dominant. Then, in the 1980s, U.S. corporate executives embraced the ideology of "maximizing shareholder value" to legitimize downsizing of their labor forces and increasing distributions to shareholders in the form of not only dividends but also stock buybacks (Lazonick and O'Sullivan 2000; Lazonick 2007b). Among the prime beneficiaries of this "downsize-and-distribute" regime were the top corporate executives themselves, who over the course of the 1980s and 1990s saw their remuneration explode, mainly because of the gains on the bountiful stock options that their boards of directors bestowed upon them.

Yet, amid the restructuring of the 1980s and the employment insecurity that it brought with it, most of the top 20 Old Economy ICT companies listed in Table 2 still held out the expectation to their employees of career employment with one company and, in fact, offered a high degree of employment security. Table 4 shows the types of pensions that these 20 companies had in 1985, as well as estimates of their union membership in both the last half of the 1980s and in 2005. Comcast is the only company on the list that that did not have a DB plan in 1985. It inherited a DB plan when it acquired AT&T Broadband in 2002—an acquisition that made it one of the top 20 Old Economy ICT companies. Note that both Qwest Communications and IAC/InterActiveCorp were founded in the 1990s, but had their origins in Old Economy companies that in 1985 had DB plans. Qwest, moreover, became a major ICT company in 2000 as a result of its acquisition of the former Bell operating company US West, with a highly unionized labor force and DB pension plan.

In the mid-1980s, amid widespread downsizing, two Old Economy ICT companies that were among the top 20 in 2005 stood out as having "no-layoff" policies. They were IBM and HP—the two largest ICT companies by revenues in 2005. In 1985, with revenues of $50.1 billion and more than 405,000 employees, IBM was by far the largest ICT company, ranked 5th on the Fortune 500 list; the next largest ICT company in revenues was AT&T. In 1985 HP had revenues of $6.5 billion, placing it at number 58 on the Fortune 500 list. HP employed over 90,000 people at that time.

Neither IBM nor HP had unions. Indeed, as Table 4 shows, among the top 20 Old Economy ICT companies in 2005, the only ones with a substantial union presence were those that had evolved out of the Bell System: Verizon, AT&T Inc., BellSouth, and Qwest Communications. Before its breakup at the beginning of 1984, the Bell System, with about one million employees, had about 675,000 union workers, including about 525,000 in the Communications Workers of America (CWA), 100,000 in the International Brotherhood of Electrical Workers (IBEW), and 50,000 in the Telecommunications International Union.

The breakup of the Bell System on January 1, 1984, created a much smaller AT&T, focused on long-distance telephony and supported in-house by the research capabilities of Bell Labs and the manufacturing capabilities of Western Electric. AT&T Technologies, of which Western Electric formed the core, accounted for well over 60% of AT&T's employees. In 1984 AT&T and the seven regional Bell operating companies had $118 billion in revenues and 933,000 employees.

Between 1985 and 2005, unions also played a role in two other companies in Table 2. One was Lucent Technologies, in which unions represented 36% of 124,000 worldwide employees and 46% of 98,000 U.S. employees when the company was spun off from AT&T in 1996, but only 10% of 30,500 worldwide employees and 16% of 18,500 U.S. employees in 2005. Adding in Lucent's major spinoffs in calculating these percentages, the 6,610 union members at Lucent, Avaya, and Agere in 2005 represented only 12% of the 55,800 worldwide employees for the three companies combined and 16% of the 40,640 U.S. employees.

The other important unionized ICT company in 1985 was Xerox. The Amalgamated Clothing and Textile Workers Union (ACTWU) organized only about 5% of Xerox's total labor force in 1985. About 60% of the union members, however, belonged to Local 14A, working at Xerox's main manufacturing facility in Webster, New York. In the 1980s and 1990s, employment relations between Local 14A and Xerox provided a textbook case of union–management cooperation in finding ways to improve productivity while collectively bargained contracts provided workers with employment guarantees. The experience at Xerox stands in sharp contrast to that at NCR, where in the 1970s the company deliberately decimated a 16,000-member union based in Dayton, Ohio, by locating work on its new electronic business machines in other parts of the United States.

TABLE 4

1985 Retirement Plans of 2005 Top 20 Old Economy ICT Companies

	Employees, 1985	U.S. union members, 1985	Employees, 2005	U.S. union members, 2005[1]	Retirement plan(s), 1985[2]
IBM	405,535	None	329,373	None	DB (92%); 401(k) (8%), 30% to 5%[3]
Hewlett-Packard	84,000	None	150,000	None	Profit-sharing DB (69%); supplemental DB (19%); 401(k) (12%), 33% to 12%
Verizon Communications[4]	79,285	See footnote 3	217,000	CWA 68,492; IBEW 65,600; (99,800)	*Bell Atlantic, NYNEX:* Bell System DB
AT&T Inc.[4]	71,400	See footnote 3	189,950	CWA 110,723; IBEW 12,250	*SBC, Ameritech, PacTel. AT&T Corp.:* Bell System DB
Motorola	90,200	None	69,000	None	DB (30%); contributory profit-sharing (70%)
Sprint Nextel	27,465	*GTE and United Telecom:* CWA, IBEW; *Southern Pacific:* railroad unions	79,900	CWA 3,500; IBEW 3,500; (7,000)	*GTE-Sprint:* for salaried employees, 401(k), 50% to 6%, with extra 25% match depending on performance of company stock, with match in company stock; *GTE, Southern Pacific, United Telecommunications:* DB
Comcast	1,318	None	80,000	CWA (4,000)	None[5]
Bellsouth[4]	92,500	See footnote 3	63,066	CWA 51,005	Bell System DB
Electronic Data Systems	40,000	None	117,000	None	General Motors division, 1984–96: DB
Xerox	102,396	ACWTU 5,500	55,200	UNITE HERE 2,325 IAM and IUOE 225	Profit sharing; supplemental DB
Qwest Communications[4]	70,202	See footnote 3	39,348	CWA 23,642; (23,000)	*Southern Pacific Railroad*[6]: DB
Texas Instruments	77,872	None	35,207	None	DB (59%); profit-sharing (37%); 401(k) (4%)
Directv Group	74,000	*Hughes Aircraft:* IAM 1,300; ESTU 12,000	9,200	None	*GM Hughes Electronics* as of 12/31/1985: DB[7]
First Data	NA	None	33,000	CWA (1,100)	DB
Alltel	5,590	CWA, IBEW	21,373	CWA (1,387)	DB
Lucent Technologies[4]	NA	See footnote 3	30,500	CWA 2,708 (3,000)	*AT&T Technologies, 1984–96:* Bell System DB

Cox Communications	NA	None		22,530	None	DB; TRASOP[8]; PAYSOP[9], 401(k), 25% to 5% (taken private in 2005)
IAC/InterActiveCorp	NA	None		28,000	None	*Paramount, MCA:* DB
NCR	62,000	UAW		28,200	None	DB (86%); profit-sharing (4%); 401(k) (11%) 25% to 6%; PAYSOP[9]
Freescale Semiconductor	NA	NA		22,700	None	*Motorola:* DB: contributory profit-sharing

DB: traditional noncontributory defined benefit plan; ACTWU: Amalgamated Clothing and Textile Workers Union; CWA: Communication Workers of America; ESTU: Electronic and Space Technicians Union; IAM: International Association of Machinists and Aerospace Workers; IBEW: International Brotherhood of Electrical Workers; IUOE: International Union of Operating Engineers; UAW: United Auto Workers; NA: not applicable.

[1] Figure in parentheses is the number of union members given in each company's 2005 annual report. CWA figures for 2005 are from the union's membership development report for December 2005. Given that in 2005 Cingular was 60% owned by AT&T Inc. and 40% by BellSouth, the CWA figures of each of these parent companies include these proportions of Cingular's 21,463 CWA members in 2005. Note also that the 2005 union membership for AT&T Corp. includes 4,897 employees at the formerly independent Southern New England Telephone Company (SNET), which was acquired by SBC in 1998.

[2] For IBM, HP, and Motorola, the italicized percentages in parentheses following different types of retirement plans represent assets in those plans as a proportion of total assets in 1986 ("Profiles" 1987); for TI, percentages are for 1987 (Leary 1988); for NCR, percentages are for 1988 ("Profiles" 1989).

[3] The "30% to 5%" format means that the company matches 30% of employee contributions to 5% of the employee's annual salary or wages.

[4] With the breakup of the Bell System on January 1, 1984, AT&T Inc. and the seven RBOCS all had identical noncontributory DB plans with benefits based on years of service and average career earnings for managerial employees and a flat benefit per year for union employees. At the end of 1986 these DB plans represented 85% to 90% of the total retirement assets held by these companies.

[5] Comcast became an "Old Economy" company when it acquired AT&T Broadband (with a Bell System DB plan) in 2002.

[6] Denver-based Qwest Communications emerged in 1995 when privately owned Southern Pacific Telecommunications (SPT), a 1989 spinoff from the Southern Pacific Railroad, was renamed after acquiring Dallas-based Qwest Communications in 1995. In 1985 the Santa Fe Southern Pacific Railroad had a DB plan for all employees.

[7] For salaried employees, years of service plus salary history for managers; for hourly employees, flat amount per year of service plus supplement for retirement with 30 years of service before retirement age.

[8] Tax Reduction Act Employee Stock Ownership Plan.

[9] Payroll Based Employee Stock Ownership Plan.

Sources: Bureau of Labor Statistics Collective Bargaining Agreements File, http://www.bls.gov/cba/cbaindex.htm; company 10-K filings; Compustat subscription database; Xerox Corporation 2006; information supplied by Communications Works of America (courtesy of Debbie Goldman and Tony Daley, to whom I am grateful).

For the U.S. economy as a whole, the 1980s and 1990s was an era of downsizing the labor force, one in which unions did not do well. Yet "downsizing" only attracted national media attention in the winter of 1996, after AT&T announced that it would cut its labor force by 40,000 over the next three years, targeting 24,000 salaried and 16,000 hourly employees. In March 1996 the *New York Times* ran a seven-part front-page series called "the downsizing of America," subsequently released as a paperback. By the spring of 1996, however, public interest in corporate downsizing suddenly disappeared. Americans had discovered the "New Economy."

The Rise of NEBM and the Transformation of ICT Employment Relations

When in August 1981 IBM launched its Personal Computer, Microsoft retained the right to sell the operating system and Intel the microprocessor to other companies. IBM's strategy for entering the microcomputer market consolidated and reinforced the vertically specialized structure of the industry in line with what can be viewed as the Silicon Valley model. The subsequent domination by Intel and Microsoft of their product markets created an immense barrier to entry to actual and potential competitors who would directly confront the New Economy giants while at the same time, by defining the "open access" standards for the microcomputer industry, presented countless opportunities for new entrants to develop specialized niche products that conformed to the "Wintel" architecture.

Vertical specialization, however, did not stop there. A number of Silicon Valley design-oriented chip companies that entered the industry in the 1980s, and even more so in the 1990s, did so without investing in the manufacture of semiconductors. The Taiwanese in particular took advantage of the opportunity, as Taiwan Semiconductor Manufacturing Company (TSMC) and United Microelectronics Corporation (UMC) became the largest semiconductor contract manufacturers in the world. If a layer of vertical specialization emerged in the manufacture of chips, so too did it emerge in the assembly of chip sets, printed circuit boards, and, increasingly, even finished products. In the 1980s and early 1990s contract manufacturers, which became known in the industry as electronic manufacturing service (EMS) providers, operated as job shops that took on extra work from integrated original equipment manufacturers (OEMs) in periods of peak demand. Then during the mid-1990s a few Old Economy companies—in particular IBM, Hewlett-Packard, and the Swedish company Ericsson—took the lead in selling existing plants to EMS providers. Meanwhile, the newest New Economy companies, such as Cisco and 3Com, that produced networking equipment out-sourced all of their manufacturing from the outset.

In the Internet boom of the late 1990s, the demand for EMS capac-ity soared. New Economy companies that did no manufacturing relied on EMS providers for not only assembly but also an increasing array of services, including testing, design, documentation, and shipping. From 1993 to 2003, the largest EMS provider, Flextronics, increased its rev-enues from $93 million to $13.4 billion and its employment from 2,000 to 95,000, while the second largest EMS provider, Solectron, increased its revenues from $836 million to $11.0 billion and its employment from 4,500 to 66,000.

These changes in the organization of industry had far-reaching impli-cations for the employment of labor. Vertical specialization and the startup phenomenon depended upon, and over time reinforced, the existence of industrywide standards as distinct from the in-house propri-etary standards that had characterized OEBM, with its vertically inte-grated enterprises such as AT&T/Western Electric and IBM. The existence of industrywide standards facilitated the movement of high-tech labor from one company to another over the course of a career. Indeed, while New Economy companies did not like to see valued employees leave via this highly mobile labor market, they nevertheless valued the industrywide experience, including knowledge of the latest developments in technology and product markets, that new employees often brought with them. The regional concentration of ICT firms in Silicon Valley further facilitated this movement of labor from one firm to another—one could change employment without moving house—while the networks created by both this concentration and interfirm mobility generated new learning to which participants in the regional labor force had privileged access relative to high-tech labor outside the region.

The interfirm mobility of high-tech labor led New Economy firms to use stock options to attract and retain employees. Stock options are granted to an employee as part of a compensation package that includes a salary based on one's hierarchical and functional position. Over the past two decades both academics and journalists have focused most of their attention on the excesses of *executive* stock options. Yet the vast majority of employee stock options in the United States have been issued to *non-executive* personnel as part of what have become known as "broad-based" programs. The widespread use of stock options for non-executive employees originated in the 1960s and 1970s, when Silicon Valley high-tech startups began to offer options to scientists, engineers, and managerial personnel at all levels, and not just to top executives, to lure them away from employment at established companies. Old Economy corporations could credibly promise secure employment to these employees with superior compensation taking the form of pay increases tied to promotion up the managerial hierarchy. Startups, their futures highly uncertain, could not realistically hold out the expectation of employment security. They could, however, use stock options, with exercise prices often at pennies a share, to attract educated and experienced personnel. If the startup did an IPO or was sold to an already listed company, these stock options could become very valuable.

The high concentration of startups in Silicon Valley meant that increasingly in the 1980s new ventures not only used stock options to induce high-tech labor to leave secure employment with established corporations, but also competed among themselves for personnel, with an emphasis on stock options in their compensation packages. Besides attracting "talent" and giving them a stake in getting the startup to an IPO, ample stock options could substitute to some extent for cash salaries. In their early years, some Silicon Valley startups, including Intel, Oracle, Sun Microsystems, and Cisco Systems, granted stock options to substantial proportions of their employees, and during the 1980s and 1990s they maintained, and in some cases enlarged, their broad-based stock option programs even as they grew to employ tens of thousands of people. Coming into the 1990s, non-executive employee stock options remained predominantly a Silicon Valley phenomenon, and even in the mid-2000s they are more prevalent among high-tech companies in Silicon Valley than in any other part of the United States, much less the world.

The growing importance of stock options to attract new employees placed pressure on high-tech firms to look to this form of compensation to perform a retention function as well. For this reason, the practice evolved in New Economy firms of making *annual* option grants. Without creating the Old Economy expectation among employees of "lifelong careers" with the company, the perpetual existence of unvested options functioned as a tangible retention mechanism. Indeed, the amount of options that an individual employee could expect to receive became tied to his or her position in the firm's hierarchical and functional division of labor so that the retention function of stock options became integrally related to the employee's career progress within the business organization.

In the Internet boom, characterized as it was by a highly speculative stock market, the payoffs from stock options could be enormous. Table 5 shows estimates of the average gains per employee (excluding the five highest paid executives, whose actual gains companies must report) from exercising options for the six companies from the New Economy top 20 list as well as top two companies, IBM and HP, from the Old Economy list. IBM and HP were exemplary companies in providing employment security in

TABLE 5

Average Gains per Employee (Excluding the CEO and Four Other Highest Paid
Executives) from the Exercise of Stock Options for Selected ICT Companies,
1995–2005

	Cisco ($)	Dell ($)	HP ($)	IBM ($)	Intel ($)	Microsoft ($)	Oracle ($)	Sun ($)
1995	60,894	3,833	2,362	671	1,116	51,829	NA	2,468
1996	93,399	7,194	2,213	1,823	0[1]	79,022	7,367	7,992
1997	85,159	11,219	3,156	3,615	5,044	154,196	6,588	7,626
1998	92,947	40,547	2,676	4,066	11,596	238,377	5,019	10,799
1999	193,476	126,639	6,613	5,790	8,380	369,693	5,650	27,477
2000	290,870	84,818	17,987	4,200	17,375	449,142	37,214	60,431
2001	105,865	76,122	1,498	4,011	5,410	143,772	88,723	46,763
2002	13,596	33,167	838	1,195	8,654	95,310	6,950	4,550
2003	8,917	10,739	936	1,553	9,007	80,283	6,193	1,182
2004	32,804	12,216	638	1,842	8,232	50,690	7,908	1,960
2005	24,432	11,297	1,816	1,256	6,549	14,500	6,926	1,187

[1] When the $123 million that Intel's top 5 executives gained from stock options in 1996 is
subtracted from the total estimated gains for all company employees, the average gains per
employee for the other 45,047 employees is -$278. Since no one would exercise a stock
option with the market price below its exercise price, I set average earnings per executive
to zero. Note, however, that had I used the highest monthly market price for these estimates, the average gains per executive in 1996 would have been $556.
NA: not available (Oracle did not report a weighted average exercise price for 1995).
Source: Company 10-K filings.

the Old Economy. As I discuss in the next section of this paper, however, in
the 1990s and 2000s IBM and HP made the transition to NEBM.

While the gains from stock options were always highly uncertain,
employees at these New Economy companies could view them as a way
to accumulate capital to fund their retirements, thus reducing or eliminating the need for a retirement savings plan. Insofar as 17 New Economy companies on the top 20 list have offered employees a pension plan
alongside stock options, it has been portable, reflecting the labor market
reality of interfirm mobility. As Table 6 shows, 15 of these companies
have had only DC plans for U.S. employees throughout their histories.
Two others—EMC and Sanmina—found themselves with DB plans
when they acquired other companies, but on completion of the acquisi-
tions, they immediately froze those plans. The New Economy business
model, against which Old Economy ICT companies had increasingly to
compete in the 1990s, was one in which DC pensions had become the
overwhelming norm.

The Transition of Old Economy ICT Companies to NEBM

Of the top 20 New Economy companies, only two—Intel, founded in
1968, and Computer Sciences, founded in 1959 (the oldest company on

TABLE 6
U.S. Pension Plans in 2005 of Top 20 New Economy Companies

Company	Year founded	U.S. pension plan	Company 401(k) match	
			% of employee contribution that company matches	Maximum % of employee compensation matched
Dell	1984	401(k)	100	4
Microsoft	1975	401(k)	50	3
Intel[1]	1968	DB		
Cisco Systems	1984	401(k)	50	3
Computer Sciences[2]	1959	DB		
Apple[3]	1977	401(k)	50–100	6
Oracle	1977	401(k)		6
Sanmina-SCI[4]	1980	401(k)		Discretionary
Sun Microsystems	1982	401(k)		4
Solectron	1977	401(k)		Discretionary
EMC[5]	1979	401(k)	Limited to $750/quarter	6
Amazon.com	1994	401(k)	From 2003, using stock	Discretionary
SAIC	1969	ESOP		
EchoStar	1993	401(k)	50, up to $1,000	Plus discretionary contribution
Jabil Circuit	1966	401(k)		Discretionary
Applied Materials[6]	1967	401(k)	"A percentage"	
Google	1998	401(k)	Up to $2,200	
AMD[7]	1969	401(k)	50	6
Qualcomm	1985	401(k)	"A portion"	
Yahoo![8]	1995	401(k)	25	

Most of these companies do not provide postretirement medical benefits. In 1998 Intel began offering such benefits in the form of dollar credits based on years of service. In 1999 Applied Materials began providing medical and vision benefits to retirees who are at least age 55 and whose age plus years of service is at least 65 at date of retirement, and coverage for a spouse or domestic partner, until they become eligible for Medicare. Computer Sciences provided medical benefits and life insurance for employees until 1992.

[1] Includes profit-sharing retirement plan begun in 1979.

[2] In 1988 replaced a DB plan with a DC plan for its principle subsidiary, Associated Credit Services.

[3] Percentage contribution depends on years of service.

[4] SCI had a noncontributory DB plan that was frozen when Sanmina acquired SCI in 2000. Unvested SCI employees were credited with years of service until vesting occurred but no additional benefits.

[5] Includes profit-sharing plan from 1983, supplemented by 401(k) from 1991. In 1999 EMC acquired Data General and then froze its DB plan.

[6] Company match vests 20% after the second year to fully vest in 6 years.

[7] Company match was 50% of employee contribution to a maximum of 3% of compensation from 1992 to 1999.

[8] Employer contribution vests 33% per year of employment.

the list)—have traditional noncontributory DB pension plans. In the manner of its Silicon Valley neighbor, Hewlett-Packard, Intel's DB plan was originally meant to supplement its deferred profit-sharing scheme. One company on the list, SAIC, founded in 1969, has been one of the largest employee-owned companies in the United States. In October 2006 SAIC did a $1.1 billion IPO that enables its employees to sell their shares, which serve as their pensions, on the open market rather than to the company.

In the mid-1980s all but one of the companies (or their predecessors) that would be in the top 20 Old Economy ICT companies in 2005 had traditional DB plans (see Table 4 above). The one exception was Comcast, which would acquire DB plans for union workers along with its purchase of AT&T Broadband in 2002. IAC was not in existence in 1985, but its predecessors, Paramount and MCA, had DB plans. In the 1990s and 2000s, however, these Old Economy companies found themselves competing against New Economy companies, the vast majority of which never contemplated the adoption of DB pension plans.

How did the Old Economy companies respond? In 2005, as can be seen in Table 7, 12 companies—HP, Verizon, AT&T Inc. (SBC before it acquired the AT&T Corp.), Motorola, Comcast, Xerox, Qwest, TI, Directv, Lucent, Cox, and NCR—still had DB plans for some or all of their existing employees, as distinct from new hires. But at only three of these companies—Motorola, Xerox, and Cox—did all existing employees have the option to be on a DB plan. At four others—HP, Qwest, TI, and Lucent—only employees with a certain level of seniority or who had been employed with the company before a stipulated date—prior to December 1997 in the case of TI—remained eligible for DB plans. At Qwest, however, the cutoff date for a DB plan applied only to salaried employees; all union members at Qwest, numbering over 23,000, had a DB plan. At NCR, "certain hourly employees" (quote taken from the NCR 2005 Annual Report, p. 43)—that is, union members—were eligible for DB pensions, but given that the company had become non-union, NCR essentially offered all employees a 401(k). At Directv, the information provided in the 10-K filings only states vaguely that "many of our employees" have DB pensions (quote taken from Directv 2005 10-K, p. 90), with the alternative for those who do not being a 401(k). At two others—Verizon and Comcast—only union members had DB plans, while at AT&T Inc., former SBC employees, both salaried and union, had a DB plan, while former AT&T Corp. employees, also both salaried and union, had a cash balance (CB) plan.

In the 1990s some ICT companies with DB plans made the transition to CB plans because in the new world of industrywide technology standards and interfirm mobility of high-tech personnel, they wanted to be

TABLE 7

Retirement Plans of Top 20 Old Economy ICT Companies, 1985 and 2005–2006

Company	Retirement plans in place, 1985	Retirement plan(s) in place, 2005–2006
IBM	DB	1/1/2005: new hires not eligible for PPA, only 401(k), enhanced to 100% to 6%, still 50% to 6% for previous employees
Hewlett-Packard	Deferred profit-sharing DB plan plus supplemental DB; 401(k), 33% to 12%	1/1/2006: no DB pension or medical benefits to new U.S. hires; freeze on pension and medical benefits for employees without sufficient seniority; increase 401(k) match to 6%
Verizon Communications	*Bell Atlantic, NYNEX:* Bell System DB	1/1/2006: new management hires not eligible for pension benefits; 6/30/2006: salaried no longer earn pension benefits or service toward company retiree medical subsidy; salaried with less than 13.5 years of service not eligible for company-subsidized retiree healthcare or retiree life insurance benefits; 7/1/2006: salaried employees receive increased company match on 401(k)
AT&T Inc.	*SBC, Ameritech, Pacific Telesis, AT&T Corp.:* Bell System DB; DC, 100% to 6%, for salaried	2005: SBC acquires AT&T Corp., and renames itself AT&T Inc; SBC changes from CB to DB for salaried; AT&T Inc. changed back to DB for 55,000 salaried; AT&T Corp. keeps CB for both salaried and union workers (in 1998 CWA had agreed to a CB favorable to members of all ages)
Motorola	DB and contributory 401(k) profit-sharing plan	1/1/2005: DB plan closed to new hires; profit-sharing component of 401(k) terminated; new hires get 401(k) match of 67% to 6% compared with 50% to 6% for those hired previously
Sprint Nextel	*GTE-Sprint:* for salaried, 401(k), 50% to 6%, with extra 25% match depending on performance of company's stock, with match in company stock; GTE, Southern Pacific, United Telecommunications: DB	12/31/2005: in wake of the merger with Nextel, Sprint DB plan amended to freeze benefit accruals for current employees, except those designated to work for Embarq (local telephone spinoff from Sprint) and Sprint employees who were unvested prior to August 2005—they will be permitted to accumulate the five years of service credit needed for vesting, but pension accruals frozen after that. 1/1/2006: only Sprint Nextel pension plan is 401(k), 100% to 5%, no longer paid in company stock
Comcast	None	AT&T Broadband DB for "some union groups" (12/31/2005: Comcast had 4,000 union members); 401(k), "we match a percentage of the employees' contributions up to certain limits"
Bellsouth	Bell System DB	CB (in 1998 CWA agreed to a CB favorable to members of all ages); 401(k)
Electronic Data Systems	DB	CB; 401(k)

48

Company	Plan Description
Xerox	DB with deferred profit-sharing component	Choice of DB or CB (in place since 1990); 401(k) 6% match 03/14/2005: only 401(k) for new union hires
Qwest Communications	*Southern Pacific Railroad*: DB	DB for all union and salaried with 20 years of service by 12/31/2000 or service pension eligible by 12/31/2003; CB for all others, based on 3% of pay while employed plus investment return
Texas Instruments	DB; deferred profit-sharing plan, invested in company stock	For employees as of 11/1997 who declined enhanced DC plan: DB plus DC, 50% to 4%. For employees as of 11/30/1997 who chose enhanced DC plan and employees hired 12/1/1997 through 12/31/2003: DC, 2% of salary plus 100% to 4%. For employees hired after 12/31/2003: DC, 100% to 4%
Directv Group	*GM Hughes Electronics* as of 12/31/1985: DB	DB plans for "many of our employees"; 401(k)
First Data	DB	DC
Alltel	DB	Noncontributory profit-sharing DC plan and 401(k); DB plan frozen: no further accruals for salaried employees if under 40 as of 12/31/2005, or if 40 years old or more and with at least 2 years of service as of 12/31/2010
Lucent Technologies	*AT&T Technologies*: Bell System DB; DC, 100% to 6%, for salaried	CB for new hires; DB for employees on DB plan prior to 1/1/1999
Cox Communications	DB; TRASOP; PAYSOP; 401(k), 25% to 5%	DB, 401(k); 2005: Cox went private
IAC/ InterActiveCorp	*Paramount, MCA*: DB	401(k)
NCR	DB; deferred profit-sharing plan; 401(k) 25% to 6%; PAYSOP	2005: DC plan for all new hires; certain hourly employees will still get DB based on years of service.
Freescale Semiconductor	*Motorola*: DB	401(k)

The term "salaried" is used to mean managerial employees, non-bargaining unit employees, non-union employees, unrepresented employees, and the like.

Company names in italics listed in the second column are antecedent companies of the current companies listed in the first column.

DB: defined benefit pension plan; CB: cash balance pension plan; DC: defined contribution pension plan.

49

able to attract younger workers with education and experience in new technologies, and, by the same token, they found it less beneficial to retain older workers who had the Old Economy expectation of "lifelong" employment. CB plans have two features that are attractive to younger workers. First, they can be structured to increase the accrual of pension benefits to younger employees, although if the company's total pension costs are to remain the same, this increase will be at the expense of the company's older employees. Second, CB plans are "portable," meaning that workers are not penalized by loss of vesting rights when they change employers, while at the same time these plans are defined benefit, with the company guaranteeing a specified rate of return on the accrued cash balances of the employee. At the end of 2004, four companies—IBM, BellSouth, EDS, and Xerox—offered all existing employees CB, along with 401(k) plans, although Xerox employees could also opt for a DB plan.

Finally, five companies—Sprint Nextel, First Data, Alltel, IAC, and Freescale (recently spun off from Motorola)—offered all employees, both existing employees and new hires, a 401(k), with varying company matches. When it came to new hires, however, 10 of the companies—the five just mentioned plus IBM, HP, Motorola, TI, and NCR—offered only 401(k) plans. In addition, at Xerox, under the collective bargaining agreement concluded in March 2005, new union employees can only expect a 401(k). TI had instituted this "new hires" rule toward the end of 1997, while NCR had made the change in 2004, IBM and Motorola at the beginning of 2005, and HP at the beginning of 2006. Directv probably had a 401(k) for most, if not all, of its new hires. At both Verizon and Comcast, new union employees continued to get a DB plan, but salaried employees got only a 401(k). By 2005–2006, therefore, the only retirement plan that 13 of the 20 Old Economy companies offered salaried employees was a 401(k). Only two companies—AT&T Inc. and Cox—offered a DB plan to all new hires in 2005. Three companies—BellSouth, EDS, and Lucent—offered all new hires a CB plan, while Qwest offered new salaried employees a CB plan.

In the 1990s and 2000s, the transitions from traditional DB to CB to DC plans in these Old Economy ICT companies were integrally related to transformations in their employment relations that reflected the adoption of some or all of the elements of NEBM. The cases of IBM and HP show how the leading ICT companies have made the transition to NEBM and consolidated it as the dominant business model. In contrast, the cases of Xerox and the companies that evolved out of the former Bell System—Verizon, AT&T Inc., BellSouth, Qwest, and Lucent—show how in the 2000s unions remain the last bulwarks against the erosion of traditional DB pension plans. Exceptions that prove the rule are the cases of AT&T

Corp. and BellSouth, where, in the 1998 contracts, the CWA agreed to CB plans that preserved or enhanced the cash benefits that would accrue to members of all ages while giving their members the added benefit of pension portability. In addition, in 2005, in the process of acquiring AT&T Corp., SBC became unique among major U.S. corporations in changing its salaried employees back from a CB to a DB plan.

IBM

IBM's organizational transformation during the 1990s and 2000s has played a major role in ensuring the dominance of NEBM in the U.S. ICT industries. IBM explicitly changed its pension system because it wanted to attract and retain younger employees who did not have the expectation of spending a career with one company. Changes in the IBM pension system from a DB plan to a 401(k) via a CB plan represented important elements in a radical transformation of the company's employment relations, and they set the trend for other high-tech firms.

IBM's decision to begin this transformation in the early 1990s was a direct result of the business model that it had adopted in making its rapid and successful entry into the microcomputer industry in the first half of the 1980s. The IBM PC, as we have seen, consolidated the vertical structure of the microcomputer industry by outsourcing the microprocessor to Intel and the operating system to Microsoft. In the process IBM played a major role in setting industrywide standards that favored cross-licensing of technology and strategic alliances rather than in-house proprietary research.

As a result, the retention of older employees with career-long experience with the company became much less valuable, and the recruitment of younger employees with experience at other companies much more valuable, to the company. In the early 1990s IBM took advantage of a slowdown in the computer industry to rid itself of its system of lifelong employment. From the end of 1990 to the end of 1994, IBM—a company that had entered this period renowned for its lifelong employment policies—reduced its employment level by 153,977 people, or 41.2% of its 1990 labor force.

Much of IBM's downsizing in the early 1990s was accomplished by making it attractive for employees to accept voluntary severance packages, including early retirement at age 55. Toward this end IBM had in 1989 decreased the vesting period for retirement benefits to the completion of five years of service from the previous 10. Of IBM's losses of $15.9 billion for 1991 to 1993—including the $8.1 billion deficit in 1993 that at the time was the largest annual loss in U.S. corporate history—$13.7 billion were because of workforce-related restructuring charges (including the cost of employee separations and relocations). This loss of $13.7 billion in effect represented the cost to the company of ridding itself of its once-hallowed tradition of lifelong employment.

During the 1990s IBM pursued a strategy of shifting its business out of hardware into services. These changes in product market strategy were accompanied by significant reductions in R&D expenditures as a percentage of sales, reflecting the company's much greater orientation toward product development rather than basic research. Integral to this strategy has been extensive patenting for the purposes of cross-licensing and IP (intellectual property) revenue generation. Cross-licensing has enabled IBM to gain access to technology developed by other companies rather than relying on in-house R&D. During the 1990s, as IBM scaled back its rate of R&D expenditure, it ramped up its patenting activity.

During the last half of the 1990s, while IBM was using its intellectual property as the basis for multibillion dollar OEM partnerships with other ICT companies such as 3Com, Acer, Cisco, Dell, and EMC, it was also taking the lead among Old Economy companies in outsourcing routine production to EMS providers. IBM's new emphasis on cross-licensing and technology partnerships as well as the vertically specialized structure of the ICT industry that IBM itself had played a major role in creating rendered the use of a fluid and flexible high-tech labor force much more desirable and possible for the company than had been the case in the 1980s. Given the absence of in-house investments in proprietary systems, the organizational and technological rationales for Old Economy lifelong employment no longer existed at IBM. The company now favored younger employees whose higher education was up to date and who had work experience at other companies within the ICT industries over older employees who had spent their careers with IBM.

Changes in IBM's retirement plans were direct reflections of these changes in employment relations. In 1989 IBM changed the vesting period for pension benefits from 10 years of service to five. Then in 1991 the company created a hybrid "Personal Retirement Plan" that included a CB feature to enable departing employees to take more pension benefits with them. In 1995, with the massive downsizing having been completed, IBM implemented a "Pension Equity Plan" (PEP) that placed a CB choice front and center in the retirement plans that the company offered.

In contrast to most CB plans, IBM's PEP offered a relatively even accrual of benefits by age that was structured to favor midcareer employees. Those employees who were close to retirement would get the higher pension benefit from the preexisting DB plan or the new PEP. Donald Sauvigne, IBM director of retirement programs, explained that in adopting PEP, "[w]e were responding to the different makeup of the workforce. The reality is that fewer people will be spending their entire careers at IBM" (Geisel 1995:11).

That labor market logic was taken a major step further in 1999, when IBM announced that it was adopting a new CB plan, dubbed a "Personal Pension Account," targeted at attracting younger, as distinct from midcareer, employees. IBM did permit some 30,000 employees who were within five years of the 30 years of service required for retirement to remain on the traditional plan, and the company also provided extra contributions to the CB plans of other employees ages 45 or older. It was estimated, nevertheless, that these midcareer employees could lose 30% to 50% of their expected pensions. Political intervention convinced IBM to permit those employees who were at least 40 years old and had at least 10 years of service—some 65,000 people—to remain on the traditional plan.

In December 2004 it became clear that the adoption of the CB plan was a first step in the eventual elimination of DB plans of any kind, as IBM announced that new employees would not be eligible for the CB plan. Instead the company would offer them a 401(k). Responding to the 2006 pension resolution at the annual shareholders' meeting, IBM's management argued the following:

> After analyzing its own workforce and the practices of the companies against which it competes for employee talent, IBM found that over 50% of its U.S. employees have 5 years or less with the Company, validating the Company's decision to change its pension plan in 1995. The Company also found that approximately 75% of its competitors did not offer a pension plan. As a result of these studies, the Company concluded that its pension plans were not delivering the kind of benefit this workforce valued, and effective in January 2005 moved forward with a new 401(k) plan for new employees, under which they would receive a new, enhanced benefit in lieu of traditional pension benefits, including an increased Company match on employee investments—from 50% to 100% of the first 6% of eligible pay. . . . These changes continue IBM's global strategy of shifting the future focus of retirement benefits toward the more predictable cost structure of defined contribution plans. (Quote taken from the *IBM 2006 Proxy Statement*, p. 28)

Hewlett-Packard

Unlike IBM, which, as we have seen, deliberately and dramatically made the transition to New Economy employment relations in the first half of the 1990s, HP sustained its commitment to employment security through the 1990s. That this commitment lasted as long as it did is testimony to the legacy of "The HP Way," a corporate philosophy whose life at the company was probably prolonged by the publication of founder David Packard's best-selling autobiography in 1995.

By the mid-2000s, however, HP, with 150,000 employees, had become what Packard would have called a "hire-and-fire" company (see Wong 2006). As was the case at IBM, HP's transition to NEBM, including the employment of a more mobile, highly educated, and flexible labor force, was encouraged by a shift from proprietary to industry technology standards that had begun to take root in the early 1980s. In the 1980s and 1990s HP found itself at the center of the microelectronics revolution not only because of its location in Palo Alto, California, where it acquired iconic status as the pioneering Silicon Valley firm, but also because of a business strategy that focused increasingly on consumer-oriented computer products and peripherals.

In the last half of the 1970s, when proprietary standards prevailed, HP derived 43% of its sales and 61% of its profits from the electronic test and measurement (ETM) business on which the engineering company had been founded. Another 44% of its sales and 45% of its profits came from electronic data products (EDP), a business that had been launched in 1966 when HP developed its first computer. In 1984, with the PC revolution in full swing, HP made a strategic decision to manufacture its computer products to comply with the open standards that had emerged in the IT industry. In building its competitive strategy around open systems, HP acquired a greater interest in employing a labor force with industrywide experience, as distinct from one with experience in proprietary technology.

In 1999 HP spun off its non-computer-related businesses—test and measurement instrumentation, medical electronic equipment, and analytical instrumentation—as Agilent Technologies. Combined these businesses had $6.5 billion of HP's $47.1 billion 1998 revenues and 43,000 of HP's 125,000 employees. As a result, without Agilent, sales per employee (in 1999 dollars) shot up 30%, from $386,000 in 1998 to $502,000 in 1999. In 1999 "imaging and printing systems" represented 43% of HP's revenues and 63% of earnings from operations, and "computing systems" 40% of revenues and 27% of earnings from operations. The only other important business segment (but one that HP was eager to expand) was IT services, with 15% of revenues and 13% of earnings from operations.

HP's dependence on printers and ink refills would have become even greater in the 2000s but for the company's controversial merger with Compaq Computer in 2002. In 2005 imaging and printing generated

29% of HP's revenues and 59% of earnings from operations, while personal systems, where Compaq made the biggest contribution, had a 30% share of revenues and 11% of earnings. Selling consumer-oriented products in markets in which price competition is intense, HP is no longer the "engineers' company" that Hewlett and Packard built. These changes in HP's product-market strategy have had far-reaching consequences for the company's employment relations. One consequence is that since the mid-1980s HP has been a leader among ICT companies in the outsourcing of employment to contract manufacturers.

In early 2001, with economic recession setting in, HP announced that it would cut 1,700 marketing jobs and 3,000 management positions. The company continued to adhere to the traditional policy that gave these employees the opportunity to find another position within HP. In late July, however, HP announced that it would chop 6,000 jobs, amounting to 6.5% of its global labor force. With 10,700 jobs being eliminated within just seven months, displaced employees faced dim prospects of finding new positions within HP. While HP's management never officially announced the demise of "The HP Way," neither would it henceforth invoke it as the prevailing corporate philosophy.

Then in September 2001 HP declared its intention to merge with Compaq Computer, the world's second largest PC producer and largest enterprise server producer, with a total of $33.6 billion in sales and 63,700 employees. It was the possibility of cost-savings through post-combination consolidation that made the merger financially attractive. One year after the merger, employment at HP had declined from 153,500 to 141,400, the net result of 18,900 layoffs and 6,800 new hires. Year-end employment increased to 151,000 in 2004 before declining to 150,000 in 2005 and remaining at that level at the end of fiscal 2006. It has been estimated that from the time of the merger with Compaq through 2006, HP laid off 45,000 employees, while hiring almost as many new employees (Wong 2006). The purpose of this "churn" has been to reduce costs. HP's employment strategy included substantial off-shoring of production to China, where the company has had a longstanding presence, as well as to India, where, with 73,000 employees between them at the end of 2006, HP and IBM have been the largest foreign employers in ICT (Kulkarni 2007).

In July 2005 HP announced that it would cut 14,500 jobs over the next 18 months. At the same time, the company announced that as of January 2006 new hires would no longer be eligible for the DB pension, while workers whose age and years of service totaled less than 62 would stop accruing benefits under the plan. Instead the company would increase its matching contribution to the 401(k) plan from 4% to 6% of employee pay. In a video message to employees, HP CEO Mark Hurd explained why the cost-cutting measures were necessary:

> Our cost structure is putting HP at a competitive disadvantage. It's simply not sustainable. When a company is structurally inefficient like we are, short-term fixes don't work. . . . I know this is not the best news you can get, but it's what's required for HP to become the great company it can be, once again (Poletti and Wong 2005).

Xerox

With 2,550 union members at 17 locations in North America at the end of 2005, Xerox's website proclaimed that "Xerox is the only union-represented office equipment manufacturer worldwide." At the time Xerox employed 36,000 people in North America, 16,000 in Europe, and 5,000 in developing countries. In its *2006 Report on Global Citizenship*, Xerox stated that "[i]n 2005, Xerox and its unions successfully negotiated new four-year contracts at all locations. The relationship fostered by Xerox and union leadership continues to be noted as a model in American industry and is a source of great pride for Xerox and our people" (Xerox Corporation 2006: 63).

The case of Xerox suggests that even a small union presence that is taken seriously by the employer can help to preserve pension benefits for all employees (for Xerox, 55,000 at the end of 2005). With the exception of new union employees (who are likely to be very few in number), all Xerox employees can still take advantage of an arrangement put in place in 1990, when the company introduced a CB plan, of choosing between a DB and a CB plan. In addition, in 2003 the company added a match of up to 6% of total pay to employer 401(k) contributions.

Nevertheless, however much the company may proclaim the value of its relationship with the union, the fact is that over the past decade, in terms of both numbers and influence, the union at Xerox has been on the decline. In 1994, when ACTWU obtained a seven-year contract with an employment guarantee for employees at Xerox's Webster plant, its Local 14A represented 3,850 employees there. That number had declined to 1,955 in 2002 when the Union of Needletrades, Industrial and Textile Employees, or UNITE—the result of the 1995 merger of ACTWU with the International Ladies Garment Workers Union—concluded its next contract with Xerox. When UNITE HERE—the product of the 2004 merger of UNITE with the Hotel Employees and Restaurant Employees International Union—signed the current four-year contract in March 2005, it covered 1,517 employees, just 39% of the membership level 11 years before. For all locations, union membership at Xerox declined from about 6,200 in 1994 to 2,550 in 2005.

In the prior three-year contract, signed in March 2002, the union got the same employment earnings guarantee that was in the 1994 contract, now applicable to the remaining 1,955 union workers at Webster. Union members also secured wage increases totaling 16.8% over the life of the contract plus cost-of-living adjustments, and retained their existing medical and dental benefits. They also obtained an increased company contribution to individual 401(k) accounts, plus some stock options and a 1.5% bonus on total pay for 2001. What the union lost, however, was the right to form joint study teams—an innovative form of union–management cooperation that dated back to 1980—to seek to find ways of keeping work in the plant that would otherwise be outsourced.

When the contract bargained in 2002 came up for renewal in March 2005, Local 14A active membership had declined to 1,517. In the new contract the union got the employment guarantee for another four years, pay increases of 10.7% over the life of the contract plus cost-of-living adjustments, and the right to retain existing medical and dental benefits. While the study-team arrangement, defunct since 2002, was not even a subject of collective bargaining at this point, the new contract did stipulate that workers at the Webster plant would continue to do final assembly and testing of specific Xerox printers, copiers, and digital presses. The one concession that the union did have to make was that any new union hires would not be eligible to receive the choice between the DB and CB plan that had been available to existing employees since 1990, but would instead be offered a 401(k) plan with the 6% company match. Given the union's employment trajectory at Webster since the early 1990s, however, it is unlikely that, going forward, there will be many new hires to whom the new pension regime will apply.

The Bell System Legacy

In 2005 the companies that evolved out of the breakup of the Bell System had a total of about 629,000 employees, 304,000 less than they had in 1984 (see Table 8). From its post-breakup peak of 950,000 in 1985, employment had already fallen to less than 681,000 in 1996. In that year the Telecommunications Act opened up competition to all comers in all telecommunications markets—local and long-distance, wired and wireless, voice (circuit-switched) and data (packet-switched)—and helped set off the Internet boom. Employment at the companies of the former Bell System increased in the boom, peaking at 893,000 in 2000. With the bursting of the Internet bubble, major new service providers such as WorldCom, Global Crossing, and Enron (with its

TABLE 8
Number of Employees in the Former Bell System Companies, 1984–2005

	SBC/ATTI	Bell South	BA/Verizon	US WEST/Qwest	ATTC	Ameritech	NYNEX	Pactel	AT&T Wireless	Cingular	Lucent	Avaya	Agere	Total
1984	71,860	96,000	79,500	70,765	365,550	77,514	94,862	76,881						932,932
1985	71,400	92,500	79,285	70,202	337,600	74,883	89,600	71,488						886,958
1986	67,500	96,900	80,185	69,375	316,900	77,538	90,200	74,937						873,535
1987	67,100	98,700	80,950	68,523	303,000	78,510	95,300	71,877						863,960
1988	64,930	100,280	81,000	69,765	304,200	77,334	97,400	69,696						864,605
1989	66,200	101,230	79,100	70,587	283,500	77,326	95,400	68,452						841,795
1990	66,690	101,945	81,600	65,469	273,700	75,780	93,800	65,829						824,813
1991	61,230	96,084	75,700	65,829	317,100	73,967	83,900	62,236						836,046
1992	59,500	97,112	71,400	63,707	312,700	71,300	81,860	61,346						818,925
1993	58,400	95,084	73,600	60,778	308,700	67,192	76,200	60,050						800,004
1994	58,750	92,100	72,300	55,246	304,500	63,594	70,600	51,590						768,680
1995	59,300	87,571	61,800	54,552	299,300	65,345	65,800	48,889						742,557
1996	61,540	81,241	62,600	51,477	130,400	66,128	68,100	48,330			124,000			693,816
1997	118,340	81,000	141,000	51,110	127,800	74,359	BA	SBC			134,000			727,609
1998	129,850	88,450	140,000	54,483	107,800	70,525					141,600			732,708
1999	204,530	96,162	145,000	58,272	147,800	SBC					153,000			804,764
2000	220,000	103,900	260,000	67,000	165,600						126,000	31,000		973,590
2001	193,420	87,875	247,000	61,000	117,800				33,000	36,000	77,000	23,000	14,400	890,495
2002	175,400	77,000	229,500	47,000	71,000				31,000	33,800	47,000	18,800	10,700	741,200
2003	168,950	76,000	203,100	47,000	61,600				31,000	39,400	34,500	16,900	6,800	685,250
2004	162,000	62,564	210,000	41,000	47,600				CING	70,300	31,800	14,900	6,600	646,764
2005	189,950	63,066	217,000	39,000	ATTI					64,000	30,500	19,100	6,200	628,816

ATTI, AT&T Inc.; ATTC, ATT&T Corp.; BA, Bell Atlantic. Since 2000, Cellphone Partnership, also known as Verizon Wireless, has been a subsidiary of Verizon Communications and is included in the parent company's consolidated accounts. At the end of 2005, 55,700 of Verizon Communications' 217,000 employees were with Verizon Wireless.
Source: Compustat subscription database.

broadband division) went down in flames, while the former Bell companies all cut back employment in order to avoid or limit losses. From 2000
to 2004, the five former Bell service providers—Verizon, SBC, Bell-
South, AT&T Corp., and Qwest—reduced their employment levels by a
combined 213,000, or 29% of the level in 2000, while the three equipment manufacturers—Lucent and its two spinoffs, Avaya and Agere—
reduced their employment by 103,000, or 66% of the 2000 level. These
employment losses were partially offset by the growth of the wireless
firms—AT&T Wireless and Cingular—owned by former Bell companies.

Between 1997 and 2005 the seven Baby Bells consolidated into four
companies: Verizon, AT&T Inc., BellSouth, and Qwest. The approval by
the Federal Communications Commission (FCC) of AT&T Inc.'s acquisition of BellSouth at the end of 2006 reduced the four to three. Cingular, the wireless company previously co-owned by AT&T Inc. and
BellSouth, is now an internal division of AT&T, renamed AT&T Mobility. Verizon (with its origins in Bell Atlantic) and AT&T Inc. (with its origins in SBC) dominate the local U.S. wireline segment of the
telecommunications industry, while Qwest, which as US West was about
the same size as SBC two decades ago, has fallen far behind the others.
Both Verizon and AT&T are now also leaders in the rapidly growing
wireless segment of the U.S. telecommunications industry; in 2005 the
wireless revenues of Cingular were $34.4 billion, Verizon $32.3 billion,
Sprint Nextel $22.3 billion, and T-Mobile $14.1 billion.

As can be seen in Table 9, since 1984 Bell Atlantic/Verizon,
SBC/AT&T Inc., and BellSouth have been profitable, as was Qwest (as
US West) until the 2000s. The traditional local wireline business has
remained a very important source of revenues and profits for all four of
these companies, although in 2005 AT&T Inc. and Qwest were far more
dependent on wireline earnings than were the other two. Indeed, in
2005 for the first time Verizon's wireless profits, at $2.2 billion, surpassed
its wireline profits at $1.9 billion. The directory (Yellow Pages) busi-
nesses of AT&T Inc., Verizon, and BellSouth, while relatively small, have
always been lucrative, with profit margins typically at 30% or more.
From 1996 through 2005, for example, SBC/AT&T Inc. raked in $21.7
billion in 2005 dollars ($19.5 billion current) from its directory listings
and advertising, with a profit margin of more than 53%.

The wireline and directory businesses of these companies are the living legacies of their regulated monopoly status in the former Bell System. The FCC and state public utility commissions regulate the return
that regional Bell operating companies (RBOCs) can obtain from their
control of local telephone infrastructures. From 1984 through 1989 the
RBOCs, as local exchange carriers, were permitted a maximum rate of

TABLE 9
Sales, Net Income, and Profit Margins for Verizon, AT&T Inc., BellSouth, and Qwest, 1984–2005

Year	Verizon			AT&T Inc.			BellSouth			Qwest		
	Sales ($m)	Net income ($m)	Profit margin (%)	Sales ($m)	Net income ($m)	Profit margin (%)	Sales ($m)	Net income ($m)	Profit margin (%)	Sales ($m)	Net income ($m)	Profit margin (%)
1984	8,090	973	12.0	7,191	883	12.3	9,519	1,257	13.2	7,280	887	12.2
1985	9,084	1,093	12.0	7,925	996	12.6	10,664	1,418	13.3	7,813	926	11.8
1986	9,921	1,167	11.8	7,902	1,023	12.9	11,444	1,589	13.9	8,308	924	11.1
1987	10,298	1,240	12.0	8,003	1,047	13.1	12,269	1,665	13.6	8,445	1,006	11.9
1988	10,880	1,317	12.1	8,453	1,060	12.5	13,597	1,666	12.2	9,221	1,132	12.3
1989	11,449	1,075	9.4	8,730	1,093	12.5	13,996	1,695	12.1	9,691	1,111	11.5
1990	12,298	1,313	10.7	9,113	1,101	12.1	14,345	1,632	11.4	9,957	1,199	12.0
1991	12,280	1,332	10.8	9,332	1,157	12.4	14,446	1,507	10.4	10,577	553	5.2
1992	12,647	1,382	10.9	10,015	1,302	13.0	15,149	1,658	10.9	10,281	1,179	11.5
1993	12,990	1,482	11.4	10,690	1,435	13.4	15,880	1,034	6.5	10,294	476	4.6
1994	13,791	1,402	10.2	11,619	1,649	14.2	16,845	2,160	12.8	9,176	1,150	12.5
1995	13,430	1,862	13.9	12,670	1,889	14.9	17,886	1,564	8.7	9,484	1,184	12.5
1996	13,081	1,739	13.3	13,898	2,101	15.1	19,040	2,863	15.0	10,079	1,215	12.1
1997	30,368	2,455	8.1	24,856	1,474	5.9	20,633	3,270	15.8	10,319	1,180	11.4
1998	31,566	2,991	9.5	28,777	4,068	14.1	23,123	3,527	15.3	12,378	1,508	12.2
1999	33,174	4,208	12.7	49,489	6,573	13.3	25,224	3,448	13.7	13,182	1,102	8.4
2000	64,826	10,810	16.7	51,476	7,967	15.5	26,151	4,220	16.1	16,610	−81	−0.5
2001	67,190	590	0.9	45,908	7,260	15.8	24,130	2,570	10.7	19,695	−3,958	−20.1
2002	67,625	4,584	6.8	43,138	7,473	17.3	22,711	2,708	11.9	15,385	−17,625	−114.6
2003	67,752	3,509	5.2	40,843	5,971	14.6	22,635	3,589	15.9	14,288	−1,313	−9.2
2004	71,283	7,261	10.2	40,787	4,979	12.2	20,350	3,394	16.7	13,809	−1,794	−13.0
2005	75,112	7,397	9.8	43,862	4,786	10.9	20,547	2,913	14.2	13,903	−757	−5.4

Source: Compustat subscription database.

return on assets of 12%, lowered to 11.25% in 1990. The following year the FCC changed the regulatory formula to a "price cap" that, after adjusting for inflation, annually lowered the maximum prices that local exchange carriers could charge by the expected rate of productivity growth. Companies that could exceed this expected rate, while maintaining quality of service, could capture additional profits. The Telecommunications Act of 1996 did not put an end to regulation of the local phone business, but only required that, as a condition for the RBOCs to enter the long-distance markets, local exchange carriers make their local networks available at reasonable rental rates to any "competitive local exchange carrier" that might want to deliver local telephone service.

In 1989 AT&T Corp., whose long-distance service had previously been subject to a rate-of-return maximum of 12.2%, had been placed under price cap regulation. Unlike local telephone service, however, which the local exchange carriers still dominate, during the 1990s long-distance service became a highly competitive segment of the telecommunications industry, rendering rate regulation irrelevant. By the 2000s the long-distance segment was subject to extreme price competition both from resellers of overabundant long-distance capacity—the result of massive overinvestment in fiber optic transmission cables by companies such as WorldCom and Global Crossing during the Internet boom—and from wireless companies that provided nationwide access as part of their service plans. Highly dependent on the long-distance segment, AT&T Corp. saw its stand-alone consumer long-distance revenues, already in decline at the end of the Internet boom, plunge from $13,973 million in 2001 to $5,161 million in 2004, while its consumer bundled services revenues (based on local voice subscribers) reached only $2,743 million from a very low base of $870 million three years earlier. From the perspective of the second half of the 2000s, the two companies that emanated from the former Bell System that came out on top—namely, Verizon and AT&T Inc.—were those that built upon their regulated monopolies over local wireline exchanges to enter the expanding wireless industry without getting caught up, as was the case of Qwest, AT&T Inc., and Lucent, in the speculative machinations of the late 1990s Internet boom.

The embeddedness of industrial unions in the Bell System in the decades prior to the breakup and the ongoing regulation of the local wireline industry in the decades since explain the extraordinary high level of unionization that still prevails in this sector. At the end of 2005, Verizon, AT&T Inc., BellSouth, Qwest, and Cingular together employed 573,016 people, of whom 253,862, or 44%, were CWA members and an estimated 77,850, another 14%, were IBEW members. The proportion of the potential labor force organized by the CWA in these companies was 94% at Verizon, 92% at AT&T Inc., 84% at BellSouth, 89% at Qwest, and 65% at Cingular. Total employment at the former Bell System telecommunications service providers was down substantially from the 735,995 people employed by these companies (including the still independent AT&T Corp. and AT&T Wireless) in 2001. Nevertheless, in the mid-2000s, these companies remained bastions of business-sector union organization in the U.S. economy.

On occasion, the CWA and IBEW have been able to secure "no-layoff" clauses in collective bargaining with former Bell System companies, including one with Pacific Telesis in 1986, NYNEX in 1994, Bell Atlantic in 1998 followed by Verizon in 2000 and 2003, and SBC in 2004. That degree of employment security, however, has been the exception rather than the rule; before the breakup of the Bell System and since, large-scale layoffs of union employees have been common at these companies. Nevertheless, seniority provisions in union contracts have meant that those union employees with the most years of service with a company have had, and continue to have, realistic expectations of continuous employment until retirement age, at which point they can count on retirement incomes secured from collectively bargained pensions. Notwithstanding the radical technological and organizational transformations that have taken place in the telecommunications industry since the mid-1990s, at Verizon and AT&T Inc. in the last half of the 2000s OEBM still prevails.

In sum, the high and steady revenues that the RBOCs have derived from their ongoing control over regulated local telephone exchanges have enabled these companies to maintain high, even if declining, levels of employment that in turn have provided employment security to very large numbers of senior union members. In addition, the secure jobs available to union members are supported by two characteristics of RBOC employment that run counter to general employment trends in the ICT industries. Firstly, the RBOCs have not as a rule outsourced or offshored employment. Secondly, RBOCs themselves are not "high-tech" companies—they do virtually no R&D—and hence the types of labor that they require are much less affected by the technological transformations that characterize ICT than is the case for companies in other segments of these industries.

While the RBOCs have not employed scientists and engineers, they have employed large numbers of managerial personnel. Rosemary Batt (1996) has shown that for the whole Bell System, excluding Bell Labs, the proportion of total employees who were managers rose from 13.7% in 1950 to 29.4% in 1980. Under the old Bell System, AT&T and its operating companies were expansive bureaucracies in which managerial personnel viewed themselves as public service employees. After the breakup the former Bell companies began restructuring their organizations to better suit the regulatory and competitive environments that each of them faced, given the resources that they had inherited from the Bell System. For example, AT&T and PacTel both downsized their labor forces significantly in the late 1980s while BellSouth, after reducing the size of its labor force by almost 4% in its first two years as an independent company, expanded it by over 10% from 1986 through 1990.

In the first half of the 1990s, however, all eight companies downsized significantly, each one laying off large numbers of salaried managers as well as unionized workers. The recession of 1990 to 1992 was widely known as a "white-collar" recession, with U.S. corporations in general downsizing their salaried workforces to an extent that had no precedent in the post–World War II decades. The recessionary conditions, however, had little impact on the RBOCS, given their regulated rates and the relatively stable demand for local telephone service over the business cycle. Probably of much more importance in their downsizing decisions was the move in 1991 to price-cap regulation, which meant that the RBOCs could reap the extra profits derived from a "leaner" labor force. As company-level research by Batt (1996) has shown, by the early 1990s RBOC lower and middle level managers were working longer and harder, pressured by their superiors and fearful of termination.

Reinforcing this corporate response to the new regulatory mechanism was the fact that, beyond salaries, the remuneration of top executives of AT&T and the RBOCs depended in part on annual bonuses and in part on gains from the exercise of stock options. For annual bonus awards, annual profitability was ostensibly the main performance criterion. In addition, in the last half of the 1980s, for the first time, some of the remuneration of the top executives of the former Bell companies took the form of stock options. For paying attention to profits and stock prices, the top executives of AT&T and the RBOCs were very well paid.

A prime way in which top executives of the former Bell companies earned their keep in the first half of the 1990s was by reducing the number of people that the company employed. After the breakup, BellSouth was the largest RBOC in terms of both sales and employees, just ahead of NYNEX. After trimming its labor force in 1985, in part through an early-retirement program, the company steadily increased both revenues and employment through 1990. From the end of 1990 to the end of 1996, however, BellSouth reduced its labor force from 101,945 to 81,241, even as its sales rose from $14.3 billion in 1990 ($17.2 billion in 1996 dollars) to $19.0 billion in 1996.

First, in 1990 and 1991, BellSouth went through two rounds of early retirement in which 4,250 managers left the company. The downsizing of BellSouth, however, had just begun. In successive layoff announcements in 1992, 1993, and 1995, the company said that it would terminate as many as 16,000 employees, and since most of the people who could be eligible for early retirement had already left in 1990 and 1991, that type of program would not be repeated. Indeed, at the end of 1996 BellSouth recorded 81,241 employees, 15,871 fewer than at the end of 1992.

Along the way, BellSouth also changed its pension plan for managers. In 1993, with the targeted reduction of 8,000 managers in process, Bell-South became the first RBOC to adopt a CB plan. Applicable only to nonrepresented workers, the BellSouth CB plan may have helped the company recruit younger salaried personnel, but given the downsizing context in which the plan was introduced, that was not its main purpose. Rather, with the stock of older managers eligible for early retirement having been substantially depleted by the departures under the 1990 and 1991 programs, BellSouth wanted to create an incentive to quit the company for midcareer managers who lacked the years of service with the company to be eligible for early retirement. When the BellSouth CB plan went into effect in July 1993, the company employed 25,000 managers with an average age of 44 and average years with the company of 24 (Wyatt 1996). In introducing the CB plan, BellSouth had a provision that employees who resigned before June 30, 1996, could have their choice of receiving the greater of the CB account balance or the present value of annuity. Those older managers who remained at BellSouth did not complain about the adoption of the CB plan because the percentage of pay credited to an employee's account increased from 3% to 8% with years of service, and employees who retired from the company before the end of 2005 would have their choice of the better of the benefits under the CB plan or the traditional DB plan (Wyatt 1996).

BellSouth would be the first of six RBOCs to move to a CB plan. Next was Ameritech in 1995 followed by Bell Atlantic and Pacific Telesis in 1996 and SBC and US West in 1997. All of these CB plans were for managerial personnel only; the RBOCs continued to bargain DB plans with the unions. Among the original seven RBOCS, only NYNEX did not make the transition from DB to some form of CB plan for managers as an independent company. After NYNEX was merged into Bell Atlantic in 1997, however, its managers also had a CB plan.

The last of the service providers from the former Bell System to transition to a CB plan was AT&T. In late January, top management announced that over the coming year the company would cut 15,000 to 18,000 jobs, of which 10,000 to 11,000 would be achieved through pension incentives to managers under what was called the "Voluntary Retirement Incentive Program" (VRIP). The expectation was that the managerial ranks would be reduced by 25%. Indeed, AT&T had adopted the CB plan specifically for the purpose of downsizing the organization (see Burlingame and Gulotta 1998).

AT&T offered the VRIP to 43,000 AT&T managers. Older workers could get a 20% increase in their pension benefits. Eligibility for lifetime health benefits required that one's age plus years of service summed up to 65, whereas previously they had to add up to 75. Up to certain limits, the pension benefits could be taken in a lump sum.

About 17,000 managers opted for the VRIP, an uptake that surpassed what AT&T's top management had hoped to achieve. The high response rate was attributable to both the value of the VRIP offer and the ease with which, in the boom conditions of 1998, a departing AT&T manager could expect to land another well-paying job. To avoid losing key people in key areas, top management had put limits on the number of people in specific departments who could be offered the VRIP. As a result of these restrictions, AT&T turned down 1,700 applications. For not being given the opportunity to quit their jobs, these people subsequently filed a lawsuit against AT&T, but it was thrown out of court.

By the end of 1998, 14,700 of the 15,300 VRIP managers had already left AT&T, with the remaining 600 leaving in early 1999. The company paid out a total of $4.6 billion in lump sum settlements, an average of more than $300,000 per VRIP recipient. AT&T's management pension fund could afford this cash flow; at the end of 1997 it had a surplus of over $12.5 billion.

With pension money so plentiful, even the unions jumped on the CB bandwagon. In mid-1988 CWA and IBEW negotiated a contract that included a CB plan. With about 50,000 union employees at AT&T, this CB plan was thought to have been the largest ever to cover union members. Morton Bahr, president of the CWA, contended that "our agreement increased the value of pension benefits for employees at every stage of their careers." Now union members had the benefit of pension portability in case of downsizing or a change in career plans (Bahr 1999). Union members with 15 years or more of service with AT&T as of June 30, 1998, could when they retired choose to receive benefits based on either a traditional DB plan, enhanced by 7% immediately and another 8% by 2000, or a CB plan. It is not clear how many union members took advantage of the negotiated CB plan to leave AT&T, but at the end of 1998 the company employed 42,036 CWA workers, down from 48,787 a year earlier. The number of CWA members employed at AT&T continued to decline steadily over the subsequent years, falling to 14,920 by 2004, after which AT&T Corp. became absorbed into AT&T Inc.

Conclusion

This chapter has shown that in a leading sector of the U.S. economy, the type of pension that one receives tends to conform to the logic of the employment relations that prevail in the place, or places, in which one works. Those employment relations are in turn embedded in distinctive business models that reflect the product markets in which a company competes and the ways that it organizes and finances the particular productive activities in which it engages to generate competitive products. Business models can change, and when they do, employment relations and the arrangements for supporting employees in retirement will change as well.

I have argued that over the past few decades there has been a profound change in the business model that prevails in the U.S. ICT industries, one that has made employment much more insecure and retirement incomes much more dependent on the savings strategies of employed individuals rather than on the highly collectivized corporate structure on which incomes at work and in old age previously depended. But for the persistence of labor unions in a particular segment of the ICT industry that still enjoys the legacy of a highly regulated industry, that collectivized structure has all but disappeared.

At the same time, however, the corporate power that had its foundation in the Old Economy business model has not disappeared. Indeed, in the absence of not only the countervailing power of unions but also an employee-oriented corporate culture that once influenced the allocation of resources at companies such as IBM and HP, corporate power has become even more centralized and concentrated in the hands of a few top executives. They claim to be running their companies for the benefit of their shareholders, but given the ways in which they are remunerated combined with the fact that in the U.S. corporate economy sharchold-ers are primarily rentiers or speculators, they are really running the corporations for themselves (see Lazonick and O'Sullivan 2000 and Lazonick 2007b).

As I have researched the evolution of employment relations in the ICT industries over the past quarter century, I have found that in virtually every instance in which corporate decisions have rendered employment and retirement more insecure, the executives who made those decisions have invoked the imperative of competition and their responsibility to shareholders. Yet such arguments do not stand up when confronted with research of the much more cooperative business models of many of the most successful global competitors that U.S. corporations face, as well as, beyond the rhetoric of competition and shareholder value, the actual ways in which successful U.S. corporations mobilize resources, human and financial, to generate competitive products (for my general perspective on these issues, see Lazonick 2007a and 2007c).

Based on such research, the U.S. labor movement could be making cogent arguments that more, not less, cooperative employment relations are needed to sustain the prosperity of the companies in which the people that they represent work—or worked—and the U.S. economy in which, even in a globalized world, those companies remain embedded. Unfortunately, in the boom of the late 1990s, in which NEBM consolidated its position as the dominant business model in U.S. high-tech industry, the U.S. labor movement was much more concerned with getting its share of "shareholder value" than with challenging the legitimacy of the institutions whereby U.S. corporations are governed. In the absence of a movement to transform the institutions of corporate governance, the result in the 2000s is ever more obscene levels of top executive pay, and what is the flip side of the "shareholder value" coin—ever more insecure employment for U.S. workers, regardless of their "salaried" or "hourly" status.

Endnotes

[1] This paper summarizes a much longer version (with much more extensive references) that will appear in a book that I am completing on the New Economy business model and employment opportunities in U.S. high-technology industry. The longer version includes detailed analyses, drastically summarized here, of the transformation of employment relations at a number of the leading ICT companies, including IBM, Hewlett-Packard, NCR, Xerox, and the companies that since the mid-1980s have evolved out of the old Bell System. To conserve space in this abridged version, I have kept bibliographic references to a minimum. A copy of the longer paper can be accessed at http://faculty.insead.edu/Lazonick.

[2] In addition, Lucent spun off, first in 2000, Avaya, an enterprise networking company that with $4.9 billion in revenues and 18,555 employees ranked 434th among the Fortune 500 in 2005, and, then in 2001, Agere Systems, a communications chips company that with $1.7 billion in revenues and 6,200 employees ranked 904th among the Fortune 1000 in 2005.

[3] With the growth of wireless communications, in 2001 AT&T Corp. spun off AT&T Wireless as a separate company, while in the same year SBC and BellSouth created the wireless company Cingular as a joint venture. In 2004 Cingular acquired AT&T Wireless. Most recently, in December 2006, AT&T Inc. (formerly SBC) acquired BellSouth, and as a result Cingular is now wholly owned by AT&T Inc.

References

Bahr, Morton. 1999. "Federal Pension Plans," *Congressional Testimony by Federal Document Clearing House*, September 21.
Batt, Rosemary. 1996. "From Bureaucracy to Enterprise? The Changing Jobs and Careers of Managers in Telecommunications Service." In Paul Osterman, ed.,

Broken Ladders: Managerial Careers in the New Economy. Oxford: Oxford University Press, pp. 55–80.

Burlingame, Harold W., and Michael J. Gulotta. 1998. "Case Study: Cash Balance Pension Plan Facilitates Restructuring the Workforce at AT&T." *Compensation and Benefits Review*, Vol. 30, no. 6, pp. 25–31.

Federal Reserve Board. 2006. *Flow of Funds Accounts of the United States, Annual Flows and Outstandings, 1985–1994 and 1995–2005*. Washington, DC: Board of Governors of the Federal Reserve System, March 9.

"The Fortune 1,000 Ranked Within Industries." 2006. *Fortune*, Vol. 153, No. 7, pp. F44–F66.

Geisel, Jerry. 1995. "Pension Equity Plans Another Option When Traditional Pension Doesn't Fit." *Business Insurance*, Vol. 29, no. 33, p. 11.

Kulkarni, Vishwanath. 2007. "IBM Headcount Crosses 50,000." *Business Line*, January 22.

Lazonick, William. 2004. "Corporate Restructuring." In Stephen Ackroyd, Rose Batt, Paul Thompson, and Pamela Tolbert, eds., *The Oxford Handbook of Work and Organization*. Oxford: Oxford University Press, pp. 577–601.

Lazonick, William. 2006a. "Evolution of the New Economy Business Model." In Eric Brousseau and Nicola Curien, eds., *Internet and Digital Economics*. Cambridge: Cambridge University Press, pp. 59–113.

Lazonick, William. 2006b. "Globalization of the ICT Labor Force." In R. Mansell, C. Avgerou, D. Quah, and R. Silverstone, eds., *The Oxford Handbook on ICTs*. Oxford: Oxford University Press, pp. 75–99.

Lazonick, William. 2007a. "Innovative Enterprise and Economic Development." in Y. Cassis and A. Colli, eds., *Business Performance in the Twentieth Century*. Cambridge: Cambridge University Press, Forthcoming.

Lazonick, William. 2007b. "The US Stock Market and the Governance of Innovative Enterprise." *Industrial and Corporate Change*, Forthcoming.

Lazonick, William. 2007c. "Varieties of Capitalism and Innovative Enterprise," *Comparative Social Research*, Vol. 24, pp. 21–69.

Lazonick, William, and Mary O'Sullivan. 2000. "Maximizing Shareholder Value: A New Ideology for Corporate Governance." *Economy and Society*, Vol. 29, no. 1, pp. 13–35.

Leary, Irene M. 1988. "TI Calculates Data." *Pensions and Investment Age*, March 21.

Pension Benefit Guaranty Corporation. 2006. *Pension Insurance Data Book 2005*. Washington, DC: Pension Benefit Guaranty Corporation.

Poletti, Therese, and Nicole C. Wong. 2005. "HP's Silicon Valley employees brace for cuts." *San Jose Mercury News*, July 20.

"Profiles." 1987. *Pensions & Investment Age*, January 26.

"Profiles." 1989. *Pensions & Investment Age*, January 23.

Whyte, William H. 1956. *The Organization Man*. Simon & Schuster: New York.

Wong, Nicole C. 2006. "HP Churn: Boot 1, Hire 1," *San Jose Mercury News*, December 21.

Wyatt, Lindsay. 1996. "'Hybrid' Plans Fit Evolving Workforce." *Pension Management*, Vol. 32, no. 13, pp. 12–19.

Xerox Corporation. 2006. *Revealing Our True Colors: 2006 Report on Global Citizenship*. Stamford, CT: Xerox Corporation. <http://www.xerox.com/downloads/usa/en/c/citizenshipreport06.pdf>. [May 29, 2007].

CHAPTER 4

Partial Retirement: Widespread Desire Among Workers, But Limited Demand by Employers

BY SHARON HERMES[1]

U.S. Government Accountability Office

The way we think about retirement is changing. Increasingly, work and retirement are no longer seen as being mutually exclusive. This reconception is a movement away from "cliff retirement," a term used to describe the steep drop-off in hours worked when one goes from full-time work to full-time retirement, and a shift toward a gradual decrease in duties and hours of work, known as partial retirement.

In fact, partial retirement is not a completely new phenomenon. In the 1970s about one fifth of older men were partially retired at a given time, and one third were partially retired at some point in their lives. Recently, though, it has become clear that there is a widespread desire or expectation among older workers to continue working in retirement. Many older workers who intend to partially retire, however, do not follow through on their plans. Recent research suggests that one of the most important factors that may be causing this gap between expectations and realizations is limited employment opportunities. This suggests that the future prevalence of partial retirement depends most critically on the extent to which employers strive to recruit and retain older workers.

The apparently low utilization of partial retirement and phased retirement, in particular, is noteworthy since aspects of it should appeal to employers, employees, and public policy makers. Older workers indicate that fewer work hours, increased flexibility, and reduced stress rank high among their priorities. Unfortunately, workers are also facing less retirement income security, so many may need to work longer out of financial necessity. Employers, on the other hand, are confronted with an aging workforce and slower labor force growth. As a result, they face the possibility of many job vacancies and skill losses, which could be mitigated by retaining older workers. Finally, policy makers and other experts advocate partial retirement as one possible solution to the fiscal pressures of an aging population, assuming it would result in greater life-time work effort. Encouraging older Americans to stay in the workforce longer through partial retirement could increase productivity and tax revenue to fund the nation's retirement programs.

Reconceiving Retirement

Traditionally, work and retirement have been seen as separate and distinct phases of life. While the idea of continuing to work in retirement may seem like a contradiction, it has become a commonly reported expectation. Recent surveys of baby boomers have found widespread expectations of working during retirement (AARP 1999; Merrill Lynch 2005). According to data from the 2004 Health and Retirement Study (HRS), though, only about 24% of people between the ages of 62 and 65 who consider themselves to be retired (partially or fully) were actually working for pay.

The overlap between work and retirement is clearly seen in the concept of partial retirement. In a general sense, partial retirement refers to a reduction in hours in transition to full retirement. For purposes of this study, I consider an individual to be partially retired if he or she classifies him- or herself as partially or fully retired but as still working for pay on a part-time basis.[2] A partial retiree may transition from full-time to part-time work by staying at the same employer or changing jobs, or may return to paid work after full retirement. Phased retirement, a category of partial retirement, refers specifically to an older worker who reduces hours at an existing job.

Using data from the Health and Retirement Study from 1992 to 2002, I can examine the incidence of partial retirement and the experience of these older workers. The data reveal that many older workers want to partially retire—about 60% of older workers express a desire to gradually reduce their hours in transition to full retirement. However, I find that only about 20% of older workers who were employed full-time in 1992 actually became partially retired at some point over a 10-year period, from 1992 to 2002. In most cases these older workers would not be considered phased retirees because more than half (55%) left their full-time employer. Across occupations, partial retirees are most commonly employed in professional and service jobs. In 2002, about 20% of partial retirees worked in professional occupations and 17% in service occupations. Within service occupations, partial retirees were most often employed in food preparation and personal services occupations, such as child care and home care assistance.

For those who do partially retire, their hours of work fall substantially but so does their pay, depending on the nature of their transition.

To examine the change in hours and wages, I compared the individual's last full-time job to the partial retirement job using Health and Retirement Study data from 1992 to 2002. On average, partial retirees reduce their full-time work hours by about half, or 22.5 hours a week. The magnitude of the decline in hourly wages depends to a great extent on the timing of partial retirement—it is much larger for partial retirees who return to work after full retirement compared to those who transition directly from full-time work. Regarding median hourly wages, older men who returned to work from retirement experienced a decline of $6.78 in hourly wage—a drop of 39.51% from the last reported full-time wage, when evaluated at the median. Older men who went directly from full-time work to partial retirement, however, earned $0.46 less per hour, which represents a 2.81% decline in hourly wages, evaluated at the median. The situation was similar for older women. Women who returned to work from retirement experienced a 17.44% drop in hourly wages, compared to an 8.68% drop for women who transitioned directly from full-time work to partial retirement.

Expectations of Working Longer

The expectation among many older Americans that they will continue to work for pay in retirement often comes from a need to supplement other traditional, declining sources of retirement income. Income in retirement has typically consisted of three basic components: employer-sponsored pensions, Social Security, and personal savings. The coverage rate for employer-sponsored pension benefits has remained roughly constant at about half of the workforce in recent years. Among people age 65 and older with employer-sponsored pension benefits, on average those benefits provided approximately 29% of their retirement income in 2004 (Social Security Administration 2004). However, the nature of employer-sponsored pension coverage is changing, and future generations of retirees are more likely to rely on defined contribution (DC) plans, such as 401(k)'s, than defined benefit (DB) plans, which provide a guaranteed monthly benefit for life. In a DC plan, the value of the pension benefit depends on employer and employee contributions as well as investment returns. Defined contribution plans have the advantage of being more portable, but because they are voluntary and participants can access them at younger ages (although with a tax penalty), they have not dramatically increased coverage. About 44% of those eligible choose not to participate[3] (Fidelity Investments 2006) and, among those who do participate, about half of those who change employers decide not to rollover their DC account (Employee Benefits Research Institute 2000). Even for those who do enroll and make contributions, account balances seem to be inadequate. According to an analysis of the 2004 Survey of Consumer Finances by the Employee Benefits Research Institute (2006), the median DC plan balance for households with a plan through their current employer was $60,000 for those near retirement (ages 55 to 64). If this balance were fully annuitized upon retirement at age 65, the monthly payment would amount to $448.[4]

The transition from DB to DC pension coverage is particularly important given increases in life expectancy. As life expectancies have increased, so have the average number of years spent in retirement. In 1950 the average male worker spent less than 12 years in retirement; in 2003 that figure had increased to 18 years (Government Accountability Office 2005). In 2006, the average remaining life expectancies for men and women at age 65 are 16 and 19 years, respectively (Bell and Miller 2005). Today's retirees thus will need to make their savings last over a longer period.

Among households without employer-sponsored pension benefits, average income in retirement is considerably smaller and Social Security is a vital source of income. More than half (57%) of people age 65 and older in 2004 relied on Social Security retirement benefits for at least 90% of their income, and almost one third have no other source of income (Social Security Administration 2004). Households without employer-sponsored pension benefits to supplement Social Security have likely always faced pressure to keep working at older ages, and this pressure would only increase with continued growth in healthcare costs, including Medicare premiums and deductibles.

Probable Labor Shortages and Job Vacancies as Baby Boomers Retire

Although it is clear that many older Americans expect to work longer, employers' demand for older workers is more difficult to gauge. Demographic trends suggest that the demand for older workers should increase out of necessity, although employers may also choose to import more labor or move production overseas. With the aging of the baby boom generation, those born between 1946 and 1964, the overall U.S. labor force is becoming more dependent on older workers. The proportion of the workforce age 55 and over is expected by the Bureau of Labor Statistics to rise from just under 13% in 2000 to slightly more than 20% in 2020 (Toossi 2002). As these older workers approach retirement, employers face the loss of many skilled workers and job vacancies that may be difficult to fill.

While the share of older workers is expected to increase in every occupational category, it should affect some areas more than others. Across occupational categories, the greatest number of workers aged 55 to 74 are employed in professional and related occupations, and this category is projected by the Bureau of Labor Statistics to have the largest growth in employment from 2004 to 2014, with an increase of 21.2% (Bureau of Labor Statistics 2005; Government Accountability Office 2005).[5] Other occupations that employ large numbers of older workers include management, business, and financial operations; office and administrative support; and services. (See Figure 1.)

Increasingly, employers will be faced with the loss of many skilled workers to retirement. According to *The Economist* (2006), as much as 40% of the workforce at some companies in the aerospace and defense industries will be eligible to retire in the next five years. This can be a critical problem because it may take years to fully train new employees in such highly skilled fields. At the national level, the proportion of teachers nearing retirement is of a similar magnitude (Shepard 2002).

Some employers have made efforts to accommodate their older workers to stay past the age of traditional retirement, including flexible work arrangements, telecommuting, and better ergonomically designed equipment. A few high-profile employers are actively recruiting older workers. For example, Home Depot has established a partnership with AARP to attract workers over age 50. By 2006, AARP has established similar partnerships with 29 other employers through its "Featured Employer" program. Many of the partner employers are in the communications, finance and insurance, healthcare, retail, or staffing sectors. Overall, though, programs to recruit or retain older employees are not widespread.

Limited Employer Use of Partial or Phased Retirement

Several surveys of employers have been conducted regarding partial or phased retirement. As a whole, they reveal that employers are interested in retaining older workers, but most have not offered partial retirement arrangements, especially not on a formal or widespread basis. For example, a recent survey of 950 employers by Robert Hutchens at Cornell University found that while 73% of firms indicated they would allow an older white-collar to shift to part-time work, only 36% actually had an employee do so in the previous three years (Hutchens and Chen, forthcoming). This same survey found that the proportion of employers who said they would allow partial retirement declined considerably, to 16%, if it were to include health insurance equivalent to that of full-time workers. Similarly, a survey by Watson Wyatt found that only 16% of employers in their sample offered phased retirement (Graig and Paganelli 2000).

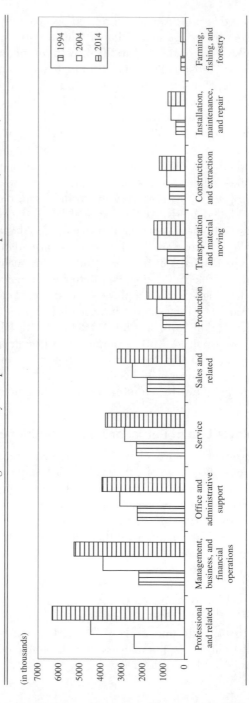

FIGURE 1

Number of Workers Aged 55 to 74 by Occupation—Historical and Extrapolated Data (1994–2014)

Source: GAO analysis of data from the Bureau of Labor Statistics and the Current Population Survey.

Note: Data for 2014 are based on GAO extrapolations using Bureau of Labor Statistics data.

Among employers that have had workers partially retire, it is typically an ad hoc arrangement that may involve rehiring a retiree as a consultant. The federal government, for example, does not broadly offer phased retirement, but it does bring back select workers as "re-employed annuitants." A study by the Conference Board (Morton, Foster, and Sedlar 2005) found that employers in the private sector who offer such ad hoc arrangements are targeting skilled workers, such as engineers, in order to promote knowledge transfer. However, none of the employers in the Conference Board study had a systematic phased retirement program.

Employers may be reluctant to hire older workers because they have higher costs. Scott, Berger, and Garen (1995) find that health insurance for older workers and retirees is the most expensive employer-provided benefit. They observe that the probability that a new hire is an older worker is significantly lower in firms that provide health care than in those that do not. Weller and Wenger (forthcoming) also find that older workers are significantly more expensive to employers because of their higher wages and costs of health care. Although age discrimination is banned under the Age Discrimination in Employment Act (ADEA), the higher cost of employing older workers may cause firms that offer health insurance to hire relatively fewer older workers.

Work Demands

Although it is commonly reported that older workers should be able to work longer because the nature of work has changed—the proportion of jobs traditionally thought of as physically demanding, such as those in construction and mining, has declined while white-collar and service sector employment has increased—it is not clear that many of the jobs available to older workers and retirees are a good match. For example, service sector jobs may involve a variety of activities that are physically challenging, such as standing for long periods, crouching to stock shelves, and lifting heavy objects. Data from the 2002 Health and Retirement Study indicate that about 52% of those employed in service occupations said their job requires much physical effort all or most of the time. Other occupations that tend to employ older workers are less likely to be physically demanding, but are more likely to involve considerable stress (see Table 1). According to the Health and Retirement Study, almost 66% of workers in managerial occupations and 63% of workers in professional occupations report that their jobs involve much stress all or most of the time, which is higher than reported for the other major occupational categories. The physical demands of service work and the stress associated with other jobs commonly held by older workers may hinder continued employment at older ages.

TABLE 1
Stress and Physical Requirements of Work by Occupation, 2002

Occupation°	Employees reporting that job involves much stress all or most of the time (%)	Employees reporting that job involves much physical effort all or most of the time (%)
White collar		
Managerial	65.5	12.7
Professional	62.9	17.9
Sales	54.4	24.5
Clerical, administrative support	55.6	15.6
Services	43.2	51.6
Blue collar		
Farming, forestry, and fishing	46.6	63.4
Mechanics and repair	55.1	53.4
Construction and extraction	42.5	66.2
Precision production	47.8	46.9
Operators	46.0	51.8

Source: GAO analysis of 2002 Health and Retirement Study data.
°*Note:* Occupational categories in the Health and Retirement Study are not exactly the same as in the Bureau of Labor Statistics and Current Population Survey data. BLS and CPS occupational categories were reclassified in 2003.

Health status is a key factor in an employee's decision to continue working or to retire. According to focus groups of retirees and near-retirees held by the Government Accountability Office (GAO; discussed below), many participants indicated they were forced to stop working and retire because of health problems. Reports of health problems were substantially higher, by a ratio of almost 2 to 1, among focus group participants without a college degree compared to those with at least a college degree. Consequently, even though older workers may intend to continue working, it is not clear that they will be physically able to do so, and lower-income workers seem likely to be more adversely affected.

Employer–Employee Mismatch in Support for Partial Retirement

To further examine the employment opportunities for older workers in light of the fact that partial retirement is not more widespread, GAO (2005) conducted focus groups of retirees and near-retirees and participated in a roundtable discussion of employers assembled by the Department of Labor's Employment and Training Administration.[6] Our research found that most older workers and retirees do not think their current or former employer provides opportunities for partial retirement. The discussion at the employer roundtable was consistent with the findings of past surveys of employers—employers stated they are concerned about the aging of the workforce, but most did not have a phased retirement program, nor did they have definite plans to establish one in the near future.

In total, GAO held 16 focus groups in four locations across the United States in June 2005.[7] In each location the participants were divided into groups as follows: retirees with a college degree, retirees without a college degree, older workers with a college degree, and older workers without a college degree. All participants were between the ages of 55 and 70, and each group had 8 to 10 participants. For the roundtable discussion assembled by the Employment and Training Administration in August 2005, the participants were 14 representatives from specific employers, as well as representatives from AARP and the U.S. Chamber of Commerce.

Employer Demand

Across all of the focus groups, very few participants felt that they had an opportunity to partially retire at their career job. The vast majority did not think their current or former employer would allow older workers to reduce their hours in transition to retirement. Based on their reports, it seemed unlikely that many of these older workers would have engaged their employer in a conversation about partial retirement. So even if an employer was willing to offer partial retirement on an ad hoc basis, the employee may not be aware of it.

Overall, most of the focus group participants felt they had limited employment opportunities for part-time work in retirement. A considerable number of retirees actually reported they had been laid off and felt forced to retire earlier than they would have otherwise. In general, though, these older workers and retirees tended to believe they could find part-time work but that such jobs would be low wage and low skilled, which is consistent with the decline in wages observed in the Health and Retirement Study. The limited employment opportunities perceived by many older workers and retirees may be the most important factor in explaining why partial and phased retirement is not more widespread.

In contrast to the focus group findings, employer representatives at the roundtable discussion agreed that the aging of the workforce is an issue of growing importance. They emphasized concerns about the eventual loss of knowledge from their organizations as highly skilled older workers retire. However, despite their awareness of challenges associated with the aging of the workforce, only about a third of employers had established any practice designed to recruit or retain older workers.

Most of the perceptions of older workers expressed by roundtable participants were favorable. Some of the most commonly cited attributes were knowledgeable, experienced, flexible, and a strong work ethic. One representative from a service sector company also observed that older workers tend to have lower turnover. Though fewer drawbacks of older workers were mentioned by the roundtable participants, the ones cited were that older workers are more expensive, less suitable for continued professional development, and less easily adaptable to change.

The employer representatives generally agreed that flexible work arrangements are essential to attracting older workers. Among employers that had taken action to recruit or retain older workers, such flexible practices included allowing work at different locations during the course of the year, providing the opportunity to switch to less demanding or stressful roles, and using older workers as mentors for younger workers.

Pension Regulations

Interestingly, although DB pension regulations are often cited as a barrier to phased retirement, they were not often mentioned by focus group participants. The vast majority of older workers and retirees in GAO's focus groups were unaware of any complications presented by their pension rules, which further suggests that there is insufficient communication between employers and their older workers regarding retirement transitions.

Several of the roundtable participants did mention barriers to retaining or hiring older workers. In particular, some employer representatives expressed concern about hiring older workers because of the additional legal protections afforded to them by the Age Discrimination in Employment Act (ADEA). Employers believed it would be more difficult to dismiss an older worker who was not performing well. In addition to the ADEA, pension regulations that prohibit in-service distributions were cited by several participants as an obstacle to phased retirement.

Changing Regulations Affecting Phased Retirement

Employers and others have suggested that regulations that prohibit in-service pension distributions create a barrier to phased retirement, which may explain why such arrangements are not more widespread. According to these rules, an older worker with a defined benefit pension plan who has reached the plan's early retirement age but not the normal retirement age is not allowed to begin receiving the pension benefit while still working for the employer sponsoring the plan.[8] Because phased retirees would be earning less income with fewer hours of work, it is likely they would need to supplement their reduced earnings with income from their pension. An older worker in this situation can gain access to a pension while continuing to work either by leaving the employer and finding a job with another firm, possibly a competitor, or by retiring and returning to work with the same employer after a break in service. There is, however, no formal guidance on what constitutes such a break—some employers require a six-month waiting period before a retiree can be rehired.

A constraint that involves a change of employer in partial retirement, as exists with the structure of DB plans, presents some immediate concerns. Older workers typically have long tenure and high levels of firm-specific human capital. Both of these factors contribute significantly to the worker's wage. If an older worker leaves a career job to partially retire, wage and fringe benefits may fall dramatically. Additionally, the departure of older workers represents a loss of human capital for the firm if it has invested in on-the-job training. As the labor force ages and a disproportionately high percentage of skilled workers approach retirement, this problem will be of increasing importance to employers.

A high rate of job change is observed among partial retirees. Data from the Health and Retirement Study reveal that the majority of partial retirees (55%) leave their full-time employer. It is not clear from the data, though, what is causing so many partial retirees to change jobs. In addition to the restrictions against in-service distributions, it is also possible that these workers wanted to try something new or that their employers simply did not offer opportunities for phased retirement. Approximately 38% of partial retirees who change jobs do not have a DB pension and would not be affected by the regulations on in-service distributions. In fact, I find that 15% of partial retirees who change jobs were actually laid off or lost the job due to a business closure.

In order to eliminate this incentive to change employers, the Internal Revenue Service (IRS) proposed changes to its regulation of in-service distributions in November 2004 to accommodate formal phased retirement programs. The proposed regulations would allow firms to pay phased retirees an in-service distribution of their pension benefits prior to the plan's normal retirement age, subject to certain requirements. The requirements include that there be a written agreement between the employer and employee, entered into on a voluntary basis by both parties, under which the employee would reduce work hours from full-time by at least 20%. The amount of the pension benefit the employee would be paid as an in-service distribution is proportional to the percent reduction of hours worked. For example, a former full-time worker who reduces work hours by 25% would be entitled to begin receiving 25% of the accrued pension benefit. Employees must also be over age 59-1/2 and eligible for early retirement under the pension plan. During the phased retirement period, the worker would continue to accrue pension benefits proportionate to the hours worked.

The IRS requested comments on their proposed changes and held a hearing on March 14, 2005. Of the seven groups that testified, three represented employers, two represented consulting or law firms, one represented the American Society of Pension Professionals and Actuaries, and one (AARP) represented retirees. The consensus among the employer, consulting, and legal representatives was that the proposed regulations are a step in the right direction but are too administratively burdensome for employers (Bureau of National Affairs 2005). Some also said that age 59-1/2 was too high; they would prefer to offer phased retirement to even younger workers. This suggests that employers might see these programs as an opportunity to phase workers out earlier, rather than retain them at older ages. AARP was the only group to advocate raising the age of eligibility—to 62, reflecting the most common age at which people commence Social Security retirement benefits. Raising the age to 62 makes it more likely that phased retirement would increase employment at older ages. A concern with offering phased retirement at younger ages is that older workers would spend less time in the workforce, have lower savings for retirement, and access their pensions earlier, thereby reducing their income in retirement.

The Congressional Research Service (CRS) has also outlined concerns about permitting in-service distributions (Purcell 2005). As CRS emphasizes, the effect of in-service distributions on total lifetime work hours is uncertain. If in-service distributions are permitted, some older workers may stay in the workforce longer and increase total lifetime work hours. Other older workers, though, may choose to reduce their hours when they would have otherwise continued working full-time until reaching their plan's normal retirement age, which could reduce their total lifetime work hours. In addition, CRS notes that some observers believe permitting in-service distributions would make the pension benefit the equivalent of a tax-subsidized wage supplement.

The passage of the Pension Protection Act (PPA) in August 2006 may have an even greater effect on partial retirement than the changes to the Internal Revenue Code. The PPA permits in-service distributions to workers aged 62 and older and applies to pension distributions starting in 2007. As a result of this change, it should be much easier for employers to offer phased retirement to employees aged 62 and older who have DB pension plans. However, as noted earlier, employer groups have been advocating for a much lower age of eligibility for phased retirement.

It remains to be seen to what extent these new regulations will result in a more widespread availability of phased retirement.

Conclusion

Some policy makers advocate partial retirement as one solution to the fiscal pressures of an aging population. They argue that working longer is a fair trade-off for longer, healthier lives and that it will help mitigate slow labor force growth as the baby boom generation exits the workforce to retirement. Workers' expectations seem to be compatible—recent survey data show that most boomers expect to continue working in retirement. However, currently only a minority of older workers ever become partially retired.

Although there is a widespread expectation among older Americans to work in retirement, employers' demand for older workers is less clear. Despite the well-known fact that the workforce is aging and the large number of impending retirements, most employers have not yet taken action to retain their older workers. Surveys of employers indicate that even when phased retirement is offered, it is typically done on an ad hoc basis and targeted to a few highly skilled workers.

In focus groups conducted by the GAO, older workers and retirees indicated they face several hurdles to extending their working life. Very few participants were aware of opportunities to partially retire at their career employer, and the majority did not believe their employer had interest in retaining older workers. In addition, many of the older workers and retirees, all between the ages of 55 and 70, mentioned health problems that limit their ability to work, especially those without a college degree. Overall, the majority felt that their work opportunities were limited to low-wage, low-skilled jobs. Proposed changes to the Internal Revenue Code and the passage of the Pension Protection Act will alleviate legal barriers to phased retirement commonly cited by employers and other experts. However, feedback provided to the IRS by employer representatives indicates they would prefer to be able to offer phased retirement for workers younger than age 59-1/2, which raises the concern that such programs may be used to phase workers out earlier rather than to retain them at older ages. The continued aging of the workforce and recent changes to the law are likely to encourage greater use of partial and phased retirement, but available evidence indicates that most older workers do not have the opportunity to partially retire at their existing job.

Endnotes

[1] The views of the author do not necessarily reflect those of the GAO.

[2] Retirement and partial or phased retirement may mean different things to different people. Individuals may consider themselves to be retired when they leave a career job, start receiving pension or Social Security benefits, stop working for pay, or choose some combination of these. Because of the possibility for ambiguity between partial and full retirement, I use a hybrid definition for partial retirement, as suggested by Gustman and Steinmeier (2001/2002), which relies on both self-reported labor force status and actual earnings from work.

[3] The Fidelity study uses data from their proprietary sample of more than 11,700 corporate DC plans with more than 9 million participants and approximately 5 million plan-eligible nonparticipants.

[4] The annuity estimate is based on a 50% joint-survivor annuity starting when both spouses are age 65 using the annuity calculator at http:www.tsp.gov.

[5] Jobs in the professional and related occupations category include computer and mathematical; architecture and engineering; life, physical, and social sciences; community and social services; legal, education, training, and library; arts, design, entertainment, sports, and media; healthcare practitioner and technical.

[6] GAO used a contractor, IQ Solutions, to screen participants, select locations, and moderate the focus groups.

[7] The four locations were Chicago, Illinois; Phoenix, Arizona; New York, New York; and Washington, DC.

[8] The regulations prohibiting in-service distributions do not apply to DC pensions, such as 401(k)'s. A worker with a DC plan may access his or her account without penalty after reaching age 59-1/2, regardless of employment status.

References

AARP. 1999. *Baby Boomers Envision Their Retirement: An AARP Segmentation Analysis*. Research Report Roper Starch Worldwide, February, p. 79.

Bell, Felicitie C., and Miller, Michael L. 2005. *Life Tables for the United States Social Security Area 1900–2100*. Social Security Administration, Office of the Chief Actuary, Actuarial Study No. 120, Table 10, p. 164. August.

Bureau of Labor Statistics. 2005. *Table 2: Employment by Major Occupational Group, 2004 and Projected 2014*. December. <http://www.bls.gov/news.release/ecopro.t02.htm>. [September 9, 2006].

Bureau of National Affairs. 2005. *Transcript of IRS Hearing on Proposed Regulation (REG-114726-04) on Distribution From Pension Plan Under Phased-Retirement Program*. TaxCore Transcripts, March 14.

Employee Benefits Research Institute. 2000. *Rollover Rates*. March. <http:www.ebri.org/publications/facts/james/dis_0300fact1.cfm>. [May 2, 2006].

Employee Benefits Research Institute. 2006. *Individual Account Retirement Plans: An Analysis of the 2004 Survey of Consumer Finances*. EBRI Issue Brief No. 293.

Fidelity Investments. 2006. *Building Futures, Volume VII: How Workplace Savings Are Shaping the Future of Retirement*, p. 63. <http://buildingfutures.fidelity.com/pdfs/full_version.pdf>. [December 7, 2006].

Government Accountability Office. 2005. *Older Workers: Labor Can Help Employers and Employees Plan Better for the Future.* GAO-06-80, December. Washington, DC: GAO.

Graig, Laurene, and Valerie Paganelli. 2000. "Phased Retirement: Reshaping the End of Work," *Compensation and Benefits Management*, Vol. 16, no. 2, pp. 1–9.

Gustman, Alan, and Thomas Steinmeier. 2001/2002. "Retirement and Wealth." *Social Security Bulletin*, Vol. 64, no. 2, pp. 66–91.

Hutchens, Robert M., and Jennjou Chen. Forthcoming. "The Role of Employers in Phased Retirement: Opportunities for Phased Retirement among White Collar Workers." In Teresa Ghilarducci and John Turner, eds., *Work Options for Older Americans.* South Bend, IN: University of Notre Dame Press.

Merrill Lynch. 2005. "The New Retirement Survey" *from Merrill Lynch Reveals How Baby Boomers Will Transform Retirement.* February 22. <http://www.ml.com/index.asp?id=7695_7696_8149_46028_46503_46635>. [May 2, 2006].

Morton, Lynne, Lorrie Foster, and Jeri Sedlar. 2005. *Managing the Mature Workforce: Implications and Best Practices.* <http://www.conference-board.org/utilities/pressDetail.cfm?press_ID=2709>. [May 2, 2006].

Purcell, Patrick. 2005. "Older Workers: Employment and Retirement Trends." *Congressional Research Service Report for Congress.* September 14. Washington, DC: Congressional Research Service.

Scott, Frank A., Mark C. Berger, and John E. Garen. 1995. "Do Health Insurance and Pension Costs Reduce the Job Opportunities of Older Workers?" *Industrial and Labor Relations Review.* Vol. 48, no. 4, pp. 775–91.

Shepard, Scott. 2002. "40% of U.S. Teachers Are Near Retirement." *Memphis Business Journal*, January 18.

Social Security Administration. 2004. "Importance of Income Sources Relative to Total Income." *Income of the Population 55 or Older, 2004.* <http://www.ssa.gov/policy/docs/statcomps/income_pop55/2004/sect06b.html>. [May 2, 2006].

The Economist. 2006. "Turning Boomers into Boomerangs—The Ageing Workforce," February 18, Special Report (2).

Toossi, Mitra. 2002. "A Century of Change: The U.S. Labor Force, 1950–2050." *Monthly Labor Review.* Vol. 125, no. 5 (May), pp. 15–28.

Weller, Christian, and Jeffrey Wenger. Forthcoming. "The Interaction between Health, Health Insurance, and Retirement." In Teresa Ghilarducci and John Turner, eds., *Work Options for Older Americans.* South Bend, IN: University of Notre Dame Press.

CHAPTER 5

Tales of the Dodo Bird and the Yellowstone Wolf: Lessons for DB Pensions and the Retirement Ecosystem

SYLVESTER J. SCHIEBER
Watson Wyatt Worldwide

For most of its existence, the flightless dodo bird lived on Mauritius, an uninhabited island in the Indian Ocean. The Portuguese arrived in the 16th century, and Mauritius became a port for ships carrying spices to market. Larger than a modern-day turkey, the mature dodo was a welcome source of fresh meat for sailors. Later the Dutch turned Mauritius into a penal colony and deposited convicts, pigs, and monkeys on the island. Rats—those peripatetic explorers of the world—also disembarked from ships passing through the port. With the humans feasting on the adult birds and the other mammals feasting on their eggs, the dodo was doomed. The last one died in 1681 (Endangered Earth Store 2007).

It often takes a long time for the full ramifications of a phenomenon to unfold. Recently, a scientist on Mauritius noted that one species of tree was becoming extremely rare. Indeed, he found only 13 of them on the island, all about 300 years old. The last of the living trees had germinated about the time of the dodo bird's demise. It turned out that the dodo ate the seeds of the tree, which became active and germinated only by passing through the bird's digestive system (Endangered Earth Store 2007).

The tale of the dodo bird's extinction and the consequent dwindling tree species may be good allegories for the plight of the U.S. private, employer-sponsored defined benefit pension system. Shortsighted regulations along with economic and demographic shifts have driven traditional private pension sponsorship rates down. Between 1980 and 2003, the number of plans insured by the Pension Benefit Guaranty Corporation (PBGC) declined from 114,396 to 31,135 (PBGC 2004). Some of the reduction in plans was due to consolidation—employers ceasing to sponsor multiple plans—but most was the result of plan terminations.

In 1980, PBGC-insured plans covered 35% of the private sector, wage-and-salary workforce. By 2003, that percentage had dropped to 19.7 (PBGC 2004). As traditional pensions are being edged out by defined contribution plans, some pension analysts worry that future retirees will not enjoy the retirement income security achieved by their parents and grandparents (Ferguson and Blackwell 1995).

Despite the endangered status of private defined benefit plans, rather than pursuing policies that will bolster their vitality, policy makers are making things worse. Changes in the underlying economics of defined benefit plans have made hybrid plans more attractive to employers and to many employees as well. But it could be foolhardy to establish these plans in today's unfriendly legal environment. Unless employers can safely go with the economic and demographic flow to hybrid plans, defined benefit plans may be headed for extinction.

Comparing Defined Benefit Plans, Defined Contribution Plans, and Hybrids

Traditionally, analysts have divided pension plans into two types: defined benefit (DB) and defined contribution (DC). These plan types differ substantially in benefit determination, funding, investment risk, portability, and regulatory status. DB plans typically promise an annual retirement benefit based on years of service and pay. In DC plans, employers and employees make regular contributions into employees' individual accounts.

Hybrid pensions are DB plans that combine many of the more attractive features of both traditional DB and DC plans into one plan (Table 1). In terms of contributions and participation, hybrid plans resemble traditional DB plans, in that both are automatic rather than self-directed. Like DC plans, hybrid plans largely eliminate penalties for workers who terminate employment before retirement. Benefit accumulation and lump-sum benefits in hybrid plans facilitate communication and portability, as is the case for 401(k) and similar plans.

Hybrid plans generally replace a traditional DB plan. The implications of this shift vary considerably from employer to employer and from worker to worker, but virtually all conversions to hybrid plans have eliminated the early-retirement incentives embedded in the preceding traditional plans (McGill et al. 2005).

Relative Merits of Alternative Forms of Retirement Plans

Traditional DB plans link retirement benefits to preretirement earnings and typically provide universal coverage. The plan sponsor bears the investment risk. Benefits are typically paid out in a lifetime annuity, so

TABLE 1
Features of Alternative Employer-Sponsored Retirement Plans

Plan feature	Traditional defined benefit plan	Defined contribution plan	Hybrid plan	Hybrid plan tendency
Employer contributes	Virtually always	Sometimes	Virtually always	DB
Employee contributes	Very rarely	Virtually always	Very rarely	DB
Participation	Automatic	Employee choice	Automatic	DB
Contribution level	Automatic	Employee choice	Automatic	DB
PBGC insurance	Yes, but capped	Not needed	Yes, but capped	DB
Early departure penalty	Yes	No	No	DC
Benefits easily portable	Usually not	Yes	Usually	DC
Annual communication	Benefit at end of career	Current balance	Current balance	DC
Retirement incentives	Occur at specific ages	Neutral	Most are neutral	DC
Accrual of benefits	Usually accelerates toward career end	Level over career	Level credits or increase with age/service	Mixed
Financial market risks	Employer bears	Employee bears	Shared	Mixed
Longevity insurance	Typically yes	Typically no	Available, but not often taken	Mixed

retirees don't have to worry about outliving their savings. Since the passage of the Employee Retirement Income Security Act of 1974 (ERISA), these benefits have been insured on a limited basis. However, workers who change jobs accumulate considerably smaller retirement benefits than those who remain with the same company, because benefits generally accrue very slowly until late in a worker's career.

DB plans can help employers reduce turnover rates, reward loyal workers (Ippolito 1997), and manage the orderly exit of retirement-age workers from the workforce. However, the regulatory structure for DB plans is considerably more burdensome than that for DC plans (Hustead 1998).

In DC plans, retirement benefits equal contributions plus returns on accumulated assets. If contributions are made regularly during a worker's career, benefits will accumulate faster and more evenly than they do in a DB plan, with its back-loaded accrual structure. For many participants, the best thing about DC plans is that employees can take their benefits with them when they change jobs.

A major disadvantage of DC plans is that participation and contributions are at the worker's discretion. Many workers do not participate, and many participants do not contribute enough. Moreover, the DC participant bears the investment risk. DC plan participants who make poor investment choices may end up with less money at retirement than they would have accumulated had the employer managed the investing. Finally, these plans tend to pay benefits in the form of lump sums. Unlike annuities, lump sums can run out—the participant bears the risk of longevity.

Funding is more straightforward and administration and communication are much simpler in DC versus DB plans. Ippolito (1997) sees a direct correlation between workers' willingness to save in 401(k)-type plans and their productivity. If employers matched employee contributions, this phenomenon would tend to concentrate employer contributions—a component of compensation—on the most valuable workers. Employers today generally regard pensions with individual accounts as a more effective human resource tool than traditional pensions. Benefit accrual is more transparent in individual-account plans, which tends to create a stronger sense of ownership and appreciation among workers. But these plans do not exert quite the same retention power as DB plans during workers' prime career years. Finally, employers cannot introduce incentives to retire into DC plans.

In hybrid plans, benefits generally accumulate at a more even pace than in traditional pensions, so today's more mobile workforce can take their benefits with them when they change jobs. Workers participating in hybrid plans tend to cash out their pension balances when they terminate employment, so they can roll the assets over and earn higher rates of return than they would typically earn in a traditional pension. In addition, these plans enhance both employers' ability to communicate the value of the retirement benefits and workers' appreciation of their accumulating benefits.

Hybrid plans tend to align pension funding obligations more closely with accounting disclosures than do traditional plans (Brown et al. 1999). And employers can accelerate benefit accruals in hybrid plans with increases in age and service to support their attraction and retention goals. Concentrating accruals toward the middle and later working years may reduce the preretirement leakages that occur with DC plans.

Participation in hybrid plans is automatic, so the typical 20% to 30% of eligible workers who decline to participate in DC plans would gain considerably under a hybrid plan approach. Account balances are credited with an annual rate of return equal to some specific rate, such as the T-bill rate, thus significantly ameliorating the financial market risks that concern many critics of DC plans. Workers retain some investment risk in that the benchmark rates used for return crediting of accounts can change over time, although the rates should remain much less volatile than those in other segments of the financial markets.

Hybrid plans are more age-neutral than traditional DB plans and rarely offer early-retirement incentives, although a hybrid plan could be structured to include such incentives. As DB plans under law, hybrid plans must offer an annuity as a benefit option, but almost all of these plans also offer a lump-sum option. Anecdotal evidence suggests that when offered a choice between an annuity and a lump sum, the over-whelming majority of workers choose the lump sum.

From an investment efficiency perspective, pooling assets in hybrid plans likely leads to more sophisticated and active management of retire-ment funds, probably reducing fees for the asset management and plan administration required in typical DC plans. Finally, participants cannot decimate their retirement savings by borrowing from hybrid plans as they can with most DC plans.

Changing Characteristics of the Workforce

Employers began sponsoring pensions to encourage superannuated workers—long-term employees who could no longer meet the strenuous demands of daily work—to retire (McGill et al. 2005). In the early decades of employer-sponsored pensions, most plans rewarded long-service workers, especially those who remained with the firm until retire-ment. In 1974, ERISA established vesting requirements that made anyone with 10 years of service under a plan eligible for benefits; the vesting standard was later lowered to five years. But most traditional pensions still structure benefit accrual to disproportionately reward long-tenure workers, especially those who stay with the employer until retirement.

Virtually all the rationales behind traditional pensions relate to employers' desire to have long relationships with workers. Twenty or more years ago, workers typically settled into a career job by their early to mid-30s and then stayed put until they retired.

But over the last 20 years or more, median tenures of men older than 35 have declined steadily, and tenures have declined somewhat more rap-idly for older workers than for younger ones (Figure 1). Women's tenures have been relatively flat and have tended to be shorter than those for similarly aged men. By 2004, however, the difference in the medians for men and women in every age group but 45-to-54 had narrowed significantly.

While there are distinct differences between the tenure patterns of men and women over the past 20 years, overall there is a general

FIGURE 1
Median Number of Years with Current Employer for
Male and Female Workers by Age

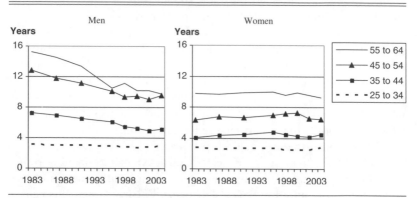

Source: U.S. Department of Labor, Bureau of Labor Statistics, news release, September 24, 1998, and Watson Wyatt tabulations of the *Current Population Survey.*

Note: Because of changes in methodology, data for 1996 to 2003 are not strictly comparable with data for 1991 and earlier years. In 1996 and later years, population controls from the 1990 census were used, adjusted for the estimated undercount. Data for the 1983 to 1991 observations were based on population controls from the 1980 census. Also, beginning in 1996, the figures reflect the 1994 redesign of the *Current Population Survey.* Data exclude the incorporated and unincorporated self-employed.

perception that worker tenures are falling. Between 1983 and 2004, median tenures declined by 27% for all workers 55 to 64 and by 23% for all workers 45 to 54. Some of this decline, shown in Figure 2, is the result of the labor force becoming increasingly female, because women have had shorter tenures at every age than men, but most of the decline reflects the sharp dropoff in the typical tenures of middle-aged and older men.

Pensions in the New Labor Market Environment

Declining tenures are important for pensions, and the following scenarios show why. Consider a hypothetical worker, Marion, who embarks on her career at age 22. She begins with earnings of $30,000 a year, and her salary increases by 4% per year over her career (this assumption is roughly in line with assumptions used by Social Security Administration [SSA] actuaries to project costs). Marion retires when she turns 60. Her pension pays an unreduced benefit at age 60 equivalent to 1.1% of average final pay based on her last three years of employment.

If Marion spends her entire career with the same employer, her pension will be roughly $51,500 per year. It will have a present value of

FIGURE 2
Median Number of Years with Current Employer for All Workers by Age

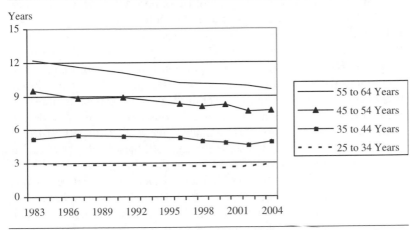

Source: U.S. Department of Labor, Bureau of Labor Statistics, news release, September 24, 1998, and Watson Wyatt tabulations of the *Current Population Survey.*

Note: Because of changes in methodology, data for 1996 to 2003 are not strictly comparable with data for 1991 and earlier years. In 1996 and later years, population controls from the 1990 census were used, adjusted for the estimated undercount. Data for the 1983 to 1991 observations were based on population controls from the 1980 census. Also, beginning in 1996, the figures reflect the 1994 redesign of the *Current Population Survey.* Data exclude the incorporated and unincorporated self-employed.

roughly $565,000 based on a unisex mortality table and 7% discount rate (this rate is roughly in line with SSA actuaries' estimates of long-term returns for individual account-type retirement plans).

Alternatively, if Marion switches jobs at ages 32, 41, and 49, but everything else—pay, benefit formula, and retirement age—remains the same, her retirement prospects would be very different. Her annual annuity would be roughly $32,500, and her pension would have an accumulated value of approximately $357,000 at retirement.

Now assume that Marion is covered by a 401(k) plan in which her employer contributes 3% of her pay plus matches 50% of her contributions up to 6% of pay. If Marion contributes the maximums, and the fund earns 7% per year, the employer-funded portion of her savings would be roughly $536,600 at retirement. In this case, Marion would retire with the same amount of money whether she worked one or four different jobs over her career, as long as she rolled over the accumulated balances into another tax-preferred account. If Marion switched jobs, her 401(k) employers would have to pay more to finance her benefits than a traditional pension plan sponsor, because 401(k) accruals are age-neutral.

As workers become more mobile, traditional DB pensions become less efficient, which partially explains the shift toward DC plans since 1980. Of course, there are several other reasons as well. Since the early 1980s, DB plans have become much more expensive to administer than DC plans (Hustead 1998). Current pension funding requirements and accounting rules are complicating the fiscal operations of some employers (Brown et al. 1999). And employment has been shifting toward industries and employers that are more likely to sponsor DC plans (Clark and McDermed 1990, Ippolito 1997). Finally, some analysts hypothesize that employers are trying to cut costs associated with back-loaded pensions as the baby boom generation nears retirement (Schultz 1999).

Some analysts believe that the shift toward DC plans is bad for workers and their retirement security. First, most of these plans require employees to contribute before the employer contributes its share. Roughly one half of private sector workers have the opportunity to join such a plan, but on average only 70% to 75% of eligible workers do so (Table 2).

To accumulate enough to retire, workers need to start saving when they're young. Most financial planners and retirement plan designers advise workers to begin saving for retirement by their late 20s or, at the

TABLE 2
Eligibility and Participation in 401(k) Plans in 2001

	Eligibility for all workers aged 20 to 64 (%)	Participation by eligible workers (%)	Participation by all workers (%)
Earnings level ($)			
Less than 20,000	27.5	49.9	13.7
20,000–39,999	56.9	70.5	40.1
40,000–59,999	70.1	78.7	55.2
60,000–79,999	76.3	83.2	63.5
80,000–99,999	77.4	87.6	67.8
100,000 or more	75.4	88.7	67.1
Age			
20–29	43.9	65.7	28.8
30–39	54.7	76.0	41.6
40–49	57.0	77.6	44.2
50–59	52.3	74.1	38.8
60–64	39.9	79.8	31.8
Total	52.1	74.1	38.6

Source: Munnell and Sunden 2004.

latest, by their early to mid-30s. Yet nearly one quarter of eligible workers in their 30s, 40s, and 50s fail to participate in their companies' 401(k) plans, with the lowest levels of participation concentrated among workers at the bottom of the pay scale.

Employers typically encourage workers to contribute up to 6% of their pay to their 401(k) plans by matching those contributions 50 cents on the dollar. A worker who takes full advantage of matching contributions would accrue benefits at a rate of 9% per year, with one third of that coming from the employer. In Marion's case, employer contributions to her 401(k) plan were estimated to be about twice the amount in the typical plan today. The higher contribution was assumed to bring the hypothetical DC benefit up to a typical DB accumulation for a full-career worker. Generally, for full-career workers, DC plans cost employers less than traditional DB plans, even if workers contribute the maximum amounts.

Many analysts worry about the investment risk for participants in DC plans. Figure 3 shows a series of hypothetical retirement benefit

FIGURE 3

Hypothetical Earnings Replacement Rates for Workers with 40-Year Careers Who Invested 6% of Their Pay in the U.S. Stock Market and Retired in 1912 through 1997

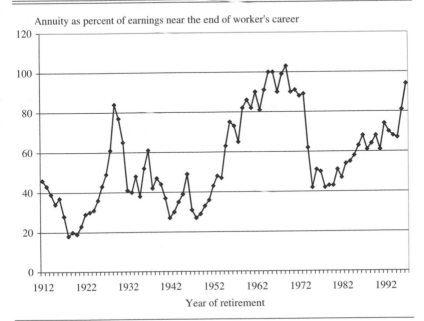

Source: Calculations by the author based on data provided by Gary Burtless at the Brookings Institution, Washington, DC.

levels as a percentage of workers' final earnings, assuming they saved 6% per year over 40 years, invested the proceeds in the U.S. stock market, and then annuitized the accumulation at age 65. The amounts are calculated on the basis of actual returns in the stock market returns and interest rates.

For example, consider what happened in the late 1950s through the early 1970s. In the late 1950s, a worker in his late 40s who started saving 6% of pay in the stock market in his mid-20s would have expected a retirement income of nearly 80% of his final earnings at 65. Indeed, if he retired at 65 in 1969, his accumulated savings would have bought him an annuity equal to 103% of his final salary. But if he turned 65 six years later, his annuity would have been only 42% of his final earnings.

Figure 3 somewhat overstates its case, because empirical evidence suggests that participants are better at diversification than the hypothetical workers in Figure 3. But many DC participants are overly cautious, playing it safe at the expense of higher returns. And even when participants invest well, they often do not actively manage their assets to meet their retirement goals.

Table 3 shows total assets and the proportion invested in equities in private DB and DC plans from 1993 through 2003. The percentage of assets held in equities remains much more stable in DB plans than in DC plans, which reflects different asset management styles. DB plan sponsors generally work with consultants and professional asset managers to

TABLE 3
Private Pension Assets and Shares Held in Equities, 1993–2003

	Defined benefit plans			Defined contribution plans		
Year	Assets ($ billions)	Equities ($ billions)	Percent in equities	Assets ($ billions)	Equities ($ billions)	Percent in equities
1993	1,195.1	577.9	48.4	1,087.9	578.6	53.2
1994	1,276.0	598.9	46.9	1,157.9	620.7	53.6
1995	1,460.5	754.4	51.7	1,428.3	850.3	59.5
1996	1,579.0	849.6	53.8	1,627.7	1,007.9	61.9
1997	1,746.8	957.4	54.8	1,942.5	1,278.8	65.8
1998	1,885.4	1,087.6	57.7	2,219.4	1,537.3	69.3
1999	2,071.7	1,192.7	57.6	2,499.6	1,786.2	71.5
2000	1,957.5	1,079.7	55.2	2,464.8	1,750.1	71.0
2001	1,762.4	916.8	52.0	2,277.3	1,557.8	68.4
2002	1,541.9	703.8	45.6	1,971.4	1,219.0	61.8
2003	1,797.4	936.5	52.1	2,378.4	1,597.3	67.2

Source: Federal Reserve Bank, *Flow of Funds.*

set investment policy and goals, and their asset managers actively implement investment plans to attain those goals. If they decide to invest 50% of assets in equities, they allocate their contributions accordingly and periodically rebalance the portfolio to stay on course. DC participants, on the other hand, seldom rebalance their portfolios after they first allocate their contributions and starting asset levels. As Choi et al. observe: "At any point in time employees are likely to do whatever requires the least current effort. . . . Almost always, the easiest thing to do is nothing whatsoever" (2001: 4).

Plan participants who failed to rebalance their portfolios during the latter part of the 1990s when rising share prices ballooned the equity share in 401(k) portfolios set themselves up to be clobbered by plunging stock prices in 2000 through 2002. Based on one estimate of median returns to plans sponsored by a set of firms that offered both DB and DC plans, assets worth $1,000 at the end of 1999 would have diminished to about $880 in the DB plans compared with $780 in the DC plans (Watson Wyatt Worldwide 2004).

Another problem with DC plans is that workers can tap their balances before retiring. Many plans allow participants to borrow from their retirement accounts, which may deplete accounts. The upside is that many would-be 401(k) participants hesitate to tie up their available cash unless they know they can borrow some of it back if necessary. The General Accounting Office estimated that participation rates are 6 percentage points higher in plans with loan provisions than in other plans (General Accounting Office 1997). Holden and VanDerhei (2001) found that participants in plans offering loans contributed 0.6 percentage points more of their salary to their 401(k), on average, than participants in other plans. Holden and VanDerhei (2004) estimated that 18% of participants had outstanding loans in 2003, and the average unpaid balance of outstanding loans was 13% of the loan holder's total account balance.

Of greater concern is that when workers switch jobs, most of them take their money out of their DC plans. While roughly three fourths of these assets are rolled over into another tax-preferred retirement savings account (Sabelhaus and Weiner 1999), 55% of workers—especially younger workers and lower-wage workers—withdraw their entire account for immediate use (Munnell and Sundén 2004).

Possibly the biggest concern about the leakage of tax-favored retirement savings is most participants self-insure against longevity risk, forgoing annuities and counting on their accumulated assets to last a lifetime. DC plans now play an increasingly central role in delivering retirement benefits to private sector workers, and these plans rarely provide annuities. In a 1997 survey of medium and large businesses conducted by the Bureau of Labor Statistics, only 25% of surveyed employers' savings and thrift plans offered an annuity option (U.S. Department of Labor 1999). Constantijn Panis (2003) found that only about 4% of DC plan participants annuitized their benefits at retirement age during the 1990s.

On top of the shift toward DC plans, more DB plans have been paying out benefits in the form of lump sums. In its most recent survey of employee benefits in private industry, the Bureau of Labor Statistics found that 43% of all private DB plans offered lump sums and that the overwhelming majority of these allowed workers to take their total benefit in this form (U.S. Department of Labor 2003). We don't know yet how many DB plan participants choose lump sums over annuities, but there is considerable anecdotal evidence suggesting that, when offered a choice, most retirees choose the lump sum. Some employers that had introduced lump-sum benefit options into their DB plans have recently begun to withdraw those options. One reason is that the low interest rates used in calculating lump-sum benefit amounts have made these options particularly expensive. Another, however, is that some employers are worried about workers losing this important traditional pension insurance against longevity risk.

To the extent that lump sums are available, retirees can convert their lump sums into steady, reliable, lifelong income streams. But the evidence so far suggests otherwise. For example, private, tax-qualified retirement plans disbursed $273 billion of benefits in 1998, nearly 60% of that from DC plans. Roughly 30% to 40% of retirees under private DB plans are taking lump sums. This suggests that as many as three quarters of private pension distributions in 1998 were cash-outs, most of them to new retirees. And by 1998, many workers who had cashed out of plans earlier and rolled their assets into IRAs had retired and were using those assets to support themselves.

In 1999, consumers paid $7 billion in premiums to life insurance companies for immediate individual annuities. That year, life insurance companies issued 134,500 new immediate annuity contracts and 2.7 million deferred annuity contracts. By the end of the year, there were only 1.6 million immediate individual contracts in force (American Council of Life Insurance 2000). By comparison, at the end of 1999 there were 27.8 million retirees receiving Social Security benefits (Social Security Administration). From a slightly earlier time frame, my tabulations of a special health and pension benefit supplement to the September 1994 *Current Population Survey* indicated that 41% of people over 55 who reported being retired also were receiving annuities from private pensions. If anything, the momentum of the move away from plans that provide annuities has picked up. If the trend continues, today's workers will be even less likely to receive private pension annuities.

Hybrid Plans: The Way Forward

Hybrid plans cannot cure all the ills that currently afflict our retirement systems. Workers would still be able to take preretirement distributions and not be required to roll their accumulations into IRAs. These plans would not resolve the annuitization problem that plagues much of the employer-sponsored system today. Shifting to hybrid plans, however, could resolve many of the concerns about retirement security, thereby allowing us to concentrate on those problems that remain.

Hybrid plans would increase the number of workers able to retire with an annuity, because these plans must offer an annuity option under DB regulations. Hybrid plans would also diminish the investment risk that surrounds DC plans, because workers' pension balances at retirement would not be based on the current value of underlying assets. These plans would not resolve the issue completely, however, because variations in interest rates would result in variations in annuity amounts at different points in time.

Hybrid plans would significantly improve participation rates in retirement savings plans. Enrollment is essentially guaranteed for covered workers because the plan is financed solely by employer contributions. While these benefits would not eliminate all financial market risks, they would minimize the investment risks associated with defined DC plans. And they would significantly improve retirement prospects for many workers by providing more portable benefits and vastly reducing the penalties for terminating employment before retirement eligibility.

But hybrid pensions have been driven to near extinction by the regulatory limbo in which they have operated in recent years. This uncertainty is one reason so many employers have frozen their DB plans and/or shifted to DC plans only. Given the potential for hybrid plans to remedy many of the problems facing traditional pensions and the DC plans that have largely replaced them, this has been foolish policy. With the passage of the Pension Protection Act of 2006, we now have a glimmer of hope that the employer-sponsored pension will not become the dodo bird of the early 21st century. With the right nourishment, the DB plan could rebound, generating benefits beyond its own immediate revival. There are examples beyond the dodo bird to which we can look for insight.

In 1914, the U.S. Congress approved funding to destroy wolves, and bounty hunters around Yellowstone National Park were paid to kill them to protect the livestock of ranchers who lived in the area. Ultimately, the wolves were eliminated from Yellowstone. As the wolf population declined, the elk population in Yellowstone Park, on which the wolves preyed, moved from their natural habitat at higher elevations down into the lower valleys and overgrazed the area as a species without predators. The elk killed the willows and cottonwoods that grew along the river-banks. The loss of these trees damaged the whole ecosystem and the wildlife in it. Birds and insects disappeared as they lost their habitat. Soil erosion silted the rivers, smothering spawning fish and reducing their populations (Oregon State University 2003).

By the early 1970s, the gray wolf was listed as an endangered species, and in 1973, Congress adopted legislation to start reintroducing it to its natural habitat. In 1995, U.S. Fish and Wildlife Services reintroduced wolves into Yellowstone National Park. Since then, the wolves have thrived, creating other ecosystem changes as well. With the return of the wolves, the elk have moved back to higher ground, where they can spot their natural predator at a distance. Along the riverbanks, willows have begun to grow to their full height for the first time in more than a half century (Robbins 2005), and cottonwoods, which were on the brink of extinction, have sprung back to life. With the return of the willows and cottonwoods, many other animals—from moose on down the chain—have returned to the area. The rivers are now cleaning themselves, and the fish are returning to normal population levels.

In the context of providing retirement security to future U.S. workers, the question we face is whether we want the employer-sponsored pension system to go the way of the dodo bird or of the Yellowstone wolf. Either way, the effects will rebound far beyond the plans themselves. Employer-sponsored pensions have become such an important element of mainstream workers' retirement portfolios that their failure could endanger the income security that millions of older Americans have been able to achieve over the past half century.

References

American Council of Life Insurance. 2000. *Life Insurers Fact Book 2000*. Washington, DC: American Council of Life Insurance.

Brown, Kyle, Gordon Goodfellow, Tomeka Hill, Richard Joss, Richard Luss, Lex Miller, and Sylvester Schieber. 1999. *The Unfolding of a Predictable Surprise: A Comprehensive Analysis of the Shift from Traditional Pensions to Hybrid Plans*. Bethesda, MD: Watson Wyatt.

Choi, James J., David Laibson, Brigitte C. Mandrian, and Andrew Metrick. 2001. *Defined Contribution Pensions: Plan Rules, Participant Decisions, and the Path of Least Resistance*. NBER Working Paper 8655. Cambridge, MA: National Bureau of Economic Research.

Clark, Robert, and Ann McDermed. 1990. *The Choice of Pension Plans in a Changing Regulatory Environment.* Washington, DC: American Enterprise Institute.

Endangered Earth Store 2007. "Extinct in the Wild: Dodo Bird." <http://www.bagheera.com/inthewild/ext_dodobird.htm>. [June 1, 2007].

Ferguson, Karen, and Kate Blackwell. 1995. *Pensions in Crisis.* New York: Arcade Publishing.

General Accounting Office. 1997. *401(k) Pension Plans: Loan Provisions Enhance Participation but May Affect Income Security for Some.* GAO/HEHS-98-5. Washington, DC: General Accounting Office.

Holden, Sarah, and Jack VanDerhei. 2004. *401(k) Plan Asset Allocation, Account Balances, and Loan Activity in 2003.* EBRI Issue Brief No. 272, August. Washington, DC: Employee Benefit Research Institute.

Holden, Sarah, and Jack VanDerhei. 2001. *Contribution Behavior of 401(k) Plan Participants.* EBRI Issue Brief No. 38, October. Washington, DC: Employee Benefit Research Institute.

Hustead, Edwin. 1998. "Trends in Retirement Income Plan Administrative Expenses." In Olivia Mitchell and Sylvester Schieber, eds., *Living with Defined Contribution Pensions: Remaking Responsibility.* Philadelphia: University of Pennsylvania Press, pp. 166–77.

Ippolito, Richard. 1997. *Pension Plans and Employee Performance: Evidence, Analysis, and Policy.* Chicago: University of Chicago Press.

McGill, Dan, Kyle Brown, John Haley, and Sylvester Schieber. 2005. *Fundamentals of Private Pensions.* Oxford: Oxford University Press.

Munnell, Alicia H., and Annika Sundén. 2004. *Coming Up Short: The Challenge of 401(k) Plans.* Washington, DC: The Brookings Institution.

Oregon State University. 2003. "Wolves Are Rebalancing Yellowstone Ecosystem." *Science Daily*, October 23. <http://www.sciencedaily.com/releases/2003/10/031029064909.htm>. [June 1, 2007].

Panis, Constantijn. 2003. "Annuities and Retirement Well Being." In Olivia S. Mitchell and Stephen P. Utkus, eds., *Money Matters: Shaping Retirement Decision-making.* Oxford: Oxford University Press, pp. 259–74.

Pension Benefit Guaranty Corporation. 2004. *Pension Insurance Data Book 2003.* Washington, DC: Pension Benefit Guaranty Corporation.

Robbins, Jim. 2005. "Hunting Habits of Wolves Change Ecological Balance in Yellowstone." *New York Times*, October 18. <http://www.nytimes.com/2005/10/18/science/earth/18wolf.html?ex=1287288000&en=76f9c712d7f50758&ei=5088>. [June 1, 2007].

Sabelhaus, John, and David Weiner. 1999. "Disposition of Lump-Sum Pension Distributions: Evidence from Tax Returns." *National Tax Journal* Vol. 52 (September), pp. 593–614.

Schultz, Ellen E. 1999. "Pension Debate Examines Aging," *Wall Street Journal*, September 22, p. C1.

Social Security Administration, Office of the Actuary. "Proposals Addressing Social Security Insolvency." <http://www.ssa.gov/OACT/solvency/index.html> [June 1, 2007].

U.S. Bureau of Labor Statistics. Various years. *Employee Benefits in Medium and Large Firms.* Washington, DC: GPO.

U.S. Department of Commerce, Census Bureau. Various years. *Current Population Survey.*

U.S. Department of Labor, Bureau of Labor Statistics. September 24, 1998. News Release.

U.S. Department of Labor, Bureau of Labor Statistics. 1999. *Employee Benefits in Medium and Large Private Establishments 1997.* Bulletin 2517. Washington, DC: Bureau of Labor Statistics.

U.S. Department of Labor, Bureau of Labor Statistics. 2003. *National Compensation Survey: Employee Benefits in Private Industry in the United States, 2000.* Bulletin 2555. Washington, DC: Bureau of Labor Statistics.

Watson Wyatt Worldwide. 2004. "Defined Benefit vs. 401(k): The Returns for 2000–2002." *Insider*, Vol. 14, no. 10, pp. 10–15.

CHAPTER 6

Multi-employer Plans:
Plan Design for the Future

BETH ALMEIDA
International Association of Machinists and Aerospace Workers

The world of retirement income is undergoing profound changes, which can have serious consequences for workers and retirees. Over the past 25 years, the proportion of workers covered by a defined benefit (DB) pension plan, the kind of plan that pays a guaranteed monthly benefit for life, has steadily declined—from about 4 in 10 workers in 1980, to just over 2 in 10 in 2004. Meanwhile, coverage under defined contribution (DC) plans, where an employer simply agrees to make a certain contribution to a retirement savings plan with no guaranteed benefits, has steadily grown. This shift away from DB plans and toward DC plans has left workers exposed to more financial risks.

Surveys suggest employer preferences for predictability in pension costs explain much of the growth of DC plans. Many observers recommend that plan sponsors and policy makers find new ways to make DC plans, with all their advantages for employers, look more like DB plans, with all their advantages for employees. But a model for this already exists—the multi-employer defined benefit pension plan.

Multi-employer DB plans are a high performing but often overlooked area of pension plan design. These plans, as the name suggests, cover employees of more than one employer, and in most cases, they encompass employees of many different enterprises. These plans have traditionally been especially important in industries where firm turnover is high but worker turnover in the occupation and industry is not. These plans offer portable benefits—as long as a worker works for an employer who participates in the multi-employer DB plan, the worker is covered by the same pension plan.

In addition to their portability, multi-employer DB plans have other advantages—economies of scale, more predictable funding for employers, and balanced governance structures that can be effective in promoting plan solvency.

Recently, multi-employer DB plans have been expanding into industries where they were less prevalent in the past, often in response to the failure of single-employer DB plans. This chapter explores the role multi-employer DB plans have played in the past and could play in the future in providing retirement security. The experience of the International Association of Machinists and Aerospace Workers (IAM) in transitioning thousands of airline members into the IAM's national multi-employer DB plan is explored to illustrate how these plans can simultaneously meet the needs of workers and employers, even in the most challenging circumstances. We also address factors driving recent trends, explore best practices for multi-employer DB plans and trustees, and offer recommendations for stabilizing multi-employer DB plan coverage in this new environment.

Background

Multi-employer DB pension plans are an important source of guaranteed monthly pension benefits in the United States. Today, close to 10 million Americans participate in such plans. Of workers and retirees who participate in a DB pension plan, about 1 in 5 is covered by a multi-employer plan (Pension Benefit Guaranty Corporation 2006).

Multi-employer DB plans are a natural fit for certain trades and industries, due to the portable nature of benefits. The construction industry, where tradespeople work for many different employers as they move from one project to the next, accounts for more than one third of U.S. multi-employer DB plan participants. The entertainment industry has also long relied on the multi-employer model for benefit provision, in large part because of the mobility of performers and stage workers who move from one production to another (Pension Benefit Guaranty Corporation 2006).[1] Typically, multi-employer DB plans are established only for workers covered under a collective bargaining agreement.

Multi-employer pension plans are a long-established feature of the retirement landscape. One of the first unions to establish such a plan was Local 3 of the International Brotherhood of Electrical Workers and Electrical Contractors in New York in 1929 (Employee Benefit Research Institute 1997). But multi-employer DB plans as we know them today grew rapidly in size and scope during the 1950s and 1960s following the passage of the Taft-Hartley Act of 1947; hence they are also referred to as Taft-Hartley plans (Weinstein and Wiatrowski 1999). The act created strict limitations on the operation of union-related health, welfare, pension, and other funds, and for that reason it was initially opposed by labor unions. Over time, though, the Taft-Hartley Act had the effect of enhancing the legitimacy of multi-employer plans, by requiring (among other things) joint labor–management oversight of these funds, which in turn fostered their growth.[2] Since that time, other regulations have come into force governing multi-employer DB plans. For instance, benefits earned in multi-employer DB plans, like their single-employer counterparts, are protected by the Employee Retirement Income Security Act of 1974 (ERISA), and funding of the plans is governed by ERISA and the Internal Revenue Code (IRC).

The multi-employer plan model has been uniquely suited to fill a coverage gap that seems to be a pervasive feature of the U.S. private and voluntary social insurance system—that is, low-income workers and employees of small and medium-sized companies, who often do not have access to a pension plan unless covered by a multi-employer plan.

Most small employers do not sponsor any kind of pension or retirement savings plan, not even a 401(k) or other DC plan. In 2005, just one fourth of full-time employees of very small businesses (those with 25 or fewer employees) participated in a retirement plan at work. And less than half of full-time employees in small firms (those with 25 to 99 employees) participated in a retirement plan (Purcell 2006). Income level is also an important determinant of pension plan coverage. In 2005, fewer than three out of 10 full-time workers in the lowest income quartile participated in a retirement plan at work (Purcell 2006). Retirement plan coverage for low-income workers in small firms is, as one would imagine, the lowest among all groups of workers.

There are various reasons for these coverage trends among small and medium-sized employers, but cost and administrative burdens are two of the primary causes of low rates of plan sponsorship (Council of Institutional Investors 2005). At the same time, some low-income workers and employees do manage to obtain pensions. How does it happen?

Many researchers have concluded that union membership is a significant, positive factor in predicting pension and other employee benefit coverage.[3] And while union membership is an important determinant of pension coverage for all workers, the effect is especially strong for those with low incomes and those who work for small employers. For example, Ghilarducci and Lee (2005) found that while just 33.8% of low-income men are covered by a pension, 70.7% of low-income male union members have a pension at work. These authors attribute the large union pension premium among low-income workers and employees of small firms to such firms' reliance on multi-employer plans.

By pooling contributions from many small and medium-sized employers, multi-employer plans can make the impossible possible. The aggregation of contributions from many different employers can create economies of scale and minimize administrative burdens, enabling employers that may be too small, too unstable, or too cash-strapped to sponsor employee benefit plans on their own to offer pensions to their employees. This means workers who might otherwise not be able to save consistently for retirement have the opportunity to accumulate substantial retirement benefits.

Certain features that have contributed to multi-employer DB plans' successful track record for small employers and lower-wage workers also make such plans the logical model to provide pension benefits in the future for employers of all sizes and workers of varying income levels. Specifically, multi-employer DB plans combine features of DB plans and DC plans, thus offering unique advantages to both employers and employees.

Important Features of Multi-employer Plans

Multi-employer DB plans are often referred to as "union plans," but this is a misnomer. They are separate, stand-alone entities that exist for a single purpose—to provide pension benefits. As described previously, pursuant to the provisions of the Taft-Hartley Act, the plans are jointly overseen by labor and management trustees. The trustees hire professionals to manage the day-to-day operations of the fund—administration, investment of plan assets, collection of contributions, and payment of benefits.

That said, unions do play an important role in the establishment and growth of multi-employer plans. They help overcome a collective action problem—that employers (especially small ones) may not be able to individually sponsor plans but also may be reluctant to cooperate with competitors to establish a joint plan (Ghilarducci 2002). Unions, as representatives, reveal worker preferences for retirement benefits that a single worker could not effectively bargain for. And where a union represents many different employers in a single sector or industry, it is uniquely positioned to encourage collective behavior among firms.

Plan Funding and Benefit Determination

The union's pivotal role in multi-employer DB plans stems from the collective bargaining process. It is through the collective bargaining agreement that the employer becomes a participating employer in a multi-employer plan. Under such an arrangement, the union and an employer negotiate a specific contribution to the pension trust, which is agreed upon by the parties for the duration of the collective bargaining agreement. This agreement represents the company's financial obligation to the plan. Except in unusual circumstances (described later in this chapter), the amount agreed to cannot fluctuate. This gives the employer the advantage of a predictable cash cost for pensions for several years. In other words, to the employer, the arrangement mimics a DC plan. However, under a multi-employer DB plan, employees are entitled to regular monthly retirement benefits. To accomplish this, the plan takes in the employer contributions, invests them, and eventually pays out benefits to retirees. Unlike in 401(k) plans, the employer must make contributions for all eligible employees, so multi-employer DB plans mimic the broad-based coverage in single-employer DB plans.

The plan, not the union or the employer, is responsible for setting the benefit level for the contributions received, based on actuarial analysis. ERISA's so-called "anti-cutback rule" applies to benefits earned in multi-employer DB plans just as it applies to single-employer plans— once a benefit is earned and vested, it cannot be taken away or reduced.[4] A multi-employer DB plan *can* change benefit levels on a prospective basis, however, just as single-employer plans can.

Benefit formulas vary and are specific to each individual plan. In addition to normal retirement benefits, other benefits, such as early retirement, disability retirement, and death benefits, may be offered. Multi-employer DB plans can tailor benefit designs to address the specific needs of the workforce covered by the plan, so long as they comport with legal requirements. For instance, just like single-employer DB plans, multi-employer DB plans must offer lifetime annuity distributions and joint-life annuity distributions for married participants, but they may also offer other benefit forms. Multi-employer DB plans must also pay premiums to the Pension Benefit Guaranty Corporation (PBGC), the government agency that insures private sector DB pension plans.[5]

From the description so far, a multi-employer DB plan looks very much like a DC plan to the employer, even though it is in fact a DB plan (but with attractive DC-like features such as portability). This combination of features means that the multi-employer model can offer the best of both worlds: predictability of contributions for employers and the security of benefits that are portable for employees.

But what is the result when reality fails to match up with a plan's actuarial assumptions? What happens when the plan finds itself in the happy circumstance of having more than enough assets to pay for earned benefits? Or in the opposite case, when the plan develops a funding shortfall? Which side bears the risk—employers or employees? Depending on the circumstances, the answer could be just employers, just employees, or both.

Risk Sharing in Multi-employer Plans

The trustees of the plan have the discretion to decide how to handle surpluses and shortfalls, consistent with plan policies and governing documents. When surpluses develop, multi-employer DB plan trustees may choose to improve benefits for employees, and in practice, this is what tends to happen. Because employer contributions are set in advance for the duration of the collective bargaining agreement, regular contributions are always coming in to the plan, so plan participants benefit from unusual investment gains.

This can be contrasted with the practice in single-employer plans—when the fund accumulates a surplus, the plan sponsor frequently stops making additional contributions. The ability of single-employer plan sponsors to take such "contribution holidays" can create tremendous volatility in the pattern of contributions. In one year or for many years in a row, the company may make no cash contributions to the plan, only to find in subsequent years that large cash contributions are now due (Government Accountability Office 2005).

When it comes to shortfalls, the situation in multi-employer DB plans is also quite different from the single-employer world. In the single-employer situation, funding rules as embodied in ERISA and IRC dictate a contribution schedule that the employer must meet to fill the gap within a certain period. When markets swing widely, that can lead to unpredictable contribution requirements. In a multi-employer plan, however, when the value of vested benefits owed to participants exceeds the plan's assets, the plan must first determine, for each contributing employer, its own pro rata share of the shortfall, an amount referred to as a company's "withdrawal liability." A participating employer is not required to immediately "fund-up" its share of the shortfall, though. As mentioned before, an employer's financial obligation to the fund is defined in the collective bargaining agreement. Therefore, it is generally the case that employers cannot be required to make larger contributions while a contract is in place, and they have no obligation per se to commit to larger contributions after the contract expires.[6]

Because employers' contributions to the fund are determined through collective bargaining and not through demands by the fund's trustees, responsible trustees will exercise options at their disposal to protect fund solvency. For instance, trustees may choose to build up a cushion of funds beyond the amounts required to pay for benefits, to guard against a negative shock from financial markets. But in the face of a shortfall that is serious and persistent enough that over time it could jeopardize the fund, a plan's trustees may take steps to reduce future benefit levels. This in turn would require a larger contribution from an employer to keep employees' benefit level constant. So when the bargaining parties negotiate for a new collective bargaining agreement, there are two possible outcomes: either the employer agrees to increase contributions to maintain employees' benefit levels, or it does not agree and employees' future benefit accruals are reduced.

Actually, there is a third possible outcome—the employer chooses to make no contributions at all. In other words, the employer withdraws from the plan entirely after the labor contract expires. This event would trigger an obligation to pay the amount of withdrawal liability assessed by the fund. Once the employer withdraws, it owes this obligation to the plan and must pay either immediately or over time with interest.

What this means is that employers and unions in effect must negotiate over the effects of a funding shortfall. Will employers pay through increased contributions? Or will employees pay through reduced benefit accruals?[7] The outcome is determined by arm's-length bargaining. Such an arrangement means that the parties must work through difficult questions together and reach a negotiated settlement that all can live with. By their design, multi-employer DB plans make sure that all parties' "handprints" are on outcomes—union, employer, and plan trustees. This gives all parties high-powered incentives to act with prudence, with an eye toward solvency and long-term benefit sustainability. The fact that PBGC benefit guarantees are lower in the multi-employer program than they are in the single-employer program reinforces these incentives.

For these reasons—steady contributions with no contribution holidays and shared governance features—well-run multi-employer plans should find that difficult situations like funding shortfalls are less likely to develop, as compared with single-employer plans. The importance of the relationship between plan governance and solvency cannot be overstated. Unlike multi-employer plan trustees, single-employer plan sponsors may face competing claims on corporate funds from various constituencies—employees, shareholders, executives, bond holders, and others. As a result, single-employer plan sponsors may face conflicting motivations—e.g., to put surplus funds into the pension plan rather than pay those funds out to shareholders—especially when times are good. This conflict may be inherent in the governance of many single-employer plans. Because the decision to fund the plan is made by individuals (most often company executives) who face conflicting objectives, it is not surprising that single-employer pension plans can find themselves in a vulnerable position when the market swings from bull to bear. For example, a recent GAO study found that, from 1995 to 2002, a significant majority of the 100 largest single-employer plans received no cash contributions, including 41% of plans that were underfunded (Government Accountability Office 2005).

Of course, trustees of multi-employer DB plans may face their own temptations in "good years." For them the risk is making overly generous benefit promises when investment returns are above average and having to roll back those promises in lean years when markets are not performing as well.

Trends in Multi-employer Plan Funding

So what has been the track record of multi-employer DB plans? Well-funded multi-employer plans are not a rarity, but recently they have been not as common as we might like. Using PBGC statistics, the picture looks gloomy indeed. In 2003, as the "perfect storm" crested, just 136 multi-employer plans with liabilities of $17 billion and a half million participants had a funded ratio of 90% or better. This represented only 8% of all plans and 5% of all participants. Just 51 plans were either fully funded or overfunded (Pension Benefit Guaranty Corporation 2006). It should be noted that PBGC measures funded status using an extremely conservative method, valuing liabilities at what it would cost to turn them over to an insurance company by purchasing an annuity contract. In other words, the methodology does not treat the plan as a "going concern" (an ongoing entity assumed to continue on into the indefinite future), but rather compares plan assets to the cost of winding the plan down immediately.

If one were to use a less conservative (going concern) method of valuation, the picture would not appear nearly as bad. For example, the Segal Company, a major consulting firm with significant multi-employer plan business, publishes an annual study of multi-employer plan funding. In 2003, it estimated that the average plan was 87% funded and that 31% of plans were fully funded for vested benefits, meaning that they had no withdrawal liability (Segal Company 2006).[8] The Segal Company uses a "going concern" measurement of plan funding in its studies.

The funded status of multi-employer plans in the early part of this decade deteriorated for the same reasons that many single-employer pension plans saw their funding drop—a sharp drop in the stock market and interest rates that fell to historic lows and stayed there for many years. Because funding patterns are cyclical, we can expect improvement for many plans as asset values recover and interest rates revert to more typical levels. Moreover, because many plans have taken steps to limit the growth of liabilities, this should also help their funded positions. For example, the Segal Company's annual survey found that 9% of multi-employer plans reduced future benefits in 2005 and that 4% had done so in 2004 (Segal Company 2006).

A well-run multi-employer plan is one that successfully balances participants' desire for benefit improvements with long-run solvency considerations. Many funds adopt practices that help with managing that balance, including using conservative interest rate and mortality assumptions, which have the effect of providing a financial cushion. They also adopt policies that prohibit benefit improvements that would create unfunded benefits or exacerbate withdrawal liability. Fund trustees who are able to strike this balance find that they can offer "the best of both worlds" to employees and employers—a DB plan that functions for employers like a DC plan.

In recent years, many unions have leveraged the advantages that well-run multi-employer plans provide to expand pension coverage. Indeed, even as the number of active employees covered by single-employer plans has continued its steady decline, the decline in coverage of active employees in multi-employer plans appears to have leveled off in recent years, as Figure 1 illustrates. And although coverage in multi-employer DB plans is not growing quickly enough to offset the continued downward trend in single-employer coverage, it does provide a glimmer of hope for those who believe that DB plans are critical to retirement security.

Indeed, the much-lamented flight of employers from DB sponsorship has presented unions with an opportunity. Unions with well run multi-employer DB plans can offer their existing members or potential new members the chance for a secure retirement, even when (or especially when) employers are reluctant to sponsor pension plans on their

FIGURE 1

Active Participants in Multiemployer Defined Benefit Plans, 1985–2003

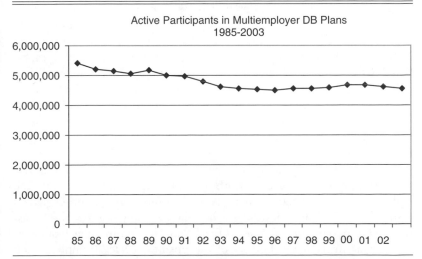

Source: Authors' calculations based on data from Pension Benefit Guaranty Corporation 2006.

own. Some unions have seized this opportunity to expand multi-employer coverage into entirely new areas. In recent years, multi-employer DB plans have played an important role in transitioning employees from, for instance, failed single-employer plans in the airline industry to benefit plans that should prove more durable in the future. The IAM is one union that has successfully achieved benefit security for members in this way.

The Airline Pension Crisis and the IAM Response

The airline pension crisis of the early 2000s was the primary wreckage of the so-called perfect storm, a sudden confluence of three events that caused many DB plans to suddenly appear underfunded. The sharp drop in the stock market followed by an extended period of extremely low interest rates conspired with general economic weakness as well as industry-specific factors (i.e., the September 11th terrorist attacks) to drive many single-employer pension plans in the airline industry to the breaking point (Almeida 2005). Researchers have observed that the countercyclical funding burdens created by pension funding rules may have the effect of increasing, not decreasing, the likelihood of single-employer pension plan terminations. This is because firms are tempted to minimize contributions when investment returns are good but must "fund-up" when times are bad, when money is less available (Weller and Baker 2005).

And indeed, the past several years have vividly illustrated the effect of countercyclical funding burdens in industries that are highly cyclical. In 2002 and 2003, the steel industry witnessed an almost wholesale abandonment of employer-sponsored DB pension plans, with the PBGC taking on $6.7 billion in claims in distress terminations at LTV Steel, National Steel, and Bethlehem Steel (Pension Benefit Guaranty Corporation 2004). A similar wave of distress terminations followed in the airline industry. In the words of Bradley Belt, former head of PBGC, "In the early 1980s, it was Braniff. In the early 1990s, it was Pan Am and Eastern. And in this decade it has been TWA, US Airways, and United. Claims from just these six airlines come to $11.7 billion, or 38% percent of the total in the history of the pension insurance program" (Belt 2005:12).

While different in many respects, the airline and steel industries share important similarities. Both are very capital intensive but face highly competitive product markets, with commodity-like pricing. As a result, for both airlines and steel, when the economy sneezes, the industry catches pneumonia. This leads to a relatively high frequency of bankruptcies as firms at the bottom of the business cycle attempt to shed fixed costs and successfully reorganize.

To the extent that an individual firm has unfunded pension liabilities, these typically have become targets for elimination in Chapter 11 bankruptcy cases. Companies, upon meeting certain standards, may move to terminate pension plans as a part of bankruptcy reorganization, discharging their liability to pay for pension underfunding. Indeed, bankruptcies in the two industries discussed here have accounted for more than 70% of claims under PBGC's single-employer insurance program (Belt 2005). Of course, it was not macroeconomic factors alone that ultimately caused the collapse of many single-employer DB plans. The fact that employers had sole control of pension funding decisions and that single-employer pension plans are exposed to the vagaries of a single industry also contributed to the pension crises in these industries. This experience suggests that the single-employer model may not be especially durable for industries highly sensitive to economic swings. And although the high-profile failures of single-employer plans in the airline industry made headlines, what happened afterward has not been as widely covered.

United Airlines

In July 2004, more than 18 months into its bankruptcy reorganization, United Airlines made a dramatic announcement that it would stop funding its pension plans. This news sent shock waves through United's workforce and indeed across America, since almost all observers predicted that ceasing funding was just a first step toward the eventual termination of United's pension plans (Williams Walsh 2004). By the following spring, United Airlines had reached an agreement with the PBGC to take over the company's four failed pension plans. These plans together were underfunded by an estimated $10 billion—making United's the biggest pension default in history (Pension Benefit Guaranty Corporation 2005a). The agency covered about two thirds of the shortfall between earned benefits and assets in the plan, but about a third was borne directly by participants, who stood to lose roughly $3 billion in earned benefits that were not covered by PBGC guarantees (Pension Benefit Guaranty Corporation 2005a).

As soon as United made the announcement it would stop funding the plans, unions representing United's employees launched a battle—in the press, in Congress, and in the courts—to save their pension plans. Because pension benefits are deferred compensation, in economic terms, the loss of benefits stemming from the termination of the pension plans was no different than if the employer had imposed a retroactive pay cut, which stretched back as far as an employee's date of hire. In the end, however, the legal and political maneuvers bore little fruit. The terminations were ultimately upheld as lawful (Alexander 2005).

While the unions at United were ultimately unable to prevent the termination of the company's pension plans, they did have the opportunity to engage in collective bargaining with the carrier over replacement plans. Early on in the process (in fact months in advance of the termination), the company proposed that the terminated plans be replaced with "competitive defined contributions plans" (United Airlines 2004:89). In an informational brief filed with the bankruptcy court, United noted several features that made DC plans "more attractive to workers." The brief cited the portability of 401(k) plans, which workers could "take with them from one job to the next," "transparency," and "control over investments" (United Airlines 2004:89). But United left out any discussion of the features of DC plans that make them *less* attractive to workers, such as increased uncertainty, investment risks, and lack of availability of a lifetime income upon retirement. It was a focus on these features that led one union, the IAM, to make clear to the company from the outset that it would not settle for a 401(k) plan as the sole source of retirement benefits for its members.[9]

The IAM was intent on having its members at United covered by a multi-employer DB plan, the IAM National Pension Fund's National Pension Plan (NPP). The NPP was established in 1960 to provide retirement benefits for employees who are represented for the purposes of collective bargaining by the IAM. From that time, the NPP has grown to cover more than 75,000 active participants working under more than 1,700 collective bargaining agreements. At the end of 2004, the fund had close to $7 billion in assets (IAM National Pension Fund 2004). Unlike some multi-employer plans that are concentrated in just one industry, the NPP's contributing employers span a range of industries. This diversification helps protect the solvency of the plan—a shock to one industry will not undermine the solvency of the entire plan.

The advantages of having airline employees join the NPP were apparent to the IAM even before this most recent crisis. As the largest airline union in North America, and having witnessed pension terminations at Eastern Airlines, TWA, and other carriers, the IAM was well aware of the fragile nature of single-employer plans in the airline industry. Indeed, the IAM had proposed in the prior round of negotiations with United (in 2000 to 2002) that the company transition IAM members out of the company-sponsored plans into the NPP. In that prior round of talks, the company did not agree to the union's proposal, making United's moves just two years later to terminate their pension plans all the more galling to the IAM. The union believed that had the company accepted its earlier proposal, the United plans would never have reached the breaking point and been terminated.

The IAM made its case, both publicly and at the bargaining table, that because the NPP had a 20-year track record of no withdrawal liability, the cost and risk to the company of participating in the multi-employer plan was no greater than that of the 401(k) plan being proposed by the airline (Wisniewski 2005). Thus, the union argued, the company ought to have no business reason to not agree to its proposal. IAM members felt strongly enough about the issue of retirement security that 94% of members voted in favor of giving the union authorization to call a strike over it (Adams 2005)—a remarkable showing when one considers the seriousness of striking a company in bankruptcy.

Ultimately, the IAM and United reached an agreement on the pension issue in early summer 2005, and the employees voted to approve the terms of the new contract in July (International Association of Machinists and Aerospace Workers 2005). The IAM was successful in achieving its demands, and today, members of the IAM are the only employees at United, including management and executive employees, to enjoy the security of a DB plan in addition to a 401(k) plan. Although benefit levels currently are lower than those under the terminated United plans, they are far more generous than what employees stood to get from the company's initial DC proposal. Moreover, now that the seed of a new DB plan has been planted, there will be opportunities in future negotiations for the parties to improve these benefits over time. Under the NPP, employees will be eligible for disability benefits, early retirement benefits, and spousal benefits that would not have been available in a DC scheme.

US Airways

Workers at US Airways were arguably the hardest hit by the events of September 11th, given the airline's concentration of operations in Washington, DC and New York City. The airline was on shaky financial footing even before the terrorist attacks, and it approached its unions in early 2002 to negotiate contract concessions as it prepared to file for bankruptcy protection. For fleet service agents at the carrier, this presented an unusual opportunity to right wrongs that had occurred a decade earlier.[10]

During the years of the last industry crisis (1992 to 1993), US Airways unilaterally froze accruals in its single-employer DB plan covering nonunion workers, substituting a 401(k) plan in its place. The fleet service agents at US Airways at that time were not represented by a union. These workers subsequently joined the IAM in 1994, due largely to their unhappiness over losing their DB plan. After the IAM was certified to represent the employees, it engaged in bargaining over an extended period with the company to reach a first collective bargaining agreement. However, when the parties finally reached an agreement in 1999, it did not incorporate the union's goal of reviving a DB pension plan for fleet service employees.

The union thus approached the prebankruptcy negotiations in 2002 with the unfinished business of reinstating a DB plan. Facing the reality of the impending bankruptcy, the IAM agreed to open up the contract to discuss certain concessions. However, the union also insisted that without agreement on the pension issue, there could be no agreement on concessions. After months of talks, the parties ultimately agreed to divert the contributions that had been going into the 401(k) plan into the NPP. In this way, the 4,000 fleet service employees at the carrier finally achieved a DB pension, and it was accomplished at a cost to the company no higher that what it had been spending for the 401(k) plan. Again, because the NPP was fully funded and had no withdrawal liability, the company's negotiated contribution represented its entire obligation to the fund.

The durability of the multi-employer model was proven when US Airways filed for bankruptcy for the second time in as many years during the fall of 2004. In this second bankruptcy proceeding, all of the company-sponsored pension plans that were still in effect—those covering mechanics, flight attendants, and the long-ago frozen plan that covered nonunion, management, and salaried employees—were all terminated and taken over by PBGC (Pension Benefit Guaranty Corporation 2005b). However, the IAM was able to maintain participation in the NPP for the fleet service agents, since the company's only obligation to the plan was its regular negotiated contribution. The lack of withdrawal liability in the plan meant that there was no debt overhang stemming from the plan that the company could seek to discharge in bankruptcy. In other words, the company had no good business reason to leave the multi-employer plan, but very good reasons to stay in. After all the lay-offs, pay cuts, and general disruption to the workforce caused by the back-to-back bankruptcies, the multi-employer plan was the means by which the company could continue to offer workers a secure DB pension at a reasonable cost, helping to retain qualified employees.

An even larger number of employees will be eligible to participate in this plan as a result of the merger of US Airways and America West. The National Mediation Board certified the IAM as the representative of fleet service agents employed by the merged carriers in the spring of 2006 (National Mediation Board 2006). As a result, 2,400 additional employees—who had no DB pension plan at America West—now can look forward to being covered by a multi-employer DB plan. Like their IAM counterparts at United Airlines, US Airways employees enjoy the protection of disability retirement benefits, the option to take early-retirement benefits, and the ability to protect their spouses after their own death with joint-and-survivor benefit options. And just like at United, IAM members at US Airways are the only employees to enjoy the security of a DB plan, on top of a 401(k) plan.

Other Airlines

As other airlines have undergone similar restructurings, the IAM has promoted participation in the NPP as a way to enhance retirement security for its members. For example, IAM members at Aloha Airlines, which terminated its pension plans in early 2006, joined the NPP later that year. At Northwest Airlines (which at the time of this writing is still under bankruptcy court protection), the IAM negotiated participation in the NPP for its members in the wake of a freeze in benefit accruals in the company-sponsored DB plan. To guard against the wave of pension terminations and freezes sweeping the industry, IAM-represented flight attendants at Continental Airlines in early 2006 negotiated a provision in their collective bargaining agreement that if the company-sponsored DB plan became endangered, they would have the option to join the NPP as well. While the pattern of pension terminations in the airline industry has been a source of great insecurity to employees, IAM members have a backup plan to safeguard their futures if and when employer-sponsored plans fail.

Success stories like these have made an important impact on the retirement prospects of tens of thousands of American workers, for whom access to a multi-employer DB plan has meant the difference between a secure, defined retirement benefit, backed up by PBGC insurance guarantees, and having to rely solely on a DC plan, with all the uncertainties that entails. When one considers the gloomy state of the DB pension landscape as a whole, the success stories profiled here are that much more impressive. These stories also show that through multi-employer DB plans, unions can achieve important things for their members. In the United case, the challenge was to transition employees from a failed single-employer DB plan while building a foundation for future retirement security. With US Airways, the multi-employer plan was a way to reinstate DB benefits in the long-ago wake of a frozen company-sponsored DB plan. In the Continental situation, the option to join the multi-employer DB plan acts as an insurance policy.

But even with their differences, there are common threads in these cases. The first has to do with timing. These stories illustrate how the IAM has taken advantage of the fact that concessionary bargaining can create opportunities, even as difficult sacrifices are required. Second, they show that success is more likely when retirement security is a high priority for employees. The strong commitment of IAM members to achieving the goal of participation in the multi-employer plan (as illustrated by the United employees' strike vote) was key to union negotiators' success in prevailing on these issues at the bargaining table. Also, the importance of the well-funded status of the NPP and the absence of withdrawal liability cannot be overstated. The ability of the IAM to convince new employers to come into the plan relied in large measure on employers' feeling that doing so was prudent. This multi-employer DB plan's track record of more than 20 years of avoiding withdrawal liability, in good times and in bad, signals a conservative approach to plan management that reassures employers that joining the fund carries few risks. The fact that the plan was made up of a highly diversified group of contributing employers, rather than being all concentrated in a single industry, also minimized the risk to employers joining the fund that a shock to one sector or region of the country could throw the fund out of balance.

What Are the Prospects for Creating Other Success Stories?

While the individual success stories we have described are impressive, they do beg the question of how widely they can be replicated. The answer is important, because recent multi-employer trends seem to point in conflicting directions.

Until a recent leveling off participation in multi-employer plans had been on the decline for a long time. The number of active participants in multi-employer plans fell to 4.6 million in 2005 from about 6 million in 1980. Coverage fell steadily through the 1980s and much of the 1990s. Active coverage hit a low of 4.5 million participants in 1996. With the strong performance of the labor market, the number of active employees covered by these plans improved in the late 1990s and has remained at roughly the same level since (Pension Benefit Guaranty Corporation 2006). Of course, when one compares these coverage statistics with the overall size of the private-sector labor force, the reach of multi-employer plans declines with each passing year. It is little consolation that the rate of decline has been slower than that of single-employer plans.

A recent report by the Government Accountability Office, formerly called the General Accounting Office (2004) identified a number of causes contributing to this decline. Of course, the overall decline in union representation and collective bargaining is a key factor that has contributed to a leveling off in multi-employer DB plan coverage. If policy makers hope to expand multi-employer pension plan coverage, steps to restore collective bargaining widely in the U.S. economy will have to be taken.

The GAO report cited other factors, some of which have to do with the design of multi-employer DB plans themselves. For example, it posited that employers' limited ability to adjust contributions from one year to the next may be a factor inhibiting multi-employer DB plan growth. However, this seems contrary to many surveys of employers that have found that predictability in pension contributions is very important to them (Hewitt Associates 2003).

The fear of withdrawal liability developing within a plan, either from poor performance or because other contributing employers fail, is a more likely factor contributing to a decline in multi-employer DB plan coverage. Also, the growth of DB plans overall is being challenged by factors that are not unique to multi-employer plans, namely, the perceived advantages of DC plans for employers—that they are cheaper and more predictable (General Accounting Office 2004).

The good news is that multi-employer plan trustees have some ability to deal with these factors. For example, they can design contribution structures workable for employers *and* for the fund. And they can take steps to avoid withdrawal liability. A plan without withdrawal liability in effect works just like a DC plan to a contributing employer. In that sense, plan trustees can use the preference for DC plans among some employers to their advantage. The healthy growth enjoyed by well-funded plans like the NPP has likely stemmed from the fact that employers are not afraid to join the fund since there is no withdrawal liability overhang. Indeed, over a five-year period plan participation grew by about 20%. The NPP had about 61,500 active participants in 1999, which grew to 73,500 by 2004. Plan assets have grown from about $5 billion to about $7 billion (IAM National Pension Fund 1999, 2004). Plans like the NPP have enjoyed a "virtuous cycle," where prudent funding and management have encouraged growth, and growth has in turn encouraged better funding. Of course, what that means for plans with large withdrawal liabilities may be less encouraging.

Some plans face problems that may be less likely to improve quickly. Plans with high ratios of retirees to active employees may find that the dual challenges of obtaining greater contributions from employers and reducing benefits prospectively conflict with each other. Because employer contributions must be bargained, active employees may be less willing to push for large contributions (which may be offset with reductions in other areas of compensation) when their own benefits have been reduced. Moreover, in plans where the majority of benefit liabilities stem from long-ago employees who are now retirees, the impact that prospective benefit cuts have may be limited.

Unlike the "virtuous cycle" enjoyed by growing, well-funded plans, some financially weak plans face a vicious cycle, whereby the cure for the underfunding problem (benefit reductions and high contributions from active employees that take away from funds available to put toward other compensation areas) could make the plan unattractive to potential new employers and new union members. Reputation effects can also be problematic—new employers and new members may be reluctant to join a plan that is viewed as being "troubled." In situations like these, it will be hard for plans to grow their way out of the problem.

Looking Ahead

The difficulties of a small number of large, very underfunded multi-employer pension plans recently prompted a major change in the rules governing multi-employer pension plan funding. The Pension Protection Act of 2006 was designed to close many of the "loopholes" that were per-ceived to have contributed to poor levels of funding of DB pension plans, whether of the single- or multi-employer variety. The law radically overhauled the rules governing single-employer DB plan funding and created a new set of regulations for multi-employer DB plans.

Under the new rules, multi-employer DB plans will be required to actively monitor plan funding and keep a sharp eye out for potential funding problems that may develop in the future. The law creates cer-tain thresholds that, if breached, will require multi-employer plan trustees and parties to collective bargaining agreements to take certain steps to protect plan solvency. For example, plans that are deemed "endangered" must develop a funding improvement plan, outlining the steps that will be taken to correct the underfunding. Bargaining parties will be notified of the options available to them (i.e., greater contribu-tions or reduced benefits) to stem the problem. Worse-off plans that are judged to be in "critical" status must develop a rehabilitation plan, but they also are given special rights to demand additional contributions from contributing employers. Plans classified as critical also have the ability to cut back certain "non-core" accrued vested benefits to help restore a fund's balance. For example, benefits at normal retirement age may not be cut back, but early-retirement benefits may be reduced. This weakening of ERISA's anti-cutback protections was the most controver-sial part of the legislation, and it prompted criticism from both active and retired members of very troubled multi-employer DB plans (Pension Rights Center 2006).

What these new provisions mean for multi-employer DB plans is not yet clear. While plans deemed in "critical" status under the new law will find that they have strong medicine available to correct plan underfunding, will the weakening of ERISA's anti-cutback protections make workers more hesitant about joining multi-employer DB plans, thus damaging the prospects of these plans over the long haul? Or will the new law's emphasis on long-term solvency spur trustees to behave more conservatively to avoid the "endangered" or "critical" label, helping more plans enjoy the virtuous cycle of growth? What is clear is that proper funding of plans is more important than ever. While it has always been true that benefit security can only be achieved through adequate funding, we may be entering a period when funding levels will mean the difference between existence or extinction for a given plan.

Even in the face of trends that would seem to paint a gloomy picture for the future of some multi-employer DB plans, plan trustees (especially union-side trustees) should remember that there is a silver lining in the clouds. The dwindling commitment among employers to sponsoring DB plans means that multi-employer DB plans have a unique growth opportunity. Because of this, unions also have a chance to grow. Increasingly in the future, union membership can be the key to benefit security, the means by which employees obtain guaranteed pension benefits in retirement. Well-funded and prudently run multi-employer DB plans and the unions they are connected to are uniquely positioned to take advantage of these opportunities.

Given what we know about the role of unions in fostering collective action, among workers as well as among firms, if we hope to grow the multi-employer model in the future, we must give equal attention to growing unions. Union membership in the private sector has fallen to historic lows, and DB pension coverage has declined along with it. Legislative initiatives like the "Employee Free Choice Act" (introduced in the 109th Congress as S.842/H.R. 1696) will be critical to rebuilding the ability of workers to bargain collectively in the United States and give effective voice to their concerns about retirement security.

Too often in the public eye, unions are painted as the problem— they are "inflexible," they are "demanding," they go on strike. But when it comes to the vexing national question of expanding pension coverage, they have an opportunity to be the solution. By combining features of DB and DC plans, multi-employer DB plans, and the unions they are connected to, have successfully delivered benefit security for millions of employees in a way that small employers and employers in volatile industries can live with. Success stories like the IAM's experience in transitioning thousands of airline workers out of failed single-employer pension plans into more durable, better funded multi-employer DB plans prove that it can be accomplished in other industries as well.

Endnotes

[1] Beyond these two sectors, the trucking industry accounts for 14% of participants in multi-employer plans, and retail trade (mostly grocery) accounts for another 13%. The remaining third of participants in multi-employer plans are spread across various manufacturing and service industries (Pension Benefit Guaranty Corporation 2006).

[2] Not all multi-employer retirement benefit plans are Taft-Hartley pension plans; TIAA-CREF, for example, is a retirement fund for teachers, researchers, and others working for nonprofit and educational institutions. Nor *must* Taft-Hartley multi-employer plans offer defined benefits. For example, a Taft-Hartley trust could be set up to accommodate a multi-employer DC plan. We restrict our scope to a discussion of Taft-Hartley DB plans.

[3] See Budd 2004 for a review of findings.

[4] Recent changes to ERISA made by the Pension Protection Act of 2006 create new circumstances and exceptions to the "anti-cutback rule." If a plan's financial position deteriorates such that certain thresholds are breached, some early-retirement and other benefits may be reduced. Normal retirement benefits, however, cannot be reduced.

[5] Coverage limits in PBGC's multi-employer program are lower than those under the single-employer program, reflecting lower premiums paid by plans. Because they do not have to rely on the financial health of a single employer, multi-employer DB plans have historically posed a lower risk of insolvency to PBGC as compared with single-employer plans. PBGC generally does not terminate troubled multi-employer plans; rather, it provides financial assistance (usually in the form of loans) to cover benefit payments. Since 1975, the agency has taken over 3,585 single-employer DB plans, representing net claims on the agency of $29.5 billion. By comparison, since 1981, only 41 multi-employer plans have received financial assistance to pay benefits, with an aggregate of $191.2 million disbursed (Pension Benefit Guaranty Corporation 2006).

[6] Plan trustees can compel payments to the fund in exceptional circumstances when the plan must cure a funding deficiency. If an employer fails to make the required payments, tax penalties are applied. This is an extremely rare event. Parties generally can foresee funding deficiencies and take steps to avoid them (by either reducing future benefits or increasing employer contributions).

[7] Some would argue that the question of "who pays" is irrelevant because contributions to a plan are just another form of compensation. This argument states that if a company increases its costs in one area of compensation—say higher contributions to a multi-employer pension plan—it will offset the expense in some other area, such as wages. The argument has weight in light of a common practice in the construction industry, whereby the employer and the union agree to a total hourly rate of compensation, and it is left to the union to allocate these amounts among cash wages and fringe benefits (Mazo 2006).

[8] Still, when one compares multi-employer plans with single-employer plans on the same basis, multi-employer plans appear to be less well funded. PBGC reported that the 2003 average funded ratio (i.e., the ratio of assets to liabilities) for multi-employer plans as a group was 64%. Single-employer plans, as a group, had an average funded status of 84% that same year. (Pension Benefit Guaranty Corporation 2006).

[9] The IAM is the largest union at United Airlines, representing about a third of the carrier's U.S. workforce. In 2006, the union represented more than 17,000 active

United employees in the ramp and stores, public contact, food service, security, fleet technical instructor, emergency procedure instructor, and maintenance instructor classifications. The IAM has represented employees at United Airlines since 1945.

[10] Fleet service agents are ground workers whose main responsibility is loading of baggage, cargo, and other material onto and off of aircraft.

References

Adams, Marilyn. 2005. "United Reports $1.1B Loss in Quarter; Labor, Airline Work on New Contracts." *USA Today*, May 12, p. B1.

Alexander, Keith. 2005. "United Can End Pensions, Judge Says." *Washington Post*, May 11, E1.

Almeida, Beth. 2005. "Weathering the Perfect Storm: Defined Benefit Pension Plans in the Airline Industry." *Proceedings of the 57th Annual Meeting*, Philadelphia, PA, January 6–9. Champaign, IL: Labor and Employment Relations Association, pp. 86–93.

Belt, Bradley. 2005. *Hearing Before the Subcommittee on Aviation, Committee on Transportation & Infrastructure, U.S. House of Representatives, 109th Congress, First Session*. Washington, DC: U.S. Government Printing Office, June 22.

Budd, John W. 2004. "Non-Wage Forms of Compensation," *Journal of Labor Research* Vol. 25, No. 4 (Fall), pp. 597–622.

Council of Institutional Investors. 2005. *Protecting the Nest Egg: A Primer on Defined Benefit and Defined Contribution Retirement Plans*. Washington, DC: Council of Institutional Investors.

Employee Benefit Research Institute. 1997. *Fundamentals of Employee Benefit Programs* (5th ed.). Washington, DC: Employee Benefits Research Institute.

Ghilarducci, Teresa. 2002. "Multi-employer Pension Plans and the Pension Coverage Problem." *Proceedings of the 54th Annual Meeting*. Atlanta, GA, January 3–6. Champaign, IL: Labor and Employment Relations Association, pp. 95–103.

Ghilarducci, Teresa, and Mary Lee. 2005. "How Lower Middle-Class Workers Obtain Employer Pensions." *Final Report for Retirement Research Foundation Grant: #2003-077*. Notre Dame, IN: University of Notre Dame.

General Accounting Office. 2004. *Multiemployer Plans Face Short- and Long-Term Challenges*. GAO-04-423. Washington, DC: General Accounting Office.

Government Accountability Office. 2005. *Recent Experiences of Large Defined Benefit Plans Illustrate Weaknesses in Funding Rules*. GAO-05-294. Washington, DC: GAO.

Hewitt Associates. 2003. *Survey Findings: Current Retirement Plan Challenges: Employer Perspectives 2003*. Lincolnshire, IL: Hewitt Associates LLC.

International Association of Machinists and Aerospace Workers. 2005. *Machinists Vote at UAL Preserves Contracts, Established Pension Plan*. Press release. Washington, DC. July 21. <http://www.goiam.org/content.cfm?cID=4971>. [February 18, 2007].

IAM National Pension Fund. 1999. *Form 5500—Annual Return/Report of Employee Benefit Plan*. As filed with the Internal Revenue Service and the U.S. Department of Labor.

IAM National Pension Fund. 2004. *Form 5500—Annual Return/Report of Employee Benefit Plan*. As filed with the Internal Revenue Service and the Department of Labor.

Mazo, Judith. 2006. *Letter to Mr. Gregory Jonas regarding Request for Comment—Multiemployer Pension Plans: Moody's Analytical Approach*. March 13. Washington, DC: Segal Company.

National Mediation Board. 2006. *Findings Upon Investigation—Determination of Certification—Case No. R-7077*. 33 NMB No. 35. May 11.

Pension Benefit Guaranty Corporation. 2004. *Pension Insurance Data Book 2003*. No. 8, Spring 2004. Washington, DC: Pension Benefit Guaranty Corporation.

Pension Benefit Guaranty Corporation. 2005a. *2005 Annual Report*. Washington, DC: Pension Benefit Guaranty Corporation.

Pension Benefit Guaranty Corporation. 2005b. *PBGC Takes $2.3 Billion Pension Loss from US Airways*. Press release. February 2. Washington, DC: Pension Benefit Guaranty Corporation.

Pension Benefit Guaranty Corporation. 2006. *Pension Insurance Data Book 2005*. No. 10, Summer 2006. Washington, DC: Pension Benefit Guaranty Corporation.

Pension Rights Center. 2006. *'Red Zone' Pension Cutback Provisions*. Washington, DC. <http://www.pensionrights.org/pubs/facts/red_zone.html>. [February 17, 2006].

Purcell, Patrick. 2006. *Pension Sponsorship and Participation: Summary of Recent Trends*. RL30122. Washington, DC: Congressional Research Service. August 31.

Segal Company. 2006. *2005 Survey of the Funded Position of Multiemployer Plans*. Washington, DC: Segal Group.

United Airlines. 2004. *United Airlines' Informational Brief Regarding Its Pension Plans*. Case No. 02-B-48191. United States Bankruptcy Court for the Northern District of Illinois, Eastern Division. September 23.

Weller, Christian, and Dean Baker. 2005. "Smoothing the Waves of the Perfect Storm: Changes in Pension Funding Rules Could Reduce Cyclical Underfunding." *Proceedings of the 57th Annual Meetings,* Philadelphia, PA, January 6–9. Champaign, IL: Labor and Employment Relations Association, pp. 94–101.

Weinstein, Harriet, and William J. Wiatrowski. 1999. "Multiemployer Pension Plans." *Compensation and Working Conditions*. Spring. Washington, DC: Bureau of Labor Statistics. pp. 19–23.

Williams Walsh, Mary. 2004. "U.S. Wants Details on United's Pensions." *New York Times*. July 27, p. C2.

Wisniewski, Mary. 2005. "United Machinists Seek Alternate Pension Plan." *Chicago Sun Times*. May 27, p. 69.

CHAPTER 7

How Can Defined Contribution Plans Meet Workers' Needs?

ERIC RODRIGUEZ
National Council of La Raza

LUISA GRILLO-CHOPE
National Council of La Raza

The nation's retirement income system is complex, involves many stakeholders, intersects with innumerable laws, and can influence the retirement prospects of workers in a variety of ways. The system has evolved extensively over the decades. And while there are more options today than ever before for workers to personally and privately save for retirement, the employer-based pension system remains the principal means by which American workers build a secure retirement nest egg.

In 2004 there were approximately 153 million working Americans. Of all these, more than 71 million (46%) worked for an employer with no retirement plan (private or public) of any kind, and 17 million did not participate in their employers' plan, even though they were offered one. According to the Employee Benefit Research Institute (EBRI), in 2004 nearly two in three (59.5%) of all wage and salary workers ages 21 to 64 were offered a pension plan at work, but only 48.3% participated (Copeland 2005). The participation rates for Black and Hispanic workers were lower. In 2004, Black wage and salary workers were offered a pension plan at about the same rate (59%) as all workers; however, only 45.9% participated (Copeland 2005). The pension coverage and participation situation for Hispanic[1] workers is even more grim. During that same year, 38.4% of Latino wage and salary workers were offered pension plans, but only 28.7% participated (Copeland 2005). The EBRI data also show disparities in Latino pension participation between native-born Hispanics and foreign-born Hispanics (Copeland 2005). Overall, EBRI estimates that in 2004 53% of White, 46% of Black, and 29% of Hispanic wage and salary workers between the ages of 21 and 64 were participating in a plan. The participation rate for native-born Hispanics was 41%, while foreign-born Hispanics participated at a rate of 21% (Copeland 2005).

Broadly, the focus of this chapter is on the workers in the private sector who are with employers that offer pension plans to their workers but who do not participate. More specifically, we will examine the private employer-based pension system. Over the last 30 years many private employers have changed the type of retirement savings plan they offer their workers. Increasingly, private employers are offering defined contribution (DC) pension plans rather than a defined benefit (DB) plans. In 1992, among workers participating in a pension plan, 37.5% had only a DC plan and 40% had only a DB plan. Twelve years later, in 2004, 24.1% of workers participating in a pension plan had only a DB plan, but more than half (51.9%) had only a DC plan (Copeland 2006). The dominance of the DC employer-based pension plan is to some degree a reflection of business conditions, workers' needs, and public policy incentives. In addition, the increase in DC plans and the corresponding decrease in DB pension plans can be explained by changes in pension plan regulation, in employers' and employees' respective interests in the plan, in risk regarding the funding and managing of a plan, and in global competition levels (Rajnes 2002). DB plans, however, remain very common in the public sector.

Overall pension coverage and participation rates for American workers have not improved significantly in recent decades. Workers continue to experience significant challenges in saving enough for retirement. Insufficient retirement savings can be largely explained by challenges in adequacy of asset accumulation and increased risk exposure. Some workers are just not covered and cannot access a retirement wealth-building opportunity through their employer. These gaps in coverage within the employer-based system are prevalent, particularly in the case of minority workers, who are a growing share of the U.S. workforce. Barriers to saving include the lack of targeted incentives to help low- and moderate-income workers save. Also, workers are increasingly exposed to the risk that they either do not save enough or take on inappropriate amounts of risk in the financial market.

The private employer-based system continues the trend of offering workers only DC plans despite their shortcomings. A big part of this trend involves a redistribution of risk for retirement savings from employers to workers. A DB plan places the risk on the employer that the assets may not yield high enough returns to provide a promised level of retirement benefits to a worker. The DC pension plan shifts that risk to the worker; employees are exposed to the possibility that their investment choices will yield lower-than-needed retirement income (McCourt 2006).

This shift raises larger questions about the extent to which the worker will be able to develop retirement savings and is able to make the proper investment allocations, contribute enough, and answer the innumerable questions that arise during such financial decisions. Accordingly, given the increasing role of DC pension plans in the marketplace, this chapter takes a look at the DC plan and how it could be improved to better address worker needs. We provide brief background on the evolution of the DC plan and highlight important features of the plan for today's workers. In addition, we outline the weaknesses of the DC plan and note ways to strengthen the system.

Background: Employer-Based Pension Plans

Before the 1980s, workers who received pensions through their employers were able to access a DB pension plan or some type of deferred compensation plan. The DB plan, which remains prevalent in the public sector, guarantees that participants receive a certain payment for the rest of their lives during retirement (McCourt 2006). A benefit formula generally based on compensation and years of service determines the payment (American Academy of Actuaries 2006). Private-sector employers originally adopted DB plans for a number of reasons, including the following: to use the employer tax benefit, to address the erosion of Social Security benefits by postwar inflation, and to bargain with labor unions that had begun to use pensions as part of collective bargaining agreements (Congressional Budget Office 2006).[2] As a result, between 1940 and 1970, pension coverage grew threefold from a mere 17% of full-time workers in 1940 to more than half (52%) by 1970 (Moore 2006).

Between 1974 and 1986, Congress emphasized individual decision making via pension reform legislation by providing individual workers more discretion and control over retirement savings (Congressional Budget Office 2006). DC pension plan benefits would depend on contributions and asset returns rather than factors such as salary history and tenure, as in a DB plan's formulaic structure (Gale and Iwry 2005). In the Revenue Act of 1978, Congress sanctioned salary-reduction plans, enabling employees to receive a portion of their income as deferred compensation, rather than as a direct cash payment (Employee Benefit Research Institute 2000). The Johnson Companies designed the first 401(k), which let workers defer a portion of their salaries pretax (McCourt 2006). In the early 1980s, the Internal Revenue Service (IRS) issued regulations, and the 401(k) plan took off. As a result, companies with preexisting deferred compensation pension plans added 401(k) components to make their plans tax advantaged (McCourt 2006). Many

laws and regulations enacted since then have aimed to increase participation in DC plans and overall pension plan coverage options. These
changes have also led to the decline of the private sector's DB pension
plans. The gradual decline began among small employers burdened by
the associated liability and costs of their plans (McCourt 2006). Other
employers with DB plans also began to adopt 401(k) plans to supplement retirement benefits or to offer new employees the 401(k) plan as a
primary retirement savings vehicle (McCourt 2006).

The private employer-sponsored retirement savings market is now
dominated by DC pension plans. From 1985 to 1999, the number of private DB pension plans dropped from 170,000 to 50,000, while the number of private DC pension plans increased from 462,000 to 683,000
(McCourt 2006).

This shift has raised various questions about the retirement security
of workers. The following section looks at what the shift means for pension coverage of workers, the overall adequacy of the retirement benefit
to workers, and the level of economic risk for workers.

Pension Coverage

For workers to have a secure retirement, they must be able to access
and participate in retirement savings coverage options. DC pension
plans, at first blush, appear to be well suited for the current U.S. workforce. They are appropriate for workers who experience frequent job
change or gaps in employment (Goodman and Orszag 2005). The flexibility and control provided by the DC plan appear to address worker
preferences and needs. For example, the DC plan's portability enables a
worker to roll over the balance of a retirement account to an Individual
Retirement Account (IRA) or another DC pension plan. Portability
allows workers to consolidate retirement savings and simplify portfolio
management and record keeping (Congressional Budget Office 2006).[3]
The typical DB plan, in contrast, provides less portability, which affects
workers who may not meet service requirements for plan benefits.
Although some DB plans may offer a lump sum distribution, this is not
the same level of portability offered by DC plans. In addition, the DC
plan features a tax-advantaged savings element for workers, where the
worker saves a portion of salary before taxes are deducted on gross earnings. This lowers the worker's tax liability and provides an additional
incentive for retirement saving. A DB plan enrolls workers, which obvi-
ates the need for strong tax incentives to participate.

It is also important to note that workers with DC plans have to make
numerous financial decisions, such as whether to enroll, how much to
contribute, how to invest, whether to roll over contributions when

changing jobs, and the proper fund allocations. While some of these design features are advantageous to workers who are trying to develop retirement assets, the burden of choice could push workers away from participating. In contrast, a worker who is eligible for the DB plan will not have to make the same financial choices.

Benefit Adequacy

Initially, the DC plan was designed to supplement the DB plan and increase overall retirement income adequacy. In 2004, nearly one in four families participated in both a DB and a DC plan (Copeland 2006). Participating in both plans does increase retirement income adequacy. The DB pension plan benefit level is usually a stated retirement income based upon a formula or rule that begins at a specified age (Employee Benefit Research Institute 2005). For a worker who begins participating in a DB plan at age 30 and expects to retire at age 65 with a final salary of $105,881, the DB plan would provide to the worker a nominal annual annuity of $35,989 (VanDerhei 2006). With regard to income adequacy, it would appear that a DB pension plan is more desirable than a DC plan because of the stable level of retirement income. However, given the decline in DB pension plan coverage compounded by funding challenges that have led to the freezing of these plans for current workers, adequacy of retirement income will continue to be a challenge.

Workers will also face some challenges to benefit adequacy given certain features in DC pension plans. For example, workers may be encouraged to access retirement savings coverage through DC plans because of the lump sum and loan options, so money does not appear to be locked away until retirement. The loan withdrawal feature is advantageous to workers who may need or want to leverage the plan assets for hardship[4] reasons.[5] These features could challenge retirement security as they reduce and impede the development of a worker's overall retirement assets. By permitting this leakage of resources, a depletion of retirement savings or substantial reductions from the overall account balances in the DC plan can result. In a standard DB plan, the worker has no access to the funds in the plan until retirement, thereby increasing retirement security. (However, the cash balance pension plan, a DB plan with some DC plan features, does permit the worker to take a lump sum distribution.)

Workers' Risk

DC plans expose workers to investment risk. In a DC pension plan, risks can include investment risk, market risk, and longevity risk. Investment risk means that workers have to consider the financial market's performance before retirement; in a down market, workers will be forced either to delay retirement or consume less during retirement. Market risk is also an issue, one that occurs when there is improper investment allocation or money is invested poorly for a worker's particular profile, inclusive of occupation, age, and other factors. Lastly, longevity risk is the risk of outliving one's funds during retirement. This risk can be reduced with an annuity option. However, few DC pension plans provide that option, and workers may not be prepared to buy an annuity on the private market (American Academy of Actuaries 2006). It should be noted that these risks are influenced by a worker's needs and choices in retirement planning and participation in a DC pension plan. In contrast, under a DB plan, the employer generally bears all the financial risk (i.e., the risk associated with investment of assets), though if a DB plan is underfunded, it can also force a worker to accept less than the promised benefit payment, so the worker carries some risk there too (Sonnanastine, Murphy, and Zorn 2003).

Issues and Emerging Challenges

DC plans play a more prominent role than ever before in the employer-based pension system. At the same time, a substantial share of workers remain uncovered, and retirement security remains a significant challenge for most U.S. workers, especially minority workers. Compounding this issue is the fact that the U.S. workforce in 2014 and beyond is likely to be older and more diverse (Toossi 2005). Consider these specific statistics:

- The labor force's median projected age is expected to reach 41.6 years, a historic level (Toossi 2005).
- The labor force participation rate for the 55-and-older age group will increase from 36.2% in 2004 to 41.2% by 2014. Perhaps more surprisingly, the 65-to-74 age group (retirement age) participated in the labor force at a rate of 21.9% in 2004, and that rate is expected to jump to 26.9% by 2014 (Toossi 2005).
- The Black and Hispanic share of the U.S. labor force will grow. The Black labor force will increase slightly from 11.3% in 2004 to a projected 12% by 2014 (Toossi 2005). Between 2002 and 2014, it is projected that the Latino workforce will increase from 13.1% to 15.9% (Toossi 2005).

Workers staying in the labor force longer may force policy makers, employers, and workers to reconsider retirement planning policies, reexamining how and where workers should save for retirement. Moreover, the workforce's changing composition, with more minority workers, should compel policy makers and employers to broaden their thinking about pension policy. Black and Latino workers are currently in a starkly different economic and financial position than non-Hispanic White workers. Minority and immigrant workers have distinct experiences, needs, and preferences with respect to savings. Many have little experience, or even no experience, with mainstream financial markets. For example, basic banking services provide some understanding of how the financial market works, yet accessing and using these services remain a challenge for minority and immigrant workers. As retirement risk shifts from employer to worker, more must be done to help workers save appropriately and adequately for retirement. Workers need deeper engagement in the financial marketplace to improve retirement savings and overall financial security.

Lastly, future changes to Social Security and other entitlement programs may result in a social insurance system less generous for future retirees than for current ones. Workers may have little choice but to rely more heavily than ever on employer-based pension savings for adequate income support during retirement. These broad challenges of a changing workforce, the limited participation, and the increasing strain on our entitlement systems, will play out in the context of a retirement system that increasingly depends on active worker participation and workers' assumption of investment risk.

The Shortcomings of Defined Contribution Pension Plans

From a policy perspective, a worker participating in a DB plan and personally saving in a DC plan is ideal. A workforce that increasingly can access only DC plans poses significant challenges. DC plans contain notable features that provide advantages to workers and may respond to the preferences of some workers. However, these plans are distinct from DB plans in shifting the financial risk from employer to worker. The benefit payout amount and the accumulation of assets in the retirement account are largely determined by choices that workers make during their working years. The areas in which worker discretion is greatest are also the areas of utmost concern. We discuss more than a dozen of those here

Participation. Part of the challenge with DC pension plans is that participation is, in general, voluntary. As a result, workers do not participate as much as they could. One study used behavioral explanations to analyze savings behavior and found that procrastination is an extremely important factor in the perceived inadequacy of individual savings for retirement and that it affects reallocation of retirement assets (Madrian and Shea 2001). Munnell and Sundén (2006), through calculations based on the 2004 Survey of Consumer Finances, found that 21% of eligible workers failed to participate in a pension plan. This lack of participation jeopardizes retirement income and adversely affects income levels in several ways:

- The worker does not benefit from the tax liability offset. Without participation in a DC pension plan, the worker is not able to shield assets from tax liability. The worker loses the tax advantage to saving, and any regular income saved is put aside in less tax-advantageous ways.

- The worker does not benefit from compound interest. Workers accrue the most benefits in a DC pension plan by investing long-term and allowing the money to grow on top of what is being contributed. In general, the earlier workers begin to save in a DC plan the better, even if they have to stop temporarily later on.

- The worker fails to seize "free money" for retirement. Many employers match at least some of the funds their workers allocate to a DC pension plan. The worker pays no taxes on this employer match, and it can accumulate in the pension plan, enhancing the worker's retirement security.

There are additional voluntary reasons for not participating in a DC pension plan. One study found being unable to afford the expense, having money tied up, not thinking about it, and having other plans to be among the prevalent reasons for nonparticipation (Sun 2004). The extent to which these concerns resonated with minority workers, especially Latinos, was notable. The "expense" was cited by 30% of Latino workers, compared to 27.8% of Black workers and 24.3% of non-Hispanic Whites, for not participating even when their employer sponsored a DC pension plan. More than 1 in 10 Latino workers (12%) also gave "not having thought about it" as a reason for not participating, compared to 11.1% of Black workers and 10.8% of non-Hispanic White workers.

Eligibility criteria. Sun (2004) also found that up to three in 10 workers not participating in an employer plan could not because they did not meet the eligibility criteria. The Employee Retirement Income Security Act of 1974 (ERISA) and its amendments provide that employers will vest workers in pension plans if the workers have worked more than 1,000 hours a year for five years or vest workers 20% after each year of service until the worker is fully vested. Latinos, particularly, are less likely to meet these minimum standards as they have shorter job tenures and jobs in high turnover industries (Sun 2004). Another study found that more than half of those who are not part of their employer's pension plan report that they do not meet the age and service requirements or do not work enough to qualify for the plan, and another 6% were excluded because their job was not eligible for pension coverage (Munnell, Sundén, and Lidstone 2002).

Knowledge and awareness. The lack of engagement in retirement savings and investing can be attributed to workers' various financial knowledge levels. Overall, 12% of workers say they know nothing about saving and investing for retirement, compared to 13% of African American workers and more than four in 10 Hispanic American workers (Employee Benefit Research Institute, American Savings Education Council, and Mathew Greenwald and Associates 2003). Younger and low-income workers are less likely to participate in part because they have less financial experience and thus may not be aware of or benefit from the tax savings advantages (Madrian and Shea 2001).

Market timing. A PBS *Frontline* episode has detailed the ups and downs of 401(k) investments by two different workers. After 9/11, one worker lost 60% of the value in his 401(k), but was able to bring back the value through later investment choices (Public Broadcasting Service 2006). The second worker saw his account balance cut in half, to a mere $26,000, because of the stock market downturn over 2000 and 2001. The first worker was able to recover because he did have some investment training and made almost twice the annual salary of the other worker.

Diversification. One survey found that 55% of employers offer their own stock as an investment choice, and 30% of plan assets are invested in employer stock (Goodman and Orszag 2005). This is problematic because participants are thus not allocating money appropriately, and they are staking too much of their retirement security on the possible success of one company.[6] Workers may fail to diversify the 401(k) portfolio, which increases the risk of inadequate retirement income. The Center for Retirement Research notes that in 2004, 21% of 401(k) participants had 80% or more in equity holdings in their 401(k) (Munnell and Sundén 2006). By putting a large portion of a (401)k fund to company stock, the worker may not be making the best choices to increase returns and to fit his or her own needs and risks losing income from employment and income into the defined contribution pension plan should the company become bankrupt.

Contribution amount and overconfidence. Though workers are not participating in DC plans and leveraging them to the extent they could for a secure future, they nonetheless remain confident overall that they will be able to live comfortably in retirement. Nearly seven in 10 workers (68%) surveyed in 2006 felt at least somewhat confident that they will have a comfortable retirement (Employee Benefit Research Institute and Mathew Greenwald and Associates 2006). These confidence levels may be misguided, because at the same time more than half of all workers (53%) have saved less than $25,000 for retirement (Employee Benefit Research Institute and Mathew Greenwald and Associates 2006). African American workers tend to be as confident as the general American worker population about their finances in retirement. However, Latino workers express less confidence about retirement finances than the general American worker population (Employee Benefit Research Institute, American Savings Education Council, and Mathew Greenwald and Associates 2003). Given that retirement security increasingly relies on the efforts of the individual worker, these contradictory numbers are cause for concern. Workers are not saving, yet the market has changed so that their retirement security is contingent on their savings behavior. This suggests that DC plans and retirement security policy decisions need to focus on having workers increase their savings and on educating workers about their participation and their stake in their future retirement.

Asset depletion. The DC plan has features that address some concerns about job tenure and asset liquidity. For example, account contributions can be rolled over or cashed out when an employee changes jobs. However, data suggest that few job changers save this money for retirement. Munnell and Sundén (2006) found that in 2004, almost 45% of 401(k) participants who changed jobs cashed out their accounts, despite a 10% personal income tax penalty. The workers cashing out tended to be younger, so the money they removed was not a substantial percentage of total pension assets (18%). And with younger workers, there is less focus on saving for retirement than paying for daily consumption. A second factor builds upon the first: "Cashing out even small amounts can have a detrimental effect on ultimate accumulations. . . . The prevalence of cashing out suggests that people do not get serious about saving for retirement until later in life, at which point it is very difficult to accumulate adequate amounts" (Munnell and Sundén 2006).

Even a small account balance, if saved, can increase retirement security, especially if left for the long haul, as the account benefits from the compounding of interest over time. Moreover, workers who cash out will have to catch up later in life or be forced to make decisions about the extent to which they can afford to retire.

Account fees. High fees can reduce the asset development aspect of a DC plan. DB plans do have expenses, but they are considerably less. In a 401(k), for example, investment fees alone can account for 75% to 90% of the total expenses associated with its management (Munnell et al. 2006). These fees affect the accumulation of funds in the account and the compound interest over time, lowering the account value and the overall retirement income security of the worker.

Longevity risk. The rising cost of retirement is, in part, attributable to increasing life expectancies and spending more years in retirement than anticipated. This creates a strong possibility of outliving retirement savings. For example, Social Security beneficiaries ages 80 and older have a poverty rate of 11.3%, whereas those ages 75 to 79 have a poverty rate of 9.1% (Social Security Administration 2006). The fastest-growing group of minority workers, Latinos, have longer life expectancies than the overall population. At the age of 22, Latinos can expect to live an additional 60 years, whereas non-Hispanic Whites and Blacks can expect to live an additional 57 and 52.7 years, respectively (Orszag and Rodriguez 2005). At the same time, Latinos face a larger wealth gap, which can make planning and preparing for retirement and the possibility of more years in retirement a challenge.

Varying employer policies. In addition, there are a number of policy challenges to the use of DC plans that have less to do with individual worker choices than with employer policies and institutional arrangements. Pension plan coverage and accessibility is limited for many workers by eligibility criteria and tax treatment. Different requirements to be eligible and to vest will affect a worker's coverage. These challenges diminish overall pension coverage, create inadequate retirement savings, and increase risk exposure for workers.

The development of incentives for workers to participate in pension plans is crucial to encouraging responsible retirement savings behavior. The U.S. tax code provides preferential tax treatment to employer-provided pensions and IRAs by excluding pension contributions and earnings on those contributions from income until the worker withdraws the assets (Gale, Iwry, and Orszag 2005b). The same rules do not apply for Roth IRAs. The value of this tax treatment does depend, however, on a taxpayer's marginal tax rate, which means that the incentive to participate to offset tax liability inures more to households with higher marginal tax rates. This system creates a twofold problem: the tax advantages are mismatched when it comes to subsidy and need, and as a method to promote national savings the subsidies are poorly targeted (Gale, Iwry, and Orszag 2005b). Furthermore, the tax subsidy does little to increase pension participation for workers with lower tax rates or workers who may be at greater risk for retirement insecurity. As a result, younger and low-income workers who have low or no tax liability have little tax incentive to participate in pension savings.

Adequacy of retirement savings is affected in that various policies will impede developing retirement savings. Specifically, asset tests in means-tested programs mean that some workers who may seek public assistance intermittently will not save adequately. Also, certain plan features will help to encourage participation and generate additional retirement savings to increase the overall adequacy of the benefit.

During times of unemployment or at times when earnings are not enough to make ends meet, many low-income families use means-tested programs. However, householders must meet asset tests to qualify. Asset rules in means-tested benefit programs can create an incentive to liquidate savings or abstain from saving (Orszag and Rodriguez 2005). The asset limits are fairly low and treat various retirement savings vehicles differently. For example, the Food Stamp Program tends to disregard employer-based retirement savings plans but counts IRAs. Given that a large share of IRA accounts are employer-based savings accounts that have been rolled over, this rule difference results in disparate treatment of retirement savings (Greenstein, Neuberger, and Sweeney 2005).

Optional DC plan features can increase the adequacy of retirement savings. One example is employer matching contributions, which helps increase workers' savings rates in the plan. A 2000 GAO study found that employees were 12% more likely to not participate in their firm's DC pension plan if the firm did not provide matching contributions (General Accounting Office 2000). The same report also acknowledges a Fidelity Investments study that found that a company match has a positive effect on participation rates and operates independently of a plan's size. Participation increased by nearly 19% (or one in five) in large plans, simply by including a 1.5% effective match.

Lastly, the exposure to risk means that workers, even though they are in the pension plan and making contributions, may not be assuming adequate risk to reach appropriate retirement savings. A targeted effort to address this can be brought about by providing investment advice.

Independent (i.e., with no conflict of interest) and good quality workplace-based investment advice is rare. ERISA did not provide for pension plans to offer investment advice to participants; in fact, it suggested that companies could be held liable for poor advice (Kim and Garman 2003). At the same time, DC pension plan participants must direct their account investments. In 2001, the Economic Growth and Tax Relief Reconciliation Act (EGTRRA) permitted employer-provided retirement planning advice to be treated as a *de minimis* fringe benefit. This allows the benefit to be excluded from employees' gross income and enables employers to take an income tax deduction for expenses associated with the advice. Yet the law does not provide for retirement planning services provided by independent outside providers (Kim and Garman 2003).

Recommendations

Public policy needs to improve both the opportunity and ability of workers to participate more effectively in employer-based pension savings programs. Moreover, given workforce trends, policy measures to improve the quality of participation in DC plans should be targeted to low-income and minority workers. There are many potential solutions to address the challenges that we have outlined above.

Enhancing savings through automatic features. The data show that DC pension plan participation increases if employees are forced to make an affirmative election not to participate (Rodriguez and Martinez 2004). Employers can create this situation by implementing automatic features in their plans. An automatic 401(k) changes the default options in the savings cycle so that even if a worker never makes an affirmative choice to save, sound savings and investment decisions become the norm (Gale, Iwry, and Orszag 2005a). A worker would be able to override the participation and investment options, but otherwise, con-tributions would be made, increased over time, invested appropriately, and preserved for the worker's retirement, without the worker's having to make these decisions at each 401(k) savings cycle. Results of auto-matic enrollment have been promising, boosting 401(k) plan participa-tion to 85% to 95% (Gale, Iwry, and Orszag 2005a). Moreover, participation among those most in need of greater asset development and access to assets markedly improved. Women's participation jumped from 35% to 85%, Hispanic participation increased more than threefold from 19% to 75%, and participation among workers making under $20,000 in earnings increased from 13% to 80%[7] (Gale, Iwry, and Orszag 2005a). The Pension Protection Act of 2006 does include auto-matic enrollment and automatic escalation of contribution provisions to promote pension participation.

Enhancing incentives to participate in savings. The tax code, an important means of reaching U.S. workers, should create more effective incentives for low- and moderate-income workers. Under current law, the Saver's Tax Credit provides one such option. Enacted in 2001, the credit provides a government matching contribution, in the form of a nonre-fundable tax credit, for individual contributions to 401(k) plans, other employer-sponsored plans, and IRAs (Gale, Iwry, and Orszag 2005b). This credit is claimed by middle- and lower-income households, but because it is nonrefundable, there is no incentive to save for lower-income households with no federal income tax liability (Gale, Iwry, and Orszag 2005b). Originally slated to sunset at the end of 2006, the Saver's Tax Credit was made a permanent part of the tax code in the Pension Protection Act of 2006. The credit would be improved by making it refundable so it reaches low- and moderate-income workers with no tax liability. This would increase retirement savings incentives in the tax code for more workers.

Congress should revisit the asset tests in means-tested benefit programs and modify or eliminate them when it comes to retirement savings to ensure that workers are better able to keep such savings. As previously noted, in some programs, such as the Food Stamp Program, 401(k) savings are excluded from means-testing, but IRA assets are counted (Orszag and Rodriguez 2005). However, since many workers roll over their 401(k)s into IRAs when they change jobs, Congress should reexamine the asset tests and the impact these tests have on retirement savings.

Companies should be encouraged to provide savings matches to employees, given the data showing that this increases workers' incentive to save. Moreover, there should be some exploration of tax incentives for employers who effectively encourage savings among their low-wage and asset-poor workers if DC plans are to reach those who most need them. One idea could be a targeted tax break for employers who make higher contributions to the accounts of their low-wage or asset-poor workers (Rodriguez and Martinez 2004). In addition, workers of the future may be more inclined to save with withdrawal and loan features in plans that address the concerns of low-income and minority workers. For example, one study reveals that Latinos, compared to their peers, are the most likely to give "don't want to tie up money" as the reason for not participating (Sun 2004). Withdrawal and loan features could allay that concern. Lastly, employers should consider, and policy should encourage, a loosening of eligibility criteria to enable more categories of workers to qualify for pension participation in the workplace.

Promoting Independent Advice and Retirement Savings Counseling

The evidence suggests that both the quantity and quality of worker participation in pension plans increase with the presence of effective educational services. The workforce of the future will comprise more minority and foreign-born workers with limited knowledge and experience of investment and retirement savings. Direct investment advice is rated high among workers, including Latino workers. To date, the availability of good-quality and independent investment advice in the workplace has been limited. The Pension Protection Act of 2006 would provide additional investment advice in the context of DC pension plans. Specifically, the legislation would exempt investment advice from the prohibited transaction rule, which governs potential conflict of interest and self-dealing situations, if certain protections are provided. The first protection option is that any advice must be offered under an eligible investment advice arrangement whereby the adviser does not receive different fees depending on the investment options available. The second protection is that the fiduciary adviser uses a computer model under an investment advice program that is to be developed. These changes, along with implementation of some of the earlier solutions, should help bring about greater access to advice on DC plans and might increase participation. For low-income, Latino, and immigrant workers especially, other options should be considered as well. Some possible options include the following:

Refundable retirement savings advice tax credit for workers (Grillo-Chope and Rodriguez 2005). Under current law, there is a provision for miscellaneous itemized deductions that includes investment fees and expenses and tax advice fees, among other items. The taxpayer is eligible to deduct up to 2% of the adjusted gross income limit for this purpose. Low- and moderate-income workers are less likely to have federal income tax liability, so an income tax deduction is not as useful as a tax credit. This refundable tax credit could be capped and empower low-income workers to seek out, identify, and choose their own independent retirement savings financial advisers. The qualifying limits for low- and moderate-income workers could also be modeled after Saver's Tax Credit eligibility.

Grants for community tax preparation sites for retirement savings counseling (Grillo-Chope and Rodriguez 2005). Some low- and moderate-income workers seek out and receive free tax-preparation services administered by community-based organizations. In many cases, these organizations receive either grants or in-kind support from the U.S. Treasury. Tax season is an important opportunity for workers to discuss retirement savings. If advice is provided at that point, the worker can discuss options for saving a tax refund for retirement. With the 2007 filing season as a deadline for the implementation of split refunds, this program could build upon and strengthen this new provision.

The suggestions we have outlined are by no means an exhaustive list of policy ideas and possible solutions to the challenges to DC pension participation. That said, each one holds promise to improve both the quantity and quality of engagement by workers in employer-based pension plans over time.

Finally, with respect to employer-based DC plans, even the best and most effectively designed and administered plans will leave many workers uncovered. Other options to increase overall coverage deserve greater attention. For example, one idea is to create a new type of private account that would be offered through a new privately run agency, known as a clearinghouse, but overseen by the federal government (Conversation on Coverage 2005). The purpose would be to have a retirement savings account available to all workers, whether full-time, part-time, self-employed, or contingent, providing coverage to the many workers who are not offered a plan at work. Under this account, the employer would facilitate the contributions from the employees to the account after the employees indicate on their W-4 form the level of contributions to be deducted. The employer would then transfer the money to the U.S. Treasury with the addition of any employer contributions. The U.S. Treasury would then transfer the funds to the clearinghouse (Conversation on Coverage 2005). Having a clearinghouse would reduce overall costs.

Another idea, put forth by J. Mark Iwry and David John, would improve retirement savings by building on the success of automatic retirement savings and coupling it with the IRA—usually an individual savings strategy—to bring about increased retirement savings. The automatic IRA would provide automated savings so workers could build assets and would simultaneously remove burdens that employers might face (Iwry and John 2006). Its design features include payroll-deduction direct deposit savings, along with fiduciary liability protections for employers. A temporary tax credit is available for employers who do not have pension plans or do not cover all their workers if they make regular payroll deposit available to employees. Automatic enrollment is also encouraged. In addition, the automatic IRA would have special provisions for the self-employed and workers without a regular employer, by extending direct deposit capability through enabling the IRS to direct deposit part of taxpayers' income tax refunds and by expanding access to automatic debit arrangements (Iwry and John 2006). These enhancements would bring about increased retirement savings coverage, even without an employer-sponsored DC pension plan.

Conclusion

Within the private employer-based pension system, DC pension plans are becoming the dominant type of plans offered and administered. The voluntary, worker-driven system of pension planning is likely to expand over time. Meanwhile, the workforce of the future will comprise more workers who have less experience with and knowledge of retirement savings. DC plans, as they are currently administered, maintain participation gaps and expose workers in a number of ways to significant investment and financial risk. At the same time, workers are faced with a social insurance system that is likely to provide them less economic security in the future.

As discussions continue by policy makers, financial experts, and advocates, it must be made clear that DC pension plans are a worker benefit, and features must be included and developed that make it easier for workers to access and to use these plans effectively. DC pension plans must be designed so that workers are engaged in and informed about the opportunities and financial decisions that such a pension plan can bring. Only in this way will workers be able to work toward a secure retirement, develop a critical asset, and begin to bridge the retirement wealth gap. Lastly, policies should begin to target minority and low-wage workers more effectively to put them on a path to retirement and pension wealth-building.

Endnotes

[1] The terms "Latino" and "Hispanic" are used interchangeably by the U.S. Census Bureau and throughout this document to identify persons of Mexican, Puerto Rican, Cuban, Central and South American, Dominican, and Spanish descent; they may be of any race.

[2] This information is located in "CBO's Online Guide to Tax Incentives for Retirement Saving." From the Guide, there is a link to "Employment-Based Retirement Plans" and on that page, there is a link to "History of the Employment-Based Retirement System" where this background can be found.

[3] The portability information is also found in "CBO's Online Guide to Tax Incentives for Retirement Saving." To access it, link to "Employment-Based Retirement Plans," then to "Defined-Contribution Plans." On the "Defined-Contribution Plans" page, there is a link to "Other Design Features that Can Be Customized," from here, the information can be found under "Portability Provisions."

[4] Under a 403(b) plan, the worker must demonstrate hardship by showing that there is no other financial means to make a down payment or pay tuition, medical expenses, or a mortgage if in danger of foreclosure.

[5] Borrowing against plan assets eliminates the tax advantages; the worker must supply returns to the account in the form of interest payments, and during this time the assets in the plan are not earning tax-deferred returns.

[6] The recently passed Pension Protection Act of 2006 provides that employees with DC plans may divest securities if a portion is invested in employer securities. The participant must complete three years and the plan must supply three options other than employer securities in which to divest.

[7] These numbers are the results from a study by Brigitte Madrian of the University of Pennsylvania's Wharton School and Dennis Shea of the UnitedHealth Group. This statistical information was based on a graph in *The Automatic 401(k): A Simple Way to Strengthen Retirement Savings* (Gale, Iwry, and Orszag 2005a).

References

American Academy of Actuaries. 2006. "The Value of Defined Benefit Plans." Issue Brief, American Academy of Actuaries, Washington, DC. July. <http://www.actuary.org/pdf/pension/db_july06.pdf> [December 12, 2006].

Congressional Budget Office. 2006. *CBO's Online Guide to Tax Incentives for Retirement Savings*. June. <http://www.cbo.gov/showdoc.cfm?index=4572&sequence=0>. [March 9, 2007].

Conversation on Coverage. 2005. *Covering the Uncovered: Common Ground Recommendations to Expand Retirement Savings for American Workers*. Washington, DC, Pension Rights Center. <http://www.conversationoncoverage.org/about/interim_recomendations/working_report_website.pdf> [December 12, 2006].

Copeland, Craig. 2005. *Employment-Based Retirement Plan Participation: Geographic Differences and Trends, 2004*. October. Issue Brief No. 286. Washington, DC: Employee Benefit Research Institute. <http://www.ebri.org/pdf/briefspdf/EBRI_IB_10-20051.pdf>. [December 12, 2006].

Copeland, Craig. 2006. *Individual Account Retirement Plans: An Analysis of the 2004 Survey of Consumer Finances*. May. Issue Brief No. 293. Washington, DC: Employee Benefit Research Institute. <http://www.ebri.org/pdf/briefspdf/EBRI_IB_05_3-20061.pdf>. [December 12, 2006].

Employee Benefit Research Institute. 2000. *History of 401(k) Plans*. December. <http://www.ebri.org/publications/facts/index.cfm?fa=1200fact>. [December 12, 2006].

Employee Benefit Research Institute, American Savings Education Council, and Mathew Greenwald and Associates. 2003. *2003 Minority Retirement Confidence Survey Summary of Findings*. <http://www.ebri.org/pdf/surveys/rcs/2003/03mrc-ssf.pdf >. [December 12, 2006].

Employee Benefit Research Institute. 2005. *FACTS from EBRI: The U.S. Retirement Income System*. April. <http://www.ebri.org/pdf/publications/facts/0405fact.pdf> [December 12, 2006].

Employee Benefit Research Institute and Mathew Greenwald and Associates. 2006. *Will More of Us Be Working Forever? 2006 Retirement Confidence Survey*. April. Issue Brief No. 292. Washington, DC: Employee Benefit Research Institute. <http://www.ebri.org/pdf/EBRI_IB_04-2006_1.pdf> [December 13, 2006].

Gale, William G., and J. Mark Iwry. 2005. *Automatic Investment: Improving 401(k) Portfolio Investment Choices*. May. Washington, DC: The Retirement Security Project.<http://www.retirementsecurityproject.org/File/AutomaticInvestment.pdf> [December 13, 2006].

Gale, William G., J. Mark Iwry, and Peter R. Orszag. 2005a. *The Automatic 401(k): A Simple Way to Strengthen Retirement Savings*. March. Washington, DC: The Retirement Security Project. <http://www.retirementsecurityproject.pubs/File/Automatic401(k).pdf>. [December 13, 2006].

Gale, William G., J. Mark Iwry, and Peter R. Orszag. 2005b. *The Saver's Credit: Expanding Retirement Savings for Middle- and Lower-Income Americans*. March. Washington, DC: The Retirement Security Project. <http://www.retirementsecurityproject.org/pubs/File/RSP-PB_SaversCredit.pdf>. [December 13, 2006].

General Accounting Office. 2000. *Pension Plans: Characteristics of Persons in the Labor Force Without Pension Coverage*. GAO/HEHS-00-131. Washington, DC: GPO.

Goodman, John C., and Peter R. Orszag. 2005. *Common Sense Reforms to Promote Retirement Security*. March. Washington, DC: The Retirement Security Project. <http://www.retirementsecurityproject.org/pubs/File/RSP-PB_CommonSense_3.pdf>. [December 13, 2006].

Greenstein, Robert, Zoe Neuberger, and Eileen P. Sweeney. 2005. *Protecting Low-Income Families' Retirement Savings: How Retirement Accounts Are Treated in Means-Tested Programs and Steps to Remove Barriers to Retirement Saving*. June.

Washington, DC: The Retirement Security Project. <http://www.retirementsecuri-typroject.org/pubs/File/AssetTestReport.final.pdf>. [December 13, 2006].

Grillo-Chope, Luisa, and Eric Rodriguez. 2005. *RE: Retirement Savings Financial Counseling.* Washington, DC: National Council of La Raza.

Iwry, J. Mark, and David C. John. 2006. *Pursuing Universal Retirement Security Through Automatic IRAs.* February 12. Working paper draft. Washington, DC: The Retirement Security Project <http://www.retirementsecurityproject.org/pubs/File/AutoIRAworkingpaper.pdf>. [December 13, 2006].

Kim, Jinhee, and E. Thomas Garman. 2003. "Financial Education and Advice Changes Worker Attitudes and Behaviors." *Journal of Compensation and Benefits*, September/October 2003, pp. 7–13.

Madrian, Brigitte C., and Dennis F. Shea. 2001. "The Power of Suggestion: Inertia in 401(k) Participation and Savings Behavior." *Quarterly Journal of Economics*, Vol. 116, no. 4 (November), pp. 1149–87.

McCourt, Stephen P. 2006. "Defined Benefit and Defined Contribution Plans: A History, Market Overview and Comparative Analysis." *Benefits and Compensation Digest*, Web Exclusives, Vol. 43, no. 2 (February), pp. 1–7. <http://www.ifebp.org/PDF/webexclusive/06feb.pdf>. [December 13, 2006].

Moore, James H. 2006. "Projected Pension Income: Equality or Disparity for the Baby-Boom Cohort?" *Monthly Labor Review*, Vol. 129, no. 3 (March), pp. 58–67. <http://www.bls.gov/opub/mlr/2006/03/art4full.pdf>. [December 13, 2006].

Munnell, Alicia H., Mauricio Soto, Jerilyn Libby, and John Prinzivalli. 2006. *Investment Returns: Defined Benefit vs. 401(k) Plans.* September. Issue in Brief No. 52. Chestnut Hill, MA: Center for Retirement Research at Boston College. <http://www.bc.edu/centers/crr/issues/ib_52.pdf>. [December 19, 2006].

Munnell, Alicia H., and Annika Sundén. 2006. *401(k) Plans Are Still Coming Up Short.* March. Issue in Brief No. 43. Chestnut Hill, MA: Center for Retirement Research at Boston College. <http://www.bc.edu/centers/crr/issues/ib_43.pdf>. [December 13, 2006].

Munnell, Alicia H., Annika Sundén, and Elizabeth Lidstone. 2002. *How Important Are Private Pensions?* February. Issue in Brief No. 8. Chestnut Hill, MA: Center for Retirement Research at Boston College. <http://www.bc.edu/centers/crr/issues/ib_8.pdf>. [December 13, 2006].

Orszag, Peter R., and Eric Rodriguez. 2005. *Retirement Security for Latinos: Bolstering Coverage, Savings and Adequacy.* July. Washington, DC: The Retirement Security Project <http://www.retirementsecurityproject.org/pubs/File/RSP_LaRaza.pdf>. [December 13, 2006].

Public Broadcasting Service. "Can You Afford to Retire?" *Frontline.* Air date May 16, 2006. <http://www.pbs.org/wgbh/pages/frontline/retirement/view>. [December 13, 2006].

Rajnes, David. 2002. *An Evolving Pension System: Trends in Defined Benefit and Defined Contribution Plans.* September. Washington, DC: Employee Benefit Research Institute. <http://www.ebri.org/pdf/briefspdf/0902ib.pdf>.[December 13, 2006].

Rodriguez, Eric, and Deidre Martinez. 2004. *Pension Coverage: A Missing Step in the Wealth-Building Ladder for Latinos.* Washington, DC: National Council of La Raza.

Social Security Administration. 2006. *Income of the Population 55 or Older, 2004.* Washington, DC: GPO. <http://www.ssa.gov/policy/docs/statcomps/income_pop55/2004/incpop04.pdf>. [December 13, 2006].

Sonnanastine, Alan, Brian Murphy, and Paul Zorn. 2003. "List of Advantages and Disadvantages for DB and DC Plans." November 14. GRS Research Memorandum, Gabriel, Roeder, Smith and Company. <http://www.nasra.org/resources/GRS%20DB%20DC.pdf>. [December 13, 2006].

Sun, Wei. 2004. *Latinos' Low Pension Coverage and Disenfranchisement from the U.S. Financial System*. Notre Dame, IN: Institute for Latino Studies, University of Notre Dame.

Toossi, Mitra. 2005. "Labor Force Projections to 2014: Retiring Boomers." *Monthly Labor Review*, Vol. 128, no. 11 (November), pp. 25–44. <http://www.bls.gov/opub/mlr/2005/11/art3full.pdf>. [December 13, 2006].

VanDerhei, Jack. 2006. *Defined Benefit Plan Freezes: Who's Affected, How Much, and Replacing Lost Accruals*. March. Issue Brief No. 291. Washington, DC: Employee Benefit Research Institute. <http://www.ebri.org/pdf/briefspdf/EBRI_IB_03-20063.pdf>. [December 15, 2006].

CHAPTER 8

Putting Annuities Back into Savings Plans

PAMELA PERUN
Aspen Institute

Economy does not lie in sparing money, but in spending it wisely.[1]

Every year, millions of dollars flow into 401(k)-type and other savings plans. As large numbers of baby boomers begin to retire in a few short years, millions of dollars will start to flow out. Most workers will be on their own in managing their savings during retirement because most plan sponsors deliberately restrict plans to lump sum distributions. Although annuities are a well-respected technique for managing income in retirement, they are virtually absent from savings plans in the private pension system.

This chapter analyzes why savings plan sponsors shun annuities and what might be done to change the situation. It begins with a discussion of an apparent puzzle: just as the shift to savings plans in the private pension system began to accelerate in the 1990s, annuities began disappearing from savings plans. I explain how legal reforms in the early 1990s, largely intended to protect participants in defined benefit (DB) plans, increased the risk of fiduciary liability associated with annuities. Employers responded by abandoning annuities as a distribution option in savings plans wherever possible, leaving to workers the responsibility for managing their savings in retirement. I also describe how one proposal for a federal charter option for life insurance companies could hold some promise for persuading plan sponsors to put annuities back into savings plans.

Savings Plans and the Case for Annuities

The Shift to Savings Plans

In recent years, the paramount goal of the U.S. private pension system has been to encourage saving for retirement. With the retirement of the baby boom generation approaching and other sources of retirement income such as Social Security under stress, there is a great deal of concern that millions of Americans will reach retirement without adequate resources (Employee Benefits Research Institute 2006). This concern has been prompted by a fundamental shift in the type of retirement income produced by the private pension system.

Historically, employers provided their workers with retirement benefits through DB plans. Typically financed entirely by employers, these plans provide a worker with income in retirement, usually payable for life, based on years of service and amount of compensation. But employers today prefer to offer savings plans, such as the popular 401(k) plan, to which both employers and workers contribute. Rather than generating a stream of retirement income, these plans accumulate a pool of assets based on contributions and their earnings. This trend to savings plans has largely shifted the risk of preparing for retirement from employers to workers. It is now well recognized that, in 401(k)-type savings plans, workers must take the initiative in saving. For many, their own savings will provide the bulk of retirement income along with, perhaps, some employer matching contributions. Workers must also assume investment responsibility for their savings. Now that savings plans dominate the private pension system, encouraging as many workers as possible to save as much as possible and to invest wisely has become a national priority.

A Role for Annuities in Savings Plans

The shift to savings plans, however, imposes another burden on workers that has not yet received much attention (Mitchell 2004). DB plans have traditionally provided retirement income in one standard form: monthly payments guaranteed to last for life. Workers in DB plans arrive at retirement with a known, guaranteed, lifetime stream of income. Workers in savings plans arrive instead with an account balance that must be converted into income for retirement through a process often referred to as self-annuitization. The growth in savings plans has shifted to workers the risk of living longer than their income. In order to avoid outliving their resources, workers must now learn how to manage their assets in retirement wisely.

For most workers in savings plans, it will not be obvious how to apportion and spend their accumulated assets throughout retirement. For instance,

> [i]ndividuals face a variety of risks in managing their assets, income, and expenditures at and during retirement. For

example, retirees may outlive their pension or retirement savings plan assets. In addition, inflation may erode the purchasing power of their income, investments may yield returns that are less than expected or decline in value, and large unplanned expenses, such as those to cover long-term care, may occur at some point during retirement (Government Accountability Office 2003:10).

Deciding how to allocate resources during retirement is difficult and fraught with uncertainty. It requires workers to estimate with some degree of accuracy how long they will live and how much they will need to spend. In addition, they must continue to manage their assets to generate income in retirement. This requires deciding how to invest assets appropriately for the 20, 30, or even 40 years of retirement that are becoming increasingly common.

At least some of the financial uncertainty inevitable in retirement can be mitigated through the use of a life annuity. There are many types of annuities: variable, fixed, immediate, deferred, and so on. The focus of this chapter is on the traditional form of annuity, the life annuity, either immediate or deferred. A life annuity is an investment product available from an insurance company, purchased through a single premium payment. In exchange for the payment, the insurance company contracts to pay a guaranteed amount, usually monthly, for life. Life annuities generally provide income only for the life of the annuitant, although it is also possible to purchase joint and survivor annuities that continue to provide income for the life of a named beneficiary. Purchasing a life annuity is an irrevocable decision—there are no opt-out provisions for buyers who change their minds.

According to economic theory, life annuities enable workers to manage their consumption appropriately in retirement and help mitigate financial uncertainty.

> By trading a stock of wealth for a life-contingent stream, a healthy individual is able to sustain a higher rate of consumption than in the absence of annuitization. . . . If an individual does not have access to annuitization then she must allocate her wealth in a manner that trades off two competing risks. The first is the risk that if she consumes too aggressively, she increases the likelihood of facing a future period in which she is alive with little or no income. The second is that if she self-insures by setting aside enough wealth to be certain it cannot be outlived, then she risks dying with assets that could have been used to increase consumption while alive. (Brown and Warshawsky 2004)

By purchasing a life annuity, workers transfer at least a portion of their mortality risk, that is, the risk of living longer than their assets, to the insurance company in exchange for a stream of income that continues for the rest of their lives, no longer how long they live. In addition, the amount they will receive from the insurance company is both known and guaranteed. A life annuity also helps workers reduce at least a portion of their investment risk, the risk their savings will produce less than their anticipated income in retirement.

Life annuities are one means by which workers in savings plans could obtain the lifetime, guaranteed stream of income produced by DB plans. But life annuities are not a popular or well-understood insurance product in the United States today. More popular forms of annuities are purchased as investment products, in part because they enjoy special tax benefits (Mitchell 2004). A "deferred annuity" can be obtained in either a variable form, where its value fluctuates according to the investments chosen by the policyholder, or a fixed form, where the insurance company promises a specific rate of return. Under tax law, an individual can invest any amount in an annuity contract and postpone tax on its increased value (its "inside build-up") until it is paid out to the policyholder. This gives annuities tax advantages similar to those in an employer-based savings plan but without annual limits on contributions. Few purchasers of investment annuities convert the value of those contracts into life annuities: fewer than 1% of such contracts are ever converted into fixed annuities (Beatrice and Drinkwater 2004; Bernard 2005).

Industry analysts believe that the market for life annuities holds great potential.

> [T]he annuitization market remains underdeveloped. According to one estimate, the annuitization market among the currently retired has the potential to exceed $114 billion. . . . Both the need and desire for annuitization already exist. Half of all individuals aged 50 to 75 with household financial assets of $50,000 or more will need to tap into savings during retirement in order to pay for basic living expenses. . . . Nearly half of those people are interested in converting some of their savings into guaranteed lifetime income. If all these people eventually annuitize a portion of their assets, the total amount annuitized would exceed $200 billion. (Sondergeld and Drinkwater 2004)

But at the present time, life annuities represent a small fraction of the industry's sales. For example, in 2004 there were $212.4 billion in new individual annuity sales, but fixed immediate life annuities accounted for only $5.6 billion of that amount (Bernard 2005; White-house 2005).

Research into the unpopularity of life annuities typically focuses on two sets of factors: people and their individual needs, and problems with the product itself. The research indicates that some potential purchasers have liquidity concerns and so are reluctant to commit their savings irrevocably to an annuity. Others are unsure about their health and question whether buying the lifetime income provided by an annuity is a good investment for them (Brown and Warshawsky 2004). Many potential purchasers try to conserve their assets for bequests to their families or to charity and therefore find an annuity unappealing. Still others prefer to rely on Social Security for a guaranteed income stream in retirement (Ameriks and Yakaboski 2003). The life annuity market is still developing, and the product is perceived to have a number of problems. For example, the issue of whether life annuities are fairly priced is an open one (Ameriks and Yakaboski 2003), leading some to question whether annuities are an attractive investment. And the market currently lacks an annuity product that protects against inflation (Brown and Warshawsky 2004).

Missing in Action: The Employer

These factors explain some of the unpopularity of annuities, but there could be another important but generally overlooked factor: the absence of annuity options in savings plans. For many people, the most significant source of information about and support for retirement planning is their employer's savings plan. Employers are important intermediaries in saving. They provide a plan and payroll deduction services, educate workers about the need to save, select a menu of investment options, and, often, encourage additional saving through financial incentives such as matching contributions. Most workers learn about and implement saving for retirement through their employers' plans.

Employers, however, deliberately play a hands-off role in educating workers about managing their savings in retirement. A Government Accountability Office (GAO) study observed that

> [p]lan sponsors . . . generally did not provide information on considerations relevant to managing pension and retirement savings plan assets at and during retirement. . . . [P]lan sponsors generally do not discuss the potential pros and cons of available payout options as related to managing pension assets during retirement. . . . [T]hey typically do not discuss risks retirees may face in managing their assets during retirement or provide information on how to assess needs at or during retirement (Government Accountability Office 2003:14).

TABLE 1
Savings Plans Offering Annuities

Study	Sample	Findings
Bureau of Labor Statistics (1999)	Sample of private firms employing more than 100 workers in 1997	27% of full-time employees in 401(k) plans had annuity options.
Government Accounting Office (2003)	Private firm data from the National Compensation Survey of the BLS in 2000	Annuities available to 38% of participants in defined contribution plans.
Hewitt Associates (2003)	About 500 401(k) plans surveyed in 1999, 2001, and 2003	Percentage of plans offering annuities fell from 31% in 1999 to 17% in 2003.
Profit-Sharing/401(k) Council of America (2004)	Survey of about 1,000 profit-sharing, 401(k), and profit-sharing/401(k) combination plans in 2002	26% of plans offered retirement annuities; more smaller plans offer annuities (36% of plans with 50-199 participants, 26% with fewer than 50) than large plans (19% of plans with more than 5,000 participants); in 2001, 28% of plans offered annuities (Government Accountability Office 2003).

Not only do employers not provide advice or education about managing assets in retirement, savings plans in particular typically constrain workers to a lump sum of cash when leaving (Government Accountability Office 2003). As Table 1 illustrates, the available data suggest that only a minority of savings plans offer annuities as a distribution option, and even that number appears to be shrinking over time.

The absence of annuities from savings plans does not mean that workers have lost their only opportunity to purchase one. They can always use a lump sum distribution of their plan account to buy an annuity directly from an insurance company or purchase one later through an individual retirement account (IRA). But with the employer sitting on the sidelines, both workers and the life annuity market have lost the services of an important intermediary. Workers do not learn about the benefits of annuities or receive help in obtaining one through their savings plan, and the life insurance industry has lost an important ally. If savings plan sponsors do not expand the distribution options in their plans to include annuities, the rate of annuitization may not increase significantly in the future. But, as I go on to describe, recent developments in the law have discouraged plan sponsors from offering annuities.

Why Savings Plan Sponsors Avoid Annuities

Several factors explain the absence of annuities in savings plans. First, while DB plans are required to provide annuities, savings plans are generally exempt from this requirement. Under Internal Revenue Code (IRC) § 401(a)(11)(B)(iii) and the Employee Retirement Income Security Act (ERISA) § 205(b)(1)(C), most DC plans are not required to offer annuities as long as the spouse of a deceased participant inherits the decedent's account automatically under the terms of the plan. The exception to this rule is a type of DC plan that is not a savings plan known as a money purchase plan. Most savings plan sponsors thus are not obliged to offer annuities as distribution options. Second, as researchers have observed, plan sponsors avoid annuities to minimize their administrative and regulatory burdens (Brown and Warshawsky 2004). But legal advisers know the real reason why plan sponsors don't offer annuities: because those advisers strongly counsel clients against them. In their view, annuities expose plan sponsors to a significant and long-term risk of fiduciary liability, a risk that can be avoided by not offering annuities in employee savings plans. And plan sponsors, more often than not, heed that advice.

ERISA and Fiduciary Liability

The fiduciary liability associated with savings plans arises out of the legal requirements under ERISA, administered by the Department of Labor (DOL), that set standards for savings plans. The rules set forth in ERISA control how a plan should be operated and impose penalties for breaching those standards. ERISA § 402 holds individuals with discretionary authority over the operation and administration of a plan to a high standard of conduct as fiduciaries. ERISA § 404 requires a fiduciary, when acting on behalf of a plan, to act solely in the interests of the participants and beneficiaries, for the exclusive purpose of providing benefits to participants and beneficiaries and defraying the reasonable expenses of administering the plan, and with the care, skill, prudence, and diligence that a prudent person would use under similar circumstances. Fiduciaries are personally liable to make a plan whole for any losses it suffers when they breach that standard of conduct.[2] In addition, a fiduciary involved in a settlement agreement or lawsuit as the result of a fiduciary breach is also subject to a 20% special civil penalty. The DOL is required to assess this penalty unless it finds that the fiduciary acted reasonably or in good faith, or will suffer severe financial hardship without a waiver or reduction of the penalty under ERISA § 502(l).

Under ERISA, a plan sponsor is not acting as a fiduciary when it chooses the distribution options in a plan, because plan design is considered to be a business, rather than fiduciary, decision. Plan sponsors thus have complete discretion when deciding to include or exclude annuities from their plans. Liability potentially arises only when a participant chooses an annuity in a plan that offers them, and the plan sponsor or other fiduciary must decide how the annuity will be provided. This is less of an issue with ongoing DB plans because annuities are typically paid directly from the plan. DC plans, however, are different. If a participant chooses an annuity form of distribution, the plan must purchase an annuity from an outside provider. The choice of annuity provider is an investment decision, subject to the fiduciary standards of ERISA. This distinguishes annuities from other forms of distributions, such as lump sum or installment distributions, for which the participant, not the plan, makes all investment decisions. Any plan official who makes a discretionary decision about an annuity purchase for a participant is therefore acting as a fiduciary and is liable for that decision unless he or she exercised due care when making it and put the best interests of the participant first.[3]

Executive Life and Its Aftermath

Until the early 1990s, the fiduciary liability associated with annuities did not seem particularly problematic, and many savings plans offered them. But, just as the shift to savings plans was accelerating in the late 1980s and 1990s, a number of large insurance companies failed, including Executive Life Insurance Company of California and Mutual Benefit Life of New Jersey (Government Accountability Office 1992a, 1992b; Government Accountability Office 1995). At that time, as the GAO (Government Accountability Office 1991) has estimated, about one third of all pension plan assets were invested in insurance company products, and some 3 to 4 million retirees held annuities purchased from insurance companies. The failure of these companies caused a crisis within the private pension system whose repercussions are still being felt today.

Most affected by the crisis were DB plans, primarily those that had purchased group annuity contracts for retirees or for terminating plans. Savings plans were affected only secondarily, but, ironically, not because of the annuities they provided. Instead, some savings plans became vulnerable because they or their participants had invested in such insurance company products as guaranteed investment contracts that could not pay their promised return. Even though the life annuities offered by savings plans were not generally implicated, the crisis exposed regulatory weaknesses that persuaded savings plan sponsors that annuities were too risky. In addition, although the crisis with life annuities was largely confined to DB plans, the regulatory response was overly broad, increasing the administrative burden and fiduciary risk associated with annuities even for savings plans.

The first regulatory weakness exposed was within the insurance industry itself. In the United States, the insurance industry is largely regulated by states rather than the federal government. States license insurance companies, oversee their financial health, and, when a company becomes insolvent, take charge of the liquidation process. When an insurance company fails, policyholders must turn to the relevant state guarantee associations for redress. These associations are neither state agencies nor funded by the states. Instead, they are an association of insurers in each state that have the power to assess member insurers when an insurance company becomes insolvent. Although these funds are called "guaranty" associations, they do not in fact provide a guarantee that they will have sufficient funds to cover the obligations of failed insurers. In addition, while these associations initially bear the cost of an insurance company insolvency, most states allow insurance companies to recover assessments through reductions in state premium taxes (American Council of Life Insurers 2004d) or rate increases. So ultimately the cost of an insurance company failure is borne by policyholders or taxpayers (Government Accountability Office 1992c).

The failure of Executive Life and the other companies gave employers and their employee benefits lawyers their first large-scale encounter with state guaranty associations and, for many it was a disturbing experience. There are no statistics available about the relief actually obtained from state guaranty associations, but contemporary accounts report a number of significant problems encountered by plans seeking to recoup losses:

- State guaranty funds generally did not provide coverage for guaranteed insurance contracts and similar products in DB plans, and only a few provided coverage for DC plans (Government Accountability Office 1991; Harrington 1992).

- "Variations in state rules cause gaps and significant differences in coverage," such as different rules for who is protected and the types of policies and annuities protected (Government Accountability Office 1992c).

- Coverage was "generally limited to a maximum of $300,000 for individual claimants with no more than $100,000 for cash values of life insurance and annuity contracts" (Harrington 1992). (The same limits were still in effect in 2004 [American Council of Life Insurers 2004d].)

- Some states provide coverage to all if the insurance company is headquartered in that state, but others provide coverage only for state residents of companies doing business in that state (Government Accountability Office 1991).

Although the National Association of Life and Health Guaranty Associations exists to help coordinate guaranty association activities when an insurance company operating in several states fails (American Council of Life Insurers 2004d), there is no parallel coordinating mechanism for employee benefit plans. Employers found that dealing with multiple state guaranty funds was expensive and time-consuming. In addition, the patchwork of coverage available led to uneven outcomes among participants, and even no protection for large numbers of participants. In the end, many in the employee benefits community concluded that, whatever the merits of the state guaranty association system, it is not well suited to the needs of employer plans, particularly those with employees in a number of states.

The second regulatory weakness exposed was within the private pension system itself. Some employers as well as those frustrated by the state guaranty association system chose a different route. They proposed to make additional contributions to their plans to make participants whole. On the surface, this appeared to be a simple, reasonable solution to a difficult problem. But the private pension system, never having grappled with such a situation before, had no mechanism permitting this. In addition, these contributions actually raised a number of significant legal questions. For example, under tax law, there were issues about whether these contributions would violate the exclusive benefit rule of IRC § 401(a)(2), the nondiscrimination rules of IRC § 401(a)(4), the limits on deductions under IRC § 404, and the limits on benefits under IRC § 415, as well as various excise tax provisions. Under ERISA, there was a great deal of uncertainty about whether such contributions would be an admission of fiduciary liability, triggering the special 20% civil penalty for fiduciary breaches.

After some consideration by the Internal Revenue Service (IRS) and the DOL and consultation with employer groups and benefits experts, the legal issues were resolved. Employers were given the ability to make such "restorative" payments to their DC plans, but only after they had received regulatory approval. The IRS created a special program for this purpose.[4] To participate in this program, employers also were required to obtain an exemption from the DOL for relief from fiduciary liability. This meant that employers had to provide information to the DOL about their plans, their failed contracts, and their affected plan participants. Employers who volunteered to make their participants whole found themselves involved in an expensive and time-consuming regulatory process.

By themselves, these regulatory issues would probably not have been significant enough to turn savings plan sponsors against annuities. But litigation surrounding the collapse of the Executive Life Insurance Company of California led to a major change in law with just that effect. The leading case was *Kayes v. Pacific Lumber*.[5] The Maxxam Group obtained control of the Pacific Lumber Company through a hostile takeover, then terminated its overfunded DB plan. It selected Executive Life, an insurance company whose bid was $2.7 million lower than other companies, to provide annuities to participants and received $62 million in surplus plan assets that were then used to pay off debt from the leveraged buyout. When this insurance company subsequently failed, litigation on behalf of annuitants, seeking to impose liability on plan fiduciaries for their self-interested selection of Executive Life, ran into a legal Catch-22. Because their annuities were fully guaranteed by an insurance company, they no longer satisfied the definition of plan "participant" under ERISA and therefore had no standing to sue.[6]

To many, *Kayes v. Pacific Lumber* signaled a problem with ERISA's fiduciary rules that needed to be fixed. Its holding, although legally correct, suggested that plan fiduciaries could violate with impunity ERISA's requirement that they act solely in the best interests of plan participants when purchasing annuities. Congress concurred and swiftly enacted the Pension Annuitants Protection Act of 1994 (PAPA). PAPA amended ERISA to grant annuitants standing to bring suit against plan fiduciaries for breaches of duty in connection with the purchase of insurance contracts and annuities.[7] This not only gave annuitants the right to sue, it also greatly expanded the period of time during which fiduciaries could be at risk for a claim of breach of fiduciary duty.[8] In addition, it authorized courts to award appropriate relief and money damages, including the purchase of backup annuities, remedies that are generally not available under ERISA.

In interpreting the new rules under PAPA, the DOL issued regulations about annuity purchases that were highly controversial. As the GAO (Government Accountability Office 1993) noted during the height of the Executive Life crisis, fiduciaries had no guidance from the DOL about the process they should follow or the criteria they should observe when selecting annuity providers for participants to comply with ERISA's requirements. In 1995, however, the DOL issued an interpretive bulletin for that purpose. Its central holding was that ERISA required plan fiduciaries to select "the safest annuity possible."[9] To do this, in the DOL's view, fiduciaries are required to conduct an objective and thorough search for potential providers, generally with the assistance of an independent expert. In particular, they should analyze each provider's creditworthiness and claims-paying ability. They should conduct their own evaluation of the safety of possible providers and not just rely on a rating from a commercial rating service. Factors to be considered include the quality and diversification of each company's investment portfolio, its capital level and surplus, and its lines of business and exposure to liability as well as the structure of the proposed annuity contract and its guarantees. In the DOL's view, a proper review should include analysis of the adequacy of state guaranty fund protection. In 2002, the DOL amplified that guidance by advising plan fiduciaries to examine "whether the provider and the annuity provider are covered by state guarantees and the extent of those guarantees, in terms of amounts (e.g., percentage limits on guarantees) and individuals covered (e.g., residents, as opposed to nonresidents, of a state" (Department of Labor 2002).

The DOL's attempt to add clarity was not well received. Some courts refused to apply the interpretive bulletin's guidance when evaluating the conduct of fiduciaries, even in cases related to Executive Life.[10] Moreover, Congress itself has recently rejected "the safest possible annuity" standard. In the Pension Protection Act, passed in mid-2006, Congress noted that it was not its intention that there "be a single safest annuity available contract" (Joint Committee on Taxation 2006:149).[11] Congress directed the DOL to issue new regulations within 12 months setting standards more closely tied to ERISA's general standard of prudence for fiduciaries. It also strongly indicated that the DOL's interpretive bulleting standards were too stringent by indicating its preference that new guidance not "restate all the factors contained in the interpretive bulletin" (Joint Committee on Taxation 2006:149).

The cumulative effect of the Executive Life crisis and the regulatory struggle over appropriate fiduciary standards for annuity purchases largely explains why savings plan sponsors shun annuities. This is an ironic outcome because the reforms brought about by PAPA make sense only for DB plans. Given the volume of annuities that DB plans typically purchase, it seems reasonable to require a formal evaluation process of providers to satisfy fiduciary standards. In addition, the price paid for annuities inevitably affects the funded status of DB plans, so plan fiduciaries have an inherent conflict of interest regarding the cost of the annuity provider they choose. It seems reasonable to ensure that plan participants have redress against fiduciaries that put the costs of annuities first and the safety of the annuities they purchase for participants second. It also seems reasonable to believe that annuities, given their long-term and irrevocable nature, deserve extended protection against fiduciary misconduct in ways lump sum and installment distributions do not.

But it is hard to understand why fiduciaries of savings plans should be held to the same standards as their counterparts in DB plans. Savings plans purchase annuities infrequently and usually one at a time. Many plans are sponsored by small employers who lack the staff, the expertise, and the funds to follow the procedures the DOL recommends. There is no conflict of interest when a savings plan buys an annuity because it can only use a participant's own account assets for that purpose.

In the end, savings plan participants lost more than they gained by the post–Executive Life reforms. These reforms prevented what was a small risk to plan participants by imposing a big risk on plan fiduciaries. Savings plan sponsors responded by concluding the fiduciary liability attached to annuities should be avoided wherever possible. They also observed that state guaranty associations do not provide adequate or even protection when an insurance company fails. Even volunteering to make their participants whole would be complicated, requiring cumbersome regulatory approvals. But, primarily, they decided they did not want to be the potential guarantors of private annuity providers under PAPA. They looked at their increased fiduciary liability and concluded that offering annuities was just not worth the risk when participants could always buy annuities on their own. The law offers savings plan sponsors an out, and many take it by deciding not to offer annuities. That leaves savings plan participants without the assistance of an important intermediary, their employer, and a valuable product, a life annuity, as they make the transition to retirement.

How Proposed Insurance Reforms Could Help

Proposals for Changing Pension Law

The absence of annuities from savings plans has not gone unnoticed, and various options have been proposed to reinstate them (Government Accountability Office 2003). Among the most prominent are proposals for some form of mandatory annuitization. These would change existing law to compel plans to provide and/or participants to receive annuities as distribution options. The most extreme proposal would eliminate participant choice and require all benefits, regardless of the type of plan, to be paid in the form of annuities. Under a more moderate proposal, the current exemption for savings plans under IRC § 401(a)(11) would be repealed. Savings plan participants would be required to receive their benefits as an annuity unless they, with spousal consent, chose an alternative. Another proposal would merely require savings plans to offer annuities.

These proposals are appealing in their simplicity: just amend pension law and the problem will be solved. The trend in the law, however, is moving strongly in the opposite direction, that is, to give savings plan sponsors more flexibility, not less, with respect to annuities. For example, the IRS has recently revised long-standing regulations and now permits savings plans to eliminate all forms of annuity distributions.[12] In addition, it is likely that these proposals would exacerbate the coverage problem currently facing the private pension system. Plan sponsors would be likely to respond to an annuity mandate that would expand their fiduciary liability by refusing to sponsor new plans or terminating their existing plans.

Plan sponsors' negative response to PAPA suggests that these proposals will not achieve what they intend. First, it is unrealistic to assume that plan sponsors will willingly assume responsibility for what they cannot control, namely the financial health of the insurance companies from which they purchase annuities. Plan sponsors are not eager to become potential guarantors for annuity providers, especially given the extended period under ERISA's statute of limitations during which they could be at risk for litigation. Second, pension law, by itself, cannot make annuities a safer or more appealing product to either plan sponsors or plan participants. These are issues that lie primarily within the control of the life insurance industry, not pension law.

A Proposal for Changing Insurance Law

The life insurance industry itself has recently proposed reforms with the potential to make annuities again an attractive option for savings plan sponsors. It has asked Congress to create a new model for insurance company organization and regulation: an optional federal charter for life insurance companies.[13] This initiative for change comes at a time when the traditional lines between the insurance, banking, and securities industries have been blurring. In addition, recent legislation, notably the Gramm-Leach-Bliley Act of 1999, has modernized federal regulation over most of the financial services industry. Similar reform has not yet been attempted on a broad scale within the life insurance industry, which remains a creature of state law.

As one industry spokesperson has noted, however,

> for the insurance business to remain viable and serve the needs of the American public effectively, our system of life insurance regulation must become far more efficient and responsive to the needs and circumstances of a 21st century global business. Life insurers today operate under a patchwork system of state laws and regulations that lack uniformity and is applied and interpreted differently from state to state. The result is a system characterized by delays and unnecessary expenses that hinder companies and disadvantage their customers. (American Council of Life Insurers 2004d)

Proponents believe that "insurance regulatory reform is integral to maintaining America's leading role in the international financial services marketplace. The current antiquated, state-by-state regulatory system reduces U.S. competitiveness in the global insurance arena, when competing head-to-head with more efficient and modernized foreign markets." (American Council of Life Insurers 2006). They also argue "consumers are . . . harmed because they ultimately pay the costs for a regulatory system riddled with redundancies and red tape that ultimately deprives consumers of the best possible services and product innovations" (American Council of Life Insurers 2006). A recent survey of 100 insurance companies estimated that 55% of all regulatory costs, or more than $250 million annually, are directly related to complying with the regulatory requirements of multiple jurisdictions (Computer Sciences Corporation 2005).

The solution proposed by the American Council of Life Insurers is to create an optional federal charter system for life insurance companies, modeled on the dual federal–state charter system long in effect in the banking industry (American Council of Life Insurers 2003, 2004a, 2004b). Under legislation recently introduced into Congress, the National Insurance Act of 2006 (NIA) would create an optional federal charter program for life insurers.[14] The NIA would establish a single federal regulator, the Office of National Insurers (ONI) to be housed in the Treasury Department, to license, regulate, and supervise insurance companies that opt-in to a federal charter. The legislation promises to ensure the financial stability of national insurers by requiring stringent accounting principles and audit standards and strong risk-based capital requirements. It would also safeguard insurance company assets by applying strong, uniform investment and valuation standards. The ONI would have broad powers to regulate the market conduct and perform financial examinations of national insurers. It would also license and supervise agents and approve the terms and conditions of policies.

Although the proposal creates new federal law for most functions of national insurers, it continues to rely on the existing state-based system in one important respect. The NIA does not propose a new federal guaranty system to protect policyholders in the case of insurer insolvencies. Instead, it would continue to rely on state guaranty associations but attempt to upgrade and standardize their protection. Every national insurer will be required to become a member of the guaranty association of each "qualified" state in which it does business. A qualified state is one whose guaranty association meets the NIA standards, which are based on the Life and Health Insurance Guaranty Association Model Act proposed by the National Association of Insurance Commissioners, the policy association of U.S. insurance regulators. These standards include providing protection, on a per-person basis, of $300,000 in life insurance death benefits but not more that $100,000 in net cash surrender and withdrawal values and not more than $100,000 in present value for annuity benefits, including net cash surrender and withdrawal values. Residents in a nonqualified state, however, would receive comparable protection through a new guaranty corporation chartered in the District of Columbia to which all national insurers will be required to belong. This corporation would be regulated by the ONI but would not itself be a federal agency, and its obligations would not be backed by the full faith and credit of the federal government.

The optional federal charter proposal holds a great deal of promise for making annuities more attractive to savings plan sponsors.[15] Its single most important contribution is that it achieves uniformity and standardization among annuity providers and their products. This alone significantly reduces the fiduciary exposure of plan fiduciaries. Under ERISA, to the extent that there are uniform annuity products and standardized annuity providers available, plan fiduciaries would not have to exercise discretion, and would therefore not be exposed to liability, when they select an annuity provider.

The federal charter proposal contains several elements that help minimize the discretion required of plan fiduciaries when selecting an annuity provider. First, the proposal would create standard annuity policies. Second, agents and insurance companies would be subject to uniform sales, marketing, and licensing standards. Third, the financial health of annuity providers would be monitored and supervised by a single federal regulator. National insurers would be subject to uniform accounting, investment, and valuation standards as well as risk-based capital requirements. Fourth, the proposal would be based on federal law, as are employee benefit plans, rather than on the laws of the current 50-plus different insurance jurisdictions.

But it is also important to recognize that the proposal in its current format has a significant drawback. Many plan sponsors would be dismayed by the continued reliance on state guaranty funds. In addition, the coverage amounts provided by these funds, although comparable to what is available today, could be perceived as inadequate for the large account balances often accumulated in savings plans. Even though the proposal achieves greater uniformity among state guaranty funds, as a matter of prudence under ERISA, plan fiduciaries would likely be required to investigate the adequacy of individual funds, often in several states, when selecting a provider. In the event of an insurance company insolvency, plan sponsors would still have to deal with multiple jurisdictions as well as its own federal regulators.

From the perspective of plan sponsors, it would be preferable to have a single guaranty fund under the jurisdiction of a single regulator and federal law. How significant this omission is, given the benefits of the proposal, is open to question. There are, however, some improvements, short of a single guaranty fund, that could be made to the proposal that plan sponsors might find helpful. For example, perhaps the proposal could include some sort of explicit coordination mechanism for employee benefit plans in the event of a multiple-jurisdiction insolvency. Alternatively, a single jurisdiction, perhaps that of the employer, could be designated for annuities purchased through an employee benefit plan. Changes like these could improve the efficiency of the guaranty system for plan sponsors without adversely affecting the protection available for plan annuitants.

Conclusion

At a minimum, the federal charter proposal would enable plan fiduciaries to minimize their fiduciary exposure when helping participants purchase annuities. That, by itself, might be sufficient to persuade more plan sponsors to offer annuities. From the perspective of pension law, this would be a practical and welcome solution to a problem largely created by pension law. But the federal charter proposal holds the potential for some positive changes to pension law as well. With a strong federal regulator, the risks of insolvency by national insurers would presumably be greatly reduced, and the need to give plan participants additional protection under ERISA would correspondingly decrease as well.

If so, why not make annuities more attractive to savings plan sponsors by reducing their exposure to fiduciary liability proportionately. One possible way to do that is to amend pension law so that the purchase of an annuity from a federally chartered insurance company by savings plan fiduciaries automatically satisfies ERISA's fiduciary provisions. If the federal charter proposal fulfills its promise, such a change would undo the damage that PAPA has inflicted on savings plans. It would give savings plan sponsors a more appropriate role as facilitators, not guarantors, of annuities. And it would be a helpful step toward making annuities once again a standard feature of savings plans and making workers more receptive to annuities.

Acknowledgments

This research has been funded by the Society of Actuaries. The opinions and analysis presented in this chapter are solely those of the author.

Endnotes

[1] Attributed to Thomas Henry Huxley, *The Columbia World of Quotations*. Available at http://www.bartleby.com/66/4/30104.html.

[2] See ERISA § 409(a). The concept that fiduciaries are personally liable for plan losses caused by the breach of their fiduciary duties is further emphasized in ERISA § 410(a), that any agreement or provision that attempts to relieve a fiduciary of his or her responsibilities or exculpate a fiduciary from the consequences of his or her actions or omissions is void as a matter of public policy. ERISA § 410(b) does permit a plan to purchase insurance to cover fiduciary liability or make a plan whole as long as the insurance company has a right of recourse (the right to recover any damages paid from the fiduciary).

[3] See ERISA Regulation § 2550.404a-1.

[4] This special program for plans involved in state life insurance company delinquency proceedings was originally authorized as a temporary program under Revenue Procedure 92-16, I.R.B. 1992-7 (February 18, 1992), went through several subsequent revisions, and then was extended indefinitely in Revenue Procedure 95-52, I.R.B. 1995-51 (December 18, 1995). The IRS has recently released additional guidance permitting such contributions generally, provided they "are made to restore losses to the plan stemming from fiduciary actions that could reasonably be expected to create a risk of liability for breach of fiduciary duty." See Revenue Ruling 2002-35, I.R.B. 2002-29 (July 22, 2002).

[5] *Kayes v. Pacific Lumber Co.*, 1993 U.S. Dist. LEXIS 7280 (N.D. Cal. May 17, 1993), affirmed in part, reversed in part, and remanded in 51 F.3d 1449 (9th Cir. 1995).

[6] See ERISA Reg. § 2510.3-3(d)(2)(ii)(A) and ERISA § 502(a).

[7] See ERISA § 502(a)(9), which applies to any legal proceeding pending or brought on or after May 31, 1993.

[8] In general, under ERISA § 413, participants may sue for a breach of fiduciary duty until the earlier of a) six years after the breach occurred or b) three years after the earliest date on which they have "actual knowledge" of the breach. In at least one case also associated with the Executive Life crisis, *Maher v. Strachan Shipping Co.*, 68 F3d 951 (5th Cir. 1995), the court applied the six-year statute of limitations to a claim of breach of fiduciary duty in the selection of an annuity provider.

[9] ERISA Reg. § 2509.95-1.

[10] See *Bussian v. RJR Nabisco*, 223 F3d 286 (5th Cir. 2000), reversing 21 FSupp2d 680, DC-Texas (1998).

[11] See Section 624 of the Pension Protection Act of 2006 (Public Law 109-280).

[12] Treas. Reg. §1.411(d)-4, Q&A-2(e).

[13] This chapter discusses the American Council of Life Insurers proposal for an optional federal charter for life insurance companies. A number of similar proposals also under consideration are discussed in Bair (2004) and Broome (2002).

[14] The National Insurance Act of 2006 was introduced in the Senate on April 5, 2006, by Senators John Sununu and Tim Johnson as S. 2509 and in the House on September 28, 2006, by Representative Edward Royce as H.R. 6225.

[15] A discussion of the merits of this proposal outside the qualified plan context is beyond the scope of the chapter. Interested readers can obtain a broader analysis of the proposal from Bair (2004) and Broome (2002).

References

American Council of Life Insurers 2003. *Executive Summary: American Council of Life Insurers' National Insurer Act and National Insurer Solvency Act.* <http://www.acli.com>. [November 1, 2004].

―――. 2004a. *ACLI Optional Federal Charter Proposal. Fact Sheet: Consumer Benefits.* <http://www.acli.com>. [November 1, 2004].

―――. 2004b. *ACLI Optional Federal Charter Proposal. Fact Sheet: Consumer Protections.* <http://www.acli.com>. [November 1, 2004].

―――. 2004c. *ACLI Optional Federal Charter Proposal. Q&A: Insurance Guaranty Associations.* <http://www.acli.com>. [November 1, 2004].

―――. 2004d. *Examination and Oversight of the Condition and Regulation of the Insurance Industry.* Testimony of Arthur F. Ryan before the U.S. Senate Committee on Banking, Housing and Urban Affairs. <http://www.acli.com>. [November 1, 2004].

―――. 2006. *Modernizing Insurance Regulation Remains Top Priority for Broad-Based Financial Services Coalition Members.* <http://www.acli.com/ACLI/Newsroom/News+Releases/Test+Releases/NR06-074.htm>. [February 28, 2007].

Ameriks, John, and Paul Yakoboski. 2003. "Reducing Retirement Income Risks: The Role of Annuitization." *Benefits Quarterly*, Fourth Quarter.

Bair, Sheila. 2004. *Consumer Ramifications of an Optional Federal Charter for Life Insurers.* Amherst: University of Massachusetts, Isenberg School of Management.

Beatrice, Dan Q., and Matthew Drinkwater. 2004. *The 2003 Individual Annuity Market: Sales and Assets.* Windsor, CT: LIMRA International.

Bernard, Garth. 2005. "Is Annuitization Dead?" *NAVA Outlook*, Vol. 15, no. 5. Reston, VA: National Association for Variable Annuities.

Broome, Lisa Lampkin. 2002. *A Federal Charter Option for Insurance Companies: Lessons from the Bank Experience.* Public Law and Legal Theory Research Paper No. 02-11. Chapel Hill: University of North Carolina, Chapel Hill School of Law.

Brown, Jeffrey R., and Mark J. Warshawsky. 2004. "Longevity-Insured Retirement Distributions from Pension Plans: Market and Regulatory Issues." In William G. Gale, J. Shoven, and M. Warshawsky (eds.), *Public Policies and Private Pensions*, Washington, DC: Brookings Institution.

Bureau of Labor Statistics. 1999. *Employee Benefits in Medium and Large Private Establishments, 1997.* Bulletin 2597. Washington, DC: U.S. Department of Labor.

Computer Sciences Corporation. 2005. *Economic Impact of an Optional Federal Charter on the Life Insurance Industry.* Austin, TX: Computer Sciences Corporation, Financial Services Group.

Department of Labor. 2002. *ERISA Advisory Opinion 2002-14A.*

Employee Benefits Research Institute. 2006. *Saving for Retirement in America.* 2006 RCS Fact Sheet. Washington, DC: Employee Benefits Research Institute. <http://www.ebri.org/pdf/RCS06_FS_01_Saving_Final.pdf>. [February 28, 2007].

Government Accountability Office. 1991. *Insurance Company Failures Threaten Retirement Income.* GAO/T-HRD-91-41. Statement of Joseph L. Delfico before the Subcommittee on Select Revenue Measures, Committee on Ways and Means, U.S. House of Representatives. Washington, DC: GAO.

————. 1992a. *Insurance Regulation: The Failure of Four Large Life Insurers.* GAO/T-GGD-92-13. Testimony of Richard L. Fogel before the Committee on Banking, Housing and Urban Affairs, U.S. Senate. Washington, DC: GAO.

————. 1992b. *Insurance Failures: Regulators Failed to Respond in Timely and Forceful Manner in Four Large Life Insurer Failures.* GAO/T-GGD-92-43. Testimony of Richard L. Fogel before the Subcommittee on Oversight and Investigations, Committee on Energy and Commerce, U.S. House of Representatives. Washington, DC: GAO.

————. 1992c. *Insurance Failures: Life/Health Insurer Insolvencies and Limitations of State Guaranty Funds.* GAO/T-GGD-92-15. Testimony of Richard L. Fogel before the Subcommittee on Antitrust, Monopolies and Business Rights, Committee on the Judiciary, U.S. Senate. Washington, DC: GAO.

————. 1993. *Private Pensions: Protections for Retirees' Insurance Annuities Could Be Strengthened.* GAO-HRD-93-29. Washington, DC: GAO.

————. 1995. *Insurance Regulation: Observations of the Receivorship of Monarch Life Insurance Company.* GAO-GGD-95-95. Washington, DC: GAO.

————. 2003. *Private Pensions: Participants Need More Information on Risks They Face in Managing Pension Assets At and Near Retirement.* GAO-03-810. Washington, DC: GAO.

Harrington, Scott E. 1992. "Policyholder Runs, Life Insurance Company Failures, and Insurance Solvency Regulation." *Regulation,* Vol. 15, no. 2 (Spring).

Hewitt Associates. 2003. *Survey Findings: Trends and Experience in 401(k) Plans, 2003.* Lincolnshire, IL: Hewitt Associates.

Joint Committee on Taxation. 2006. *Technical Explanation of H.R. 4, the "Pension Protection Act of 2006,"* as passed by the House on July 28, 2006, and considered by the Senate on August 3, 2006." JCX-38-06. Washington, DC: GPO.

Mitchell, Olivia S. 2004. *The Value of Annuities.* Address before the Accademia Nazionale dei Lincei, Rome, Italy. <http://cerp.unito.it/Pubblicazioni/archivio/OTHER/Mitchell-INAPrizeLecture1-9-04.pdf>. [November 9, 2004].

Profit Sharing/401(k) Council of America. 2004. *46th Annual Survey of Profit Sharing and 401(k) Plans.* Washington, DC: Profit Sharing/401(k) Council of America.

Sondergeld, Eric T., and Matthew Drinkwater. 2004. *Annuitization Doesn't Have To Be Painful, So Why Hasn't It Caught Fire?* <http://www.findarticles.com/p/articles/mi_go2013/is_200408/ai_n6289848>. [February 28, 2007].

Whitehouse, Kaja. 2005. *Annuities, Meet 401(k)s.* New York: Global Action on Aging. <http://www.globalaging.org/pension/us/private/2005/meet.htm>. [February 28, 2007].

CHAPTER 9

U.S. Federal Pension Policy: Its Potential and Pitfalls

MICHELE VARNHAGEN

U.S. House of Representatives Committee on Education and Labor

This chapter examines how U.S. federal pension policy has evolved since the enactment of the country's major pension law: the Employee Retirement Income Security Act of 1974 (ERISA; P.L. 93-406). Pension policy has had to balance the need for a reliable pension supplement to Social Security within a voluntary system of employer-provided employee benefits. Although experts have long known that tax incentive–based systems do little to promote extra savings for retirement, such incentives remain the most popular and attractive public policy tool. As individual-based retirement plans, such as 401(k) plans, have become the dominant form of retirement savings, it is becoming clearer that individuals are unreliable managers of long-term savings and that employers have an inconsistent history in managing 401(k)s and large incentives not to extend them to the lowest earners. This chapter outlines the predictable issues that arise in federal pension policy and suggests directions future policy might take. One of the current challenges is to encourage individual savings plans to adopt more traditional guaranteed benefit features to ensure needed minimum long-term retirement security.

Pension policy was largely unregulated until the enactment of ERISA, which has been described as the triumph of Congress over the affected special interest groups: employers and unions (Wooten 2004). For much of the past 30 years, congressional amendments to ERISA have tested this unusual policy dynamic, sometimes balancing and sometimes failing to find a balance between the interests of public policy, organized labor, and business.

Participant Activism to Perfect ERISA

Throughout the 1980s, participant advocates sought and fought to close the gaps in the private pension system that ERISA failed to address, including divorced and surviving spouse issues in the Retirement Equity Act of 1984 (P.L. 98-397); vesting, Social Security integration and nondiscrimination issues in the Tax Reform Act of 1986 (P.L. 99-514); age discrimination in benefit accrual standards in COBRA of 1986 (P.L. 99-509); and employer recapture of overfunded pension fund assets in the Omnibus Budget Reconciliation Act of 1990 (P.L. 101-508). The 1980s were a decade of participant activism that tipped the private system closer to delivering on the promises understood by workers and retirees. Of course, these years also were years of some degree of Democratic congressional control, though the Senate was Republican from 1981 to 1986 and Republican Ronald Reagan was president through 1988.

One of the first post-ERISA participant milestones, the Retirement Equity Act, was conceived by a variety of women's group advocates as a result of their own experiences as well as those of thousands of women who contacted women's and similar consumer advocacy–type organizations. In the liberated 1980s, increasing numbers of marriages crumbled, and tens of thousands of (primarily) women found themselves older, alone, and in financial trouble. The lucky ones had divorce lawyers who fought for a share of all of the couple's financial assets, including the husband's pension. But thousands either did not know about the employer pension plan or did not have lawyers who understood this potentially valuable financial asset. If the divorce order didn't award a share of the pension, then the pension plan likely wouldn't recognize it. Even when included in a state divorce decree, some pension plan administrators questioned whether to pay out to divorced spouses.

For the traditional homemaker, adversity also could strike. The widows of employed spouses who died before drawing retirement benefits, even though eligible, could lose all spousal rights. And retirees could waive survivor annuity benefit protection without the consent of the spouse who would be left without any retirement income. These interrelated sets of issues were not fully or adequately addressed in ERISA, and by the early 1980s they had coalesced into a legislative reform agenda that women's groups and their consumer advocates could rally around. The groups effectively made their case that these inequities were in large part the reason for the disproportionate poverty among older women and lobbied Democrats and Republicans for relief. Within three years, the Retirement Equity Act (REA) passed the House and the Senate by overwhelming bipartisan numbers—413–0 in the House (H.R. 4280) and unanimous voice vote in the Senate (P.L. 98-397).

Not only did passage of the Retirement Equity Act provide meaningful pension assistance to millions of men and women, the act's passage, unlike the passage of ERISA, showed how organizations and coalitions could successfully lobby for retirement reforms. Both ERISA and REA also served to show that key members of Congress, both Democrat and Republican, were receptive to be involved in advancing "retirement security" reforms and that large majorities of both chambers would vote for retirement security initiatives.

Once again, the Retirement Equity Act did not address all private pension problems and needs, and pension participant advocates quickly assessed what issues still faced their members and millions like them. Three quickly came to the fore—vesting, integration, and portability (acronymed "VIP"). Prior to ERISA's enactment, many employers required workers to work 20 or 30 years or be with the company on the day of retirement to have any ability to receive an employer pension. ERISA took a huge step in generally reducing vesting to 10 years. But that still left millions of shorter-service workers who likely would never vest a right to a pension, particularly women who leave the workforce during their child-bearing years.

The vesting issue provoked three philosophical debates for retirement policy stakeholders. First, if the workplace is becoming more mobile, shouldn't pensions become more mobile? Second, shouldn't everyone have the same right to receive a pension? And third, whose money is this—mine or my employer's? These questions led to both intellectual and emotional debates. Some believed that having pensions be more mobile and portable was the preferred policy result. Others raised both practical and intellectual objections. The practical issue was money. If more workers vested and took their money with them, then that itself would cost companies more money. In addition, defined benefit (DB) plans generally included in their formulas an assumption that a certain percent of participants would not vest. Reducing that percent would increase employer pension costs.

Intellectually, vesting also challenged fundamental employment and employee benefits policy. Did employers want to retain employees or not? Were long service requirements a critical aspect of employment policy and thus of pension plans? While the answer varied among employers, employers were publicly reluctant to take a firm side on these emerging employment policy issues (Retirement Income Security in the U.S. 1985, Retirement Income Policy Act 1986).

On the question of whether everyone should benefit from the company pension plan, similar views and arguments were heard. To some it seemed a fairness and antidiscrimination issue. Other proponents looked at it more economically and from a "class-based" point of view—lower income and economically disenfranchised groups would primarily benefit from increased pension receipt. The opponents again raised the practical and philosophical counterarguments—cost and employer retention needs and policy (Retirement Income Security in the U.S. 1985, Retirement Income Policy Act 1986).

Finally, on the question of whose money it is, a different debate was heard. Worker advocates advanced the deferred compensation theory of pensions. Employees had negotiated for their employer pension contributions and given up other wages, benefits, and employment opportunities for these contributions, so the contributions belonged to the employees and might as well be provided to participants sooner rather than later. Employer opponents were not so willing to concede the deferred wage argument; they primarily argued the practical cost reality— employers would not pay more, so if benefits were required to be provided to a larger group of workers, everyone would simply get less (Retirement Income Security in the U.S. 1985; Retirement Income Policy Act 1986).

Portability raised many of the same issues. To the extent that some workers became more mobile and some, especially women, worked for shorter job tenures, consumer and women's advocates realized the importance of and need for portable pensions. Portability had been considered during the enactment of ERISA but was dropped in conference (Wooten 2004). The primary hindrance to portability has been cost and complexity. It is hard for most to argue that the current system is ideal. A worker who works from ages 25 to 35 at a firm and leaves after 10 years potentially must wait until age 65 to receive the benefit earned. The unfairness is that the benefit is not indexed during the 30 intervening years and thus provides devalued and insignificant retirement income. In recent years, it has been much more common for plans to permit workers who sever service to receive a distribution of their benefits and, it is hoped, roll the funds over into a tax-deferred retirement plan that will increase with inflation. Still, even today, according to the Bureau of Labor Statistics, less than half of all workers covered by DB plans are offered distributions on separation from service (*National Compensation Survey* 2000). While making preretirement distributions to enable deferred benefit indexing was feasible in 1984, it was controversial with some groups, including some unions, whose collective bargaining agreements assume that a certain percent of participant contributions will default and be used to bolster the retirement benefits of long-service employees.

Indexing, however, was but a small part of the portability conundrum. A defined benefit based on final average pay from a single employer, calculated on 30 to 35 years of service still delivers a far higher benefit than multiple smaller benefits from several employers.

True portability believers have wanted to create a pooled fund, similar to a multi-employer plan, to equate the full potential value of multiple small pensions and a single one. For years, many worker advocates tried to articulate how to create such a true portability model. But employers resisted the idea of joining a group pool, particularly if it would be government controlled, as many proposals were conceived. And key single-employer unions were less than supportive as well.

As for Social Security integration, it raised emotional more than intellectual issues. Since the beginning of employer-based pension trusts, some employers had argued that their trusts were intended to supplement "key" employees who did not benefit much from Social Security. To the extent that the Internal Revenue Code required that employers cover a broad cross-section of their employees, employers argued passionately that their Social Security contributions should count to offset the benefit of Social Security–dependent low-paid employees (Wooten 2004). Congress considered banning integration with Social Security in ERISA, but the fight over funding and vesting took precedence (Wooten 2004). For advocates for lower wage earners, Social Security integration kept the employer-based pension system primarily a tax-avoidance device for management employees. Prior to the Tax Reform Act of 1986, employers argued that they could integrate 100% of a participant's vested pension benefit. Social Security integration, unlike the other issues, didn't really turn on cost, but rather the fundamental vision of whether tax-deferred pension trusts could benefit a few or were required to benefit all.

The tax reform debate also introduced the idea of adding specific statutory requirements limiting the ability of employer pension plans to discriminate in favor of highly compensated employees. Although supported by participant advocates, these nondiscrimination provisions were primarily advanced by tax policy purists. Tax and trust law had long required individuals who established trusts to benefit a broad cross-section of covered beneficiaries. A specific nondiscrimination provision would limit the ability of plans to favor highly compensated employees in either benefits or contributions by a specific percentage (roughly 2 to 1). Similar to employer arguments about Social Security integration, many employers primarily wanted to use tax-deferred pension trusts to benefit key highly compensated employees. ERISA had not specifically included these requirements. The huge tax reform effort provided an opportunity for the purists to obtain what on its own likely would have been a much debated and controversial provision.

While the experts and lobbyists debated these issues, members of Congress were forced to make choices. The House and Senate passed bills that were sent to a formal conference committee where appointed members of Congress negotiated compromises and reported a final conference bill. The Tax Reform Act emerged from the conference committee, and the House and Senate passed a widely hailed final bill that, with respect to pensions, shortened vesting from 10 to 5 years, limited integration with Social Security to 50% of earned benefits, and added specific nondiscrimination rules. Portability was once again dropped from the final Act (P.L. 99-514).

A final example of legislative activity during the 1980s centered on the issue of what were known as asset reversions. During the early 1980s, the economy was in transition, and numerous older companies needed new capital to expand or change direction. At some point, a handful of clever capitalists noted that many of these companies had surpluses in their pension funds. If the plan were terminated, the excess could be taken by the employer or a new buyer to fund the company changes, which might include layoffs or reductions in workforce. One problem, however, was that the law wasn't completely clear as to the ownership of the surplus. Employers argued that after paying out all "accrued benefits," the surplus was theirs. Worker advocates argued that the surplus was generated by the earnings from their deferred wages and thus belonged to them. Trust and tax law traditionally held that excess assets could revert to the settlor-employer only if the trust explicitly provided for such. The law did not address whether the plan could be amended to insert the employer's ability to recover the surplus.

A few high-profile public cases, notably at A&P, Pacific Lumber, and the American Red Cross, brought the issue to Congress's attention. Numerous congressional hearings were held, and workers and worker advocates passionately argued the injustice of their pension funds' being used to terminate their jobs. The dispute lingered for years and laid bare the myth that employers operated pension funds solely in their workers' interest. Ultimately, the budget deficit resolved the dispute. In order to raise revenue, the Omnibus Budget Reconciliation Act of 1990 imposed a tax on employers that recovered surplus pension assets (P.L. 101–508). The tax varied based on the employer's behavior. If the surplus was transferred to another pension plan, including a defined contribution (DC) plan, the tax was 20%. If no new pension plan was created, income and excise taxes could exceed 50%.

This period made significant strides in bringing pension law closer to the needs and expectations of employees. Reducing vesting periods opened up benefits to millions of workers who otherwise would not have expected to receive retirement income. Changes regarding divorced and surviving spouses expanded pension equality and women's retirement income. Funding and anti-reversion requirements forced employers to increase pension contributions and discouraged financial shenanigans. However, these advances came at a price. Employers did not expand and increase benefits for all, but rather provided lesser benefits to an expanded group. And the increased regulatory and financial costs discouraged broadened pension coverage. Pension plan sponsorship, which started the decade at under 50%, did not expand during this period.

The 1990s Employers Take the Field

After the passage of the pension asset reversion legislation, the participant advocates briefly withdrew from the congressional arena. Not that all problems had been solved from their point of view, but the remaining issues, particularly coverage and adequacy, could not be solved by modest amendments to ERISA. Pension coverage hovered above or below 50% of the workforce from year to year, but only mandated coverage could effectively redress the problem, and that would provoke an all-out war with the employers. Adequacy was equally troubling. Participant groups had failed to fully abolish integration with Social Security; setting minimum retirement benefit standards would be even more difficult. Changes in staff and purpose at the major consumer groups also created a pause in participant advocacy. And the election of Bill Clinton created an opportunity to use the regulatory, rather than the legislative, process to strengthen participant pension protections.

The Republican landslide of 1994 enabled employers to turn the tables on the consumer advocates. Suddenly there was a new majority looking for legislative opportunities and victories. The Republicans and employer groups started small. First came the Savings Are Vital to Everyone's Retirement Act of 1997 (the SAVER Act; P.L. 105-92). It was mostly a feel-good piece of legislation that required the Department of Labor to conduct public education on the need to save for retirement and convene triennial national summits on retirement savings. It was so innocuous that it garnered widespread bipartisan support. But, it started to change the debate away from "pension promises" and toward "retirement saving" (i.e., individual responsibility). The SAVER Act was part of a conscious and subconscious effort by the business and financial service communities to shift the retirement policy debate away from employers and onto individuals.

The second opportunity for the business community, primarily the life insurance industry, to move the law more closely in business's favor was an issue known as "Harris Trust." In 1993, the Supreme Court in John Hancock Mutual Life Insurance Co. v. Harris Trust and Savings Bank (510 US 86 [1993]) held that ERISA required that DB pension plans investing in certain guaranteed life insurance investment contracts had to be separately accounted for and that insurers were subject to fiduciary responsibility for each separate account. According to the life insurance industry, they had not been operating in this way, but only as fiduciaries over all of the aggregated assets they invested. It was never clearly proved what the industry might have to do differently, and it mostly was a debate over form rather than substance. But the industry did not want to change its practices and screamed loudly to the new and receptive Republican Congress that it needed a prospective and retroactive exemption from having to comply with the Harris Trust decision. The Clinton administration refused to agree to prospective relief, but reluctantly agreed that undoing existing practices might be overly burdensome and worked out a compromise with the Congress. The Harris Trust legislative fix was a narrow modification of ERISA, but it further unveiled the new dynamic in which business community requests would receive enthusiastic and almost unquestioned legislative assistance from the Republican congressional majority (the Small Business Job Protection Act, P.L. 104-188).

Business community lobbying and wish lists reached their apotheosis in what became known as the "Portman-Cardin" legislation. Republicans still uncertain in their new majority status and Democrats maneuvering to retain some legislative power in the minority found that partnerships on occasion could be advantageous. Rob Portman, a relatively ambitious but somewhat junior Republican from Ohio was looking for ways to rise in the Republican leadership by demonstrating his legislative abilities. And Ben Cardin, Democrat from Maryland, didn't want to be just a back bench member of Congress. Both served on the House Committee on Ways and Means, which has jurisdiction over the tax deferral for pensions, and were being actively lobbied by the employer pension community.

Representative Cardin had become interested in pension issues when some Maryland state employees took pension distributions that the IRS ultimately determined were subject to taxation for failure to properly meet the rollover distribution rules. Cardin's fight to assist his Maryland constituents led him to a broader interest in pension issues. Prior to 1994, he began to work with other Democrats and outside stakeholders who were promoting legislation to amend ERISA.

Representatives Portman and Cardin agreed to work together and actively sought out the major employer stakeholder groups to ask for their list of needed legislative reforms. The employer groups were more than happy to compile their lists. Now that 401(k) plans were hitting their stride, a few obstacles had begun to emerge, and the 401(k) plans and providers were ready to seek legislative relief. High on the roadblock list was the cap on the amount that employees could contribute each year to a 401(k) plan on a tax-deferred basis. Many middle and upper income managers were able and willing to contribute 10 or more percent of their income for retirement or other deferred saving. Although less than 5% reached the annual cap, they were an influential group that was unafraid to speak up and that employers wanted to appease. Also problematic was 401(k) plan nondiscrimination testing. Employers and human resource managers bemoaned the code's rules on how to ensure that pension plans, both DB and DC, satisfied the rules on nondiscrimination in favor of highly paid employees. In fairness, the tests could be perverse and require managers to return excess contributions to employees, which did not engender goodwill among either employers or employees. The employer solution, of course, would not simply address the administrative impracticalities, but rather would create exceptions to avoid the test entirely.

As Portman and Cardin began to develop legislation to address these and other issues, they structured support for the bill so that one group could only get what it wanted if it also supported or at least went along with what the other groups wanted. Portman-Cardin moved slowly for a long time. Hearings were held but not too much more occurred (H.R. 1102, 1999). Republicans were growing more enthusiastic, but Democrats stayed on the sidelines. The missing piece was a lack of any proworker provisions. Portman and Cardin had courted the employers but not the participant groups, particularly the unions.

Participant advocacy groups did not engage early or actively enough in the developing legislation. Representatives Portman and Cardin did not seek them out either. After reducing vesting, Social Security integration, and other concerns in previous legislation, participant advocates were down to the big and hard issues that were too controversial for Reps. Portman and Cardin to include—universal pension coverage and benefit adequacy. The participant groups did seek some more modest reforms, such as spousal consent for 401(k) distributions, but the employer and industry groups strongly objected. Once Portman and Cardin acquired active union support, they had less need for the support of women's groups.

Eventually a union issue emerged that would ultimately provide enormous momentum to the legislation. Some unions, particularly the multi-employer construction and trucking unions, had employees (and union officers) whose pensions were limited by the code's maximum deductibility caps, known as section 415. Section 415 limited the ability of employees to receive pension benefits greater than their final salary.

Under collective bargaining agreements, some long-service employees could earn pensions greater than their final compensation, especially if their last years of service were part-time or less than full hours worked. Also, union officers may be covered by more than one pension plan (as a company employee and as a union employee) and could earn a pension greater than their final salary. Portman and Cardin agreed to add section 415 relief to their bill, and the affected unions vigorously started to lobby members of Congress, particularly Democratic members, to cosponsor the bill.

The Clinton administration did not have its own retirement reform agenda, but Clinton appointees early on promoted initiatives to encourage socially responsible investing of pension assets and undo judicial decisions that had limited employee rights to recover for pension law violations. These efforts were vehemently opposed by the employer pension community and forced the Clinton administration to back away and focus primarily on administrative efforts, such as ensuring timely contributions by employers to 401(k) plans.

Clinton's administration was not enthusiastic about the Portman-Cardin legislation because its provisions benefited primarily upper income taxpayers, and they cautiously discouraged its passage. The Clinton staff argued that, at a minimum, the legislation needed to include a tax credit for low-income savers (what became the SAVER credit). The bill did not pass Congress while Clinton was in office. However, when George Bush took the presidency in 2001, his insistence on wide-ranging tax cuts enabled Portman-Cardin to pass as part of broad tax cut legislation (Economic Growth and Tax Relief Reconciliation Act of 2001, P.L. 107-16). For good or for bad, Cardin voted against the final provisions that he worked over a decade on but that ultimately were part of a massive $1.2 trillion unpaid-for tax cut largely for the wealthiest Americans.

The Portman-Cardin bill was a lesson in how groups with different interests could be leveraged to support legal changes. But the result was modest changes that primarily benefited those who already had retirement savings, with minimal advances for those without preexisting resources. The absence of active involvement by participant-oriented groups negatively affected the worker protections and retirement security aspects of each of the discussed bills. The employer-sought changes also did not significantly expand pension coverage or retirement savings. Pension coverage expanded briefly in the late 1990s along with the period of strong economic growth, notably for small employers as well, but the increases disappeared with the economic downturn in 2001.

Where We Are Today

From 1974 to 2006, ERISA was amended over 20 times. Most of these amendments modified the DB pension plan rules. While ERISA insiders were debating the merits of each policy reform, 401(k) plans were beginning their rise. By the mid-1980s, many insiders well understood the threat that 401(k) plans presented to DB plans. While most still assumed and argued that large employers would maintain both plans for their workforce, DB supporters also feared the powerful advantages that 401(k) plans offered over DB plans. Notably, 401(k) plans were simpler—no complicated formulas or actuarial computations, just a fixed percent of salary, and no required annuities upon retirement; cheaper—no contributions required for employees who did not make their own contributions; and less risky—no employer obligation to offset investment losses.

One response to the threat that 401(k) plans posed was the creation of what are known as cash balance plans. The consulting industry created them to provide a plan that retained key features of a DB plan but added many of the desirable features of 401(k) plans, primarily the illusion of an account balance that participants could understand, value, and theoretically cash out when needed. The challenge was how to switch workers' retirement benefits from a traditional DB final-average-pay formula to an account balance calculation. The simplest and fairest way was to grandfather participants over a certain age and/or with a certain number of years of service. According to the Government Accountability Office (GAO), 77% of large employers and 49% of all employers chose this method (Government Accountability Office 2005). For the others, the consulting industry devised a handful of methods, adjusted for each employer, that simulated accrued benefits or added conversion supplements or maybe did nothing at all. Without a grandfather or equal-cost offset, participants would lose greatly. Again, according to the GAO, without a grandfather provision some workers could lose up to 50% of expected benefits. For a cash balance plan to be equivalent to a 1.5% DB plan, it would have to provide an employer contribution of 13%. GAO could find no employer providing that level of contribution (Government Accountability Office 2005).

At some point the consultants figured out a way to overcome these dilemmas—workers wouldn't be able to determine the loss of benefits by themselves, and employers, plan administrators, and consultants wouldn't make it clear to them. Cash balance plans started slowly in the 1980s and early 1990s but began to take off in the mid-1990s. The Financial Accounting Standards Board and Wall Street analysts and lenders were starting to demand more public reporting of long-term employer obligations, including pensions. These inquiries made employers nervous about their possible long-term DB plan obligations, and they began to consider cutting back. Employers also were looking to eliminate early retirement incentives that had been needed in the 1970s but were no longer necessary. Plus the stock market was booming, making 401(k) plans attractive to both employers and employees. Termination of an overfunded DB plan would trigger the reversion tax of up to 50%. Converting to cash balance became an acceptable way to freeze long-term liabilities, eliminate early-retirement subsidies, and shift closer to a 401(k) without losing or facing a tax on the excess assets accumulated in the plan.

Employers and plan administrators, and their consulting firms, figured they could explain the change as a positive plan amendment. They could accurately explain the amendment as required under ERISA's requirement of notice of a reduction of accrued benefits as a change in plan formula from final average pay to an account balance. ERISA did not require plans to explain the monetary value of the loss, in the aggregate or on an individual basis. Participants generally would not be able to calculate the difference in the two benefits.

Cash balance plans were expanding greatly until the *Wall Street Journal* wrote a series of articles on how participants could lose under the plans. Around the same time, IBM announced its conversion to cash balance. IBM's computer-savvy employees *could* calculate the loss of benefits, and they used the newly emerging Internet to protest to each other and members of Congress. Congressional hearings were held, and legislation to stop the perceived abuses was introduced ("Pension Reform" 1999, "Hybrid Pension Plans" 1999.) There was sufficient outcry that, in late September 1999, the Clinton administration imposed a moratorium on Internal Revenue Service approval of determination letters approving plan amendments adopting cash balance features. The moratorium largely stopped the growth of cash balance plans, though significant numbers continued without IRS approval.

Cash balance plan supporters have complained that participant advocates stymied the last, best chance for the survival of DB plans. They argue that cash balance plans maintain a delicate mix of DB and DC features—employer contribution and PBGC (Pension Benefit Guaranty Corporation) guarantee combined with account balance and market return—to ensure retirement security for the long term. Participant advocates are split on this question. Some, like the Pension Rights Center, highly value the employer contribution and PBGC protection. Typically 401(k) plans have immediate or one-year vesting, whereas cash balance plans usually retain five-year vesting. The GAO estimates that almost 40% of workers never vest under a cash balance plan (Government Accountability Office 2005). A 401(k) plan provides an actual market return that is likely to be higher than the cash balance plan's more conservative "hypothetical" interest credit. Both plans are equally bad in encouraging lump sum distributions that undermine long-term retirement income. The United Kingdom considered encouraging cash balance plans, but reconsidered when actuarial analyses showed that workers fared better in 401(k)-type plans (US/UK Dialogue on Pensions 2005).

Are We Destined to Live in a 401(k) World?

As it has become clear that 401(k) plans have eclipsed DB plans, many are pointing fingers of blame or trying to understand why DB plans lost the retirement vehicle race. Some are undertaking this inquiry in hopes of proposing changes to revitalize DB plans. We may never know if the demise of DB plans was inevitable. As I noted earlier, it was clear even by the 1980s that 401(k) plans held tremendous advantages in terms of lower cost, less employer risk, and simplicity. Initially, observers hoped employers would maintain both types of plans. But by the 1990s, employers started to shift to 401(k) plans as their only retirement plan. Historically, the key reasons that employers have wanted to maintain DB plans have been tax advantage, funding flexibility, employee retention, employee demand, and alternative-use flexibility.

When DB plans were being created in the post–World War II years and when ERISA was enacted in 1974, corporate tax rates were considered to be high. Making contributions to a tax-deferred pension trust was an appealing way to reduce corporate taxation, especially since the contributions benefited employees and management. Since 1969, maximum corporate tax rates have dropped from 52.8% to 35%, greatly lessening the tax advantages. And the reduction in the top capital gains tax rate from almost 40% to approximately 20% has made equity investments more beneficial than tax-deferred retirement trusts. Some actuaries and consultants have written that corporate executives would do better investing their personal and corporate funds in investments other than pensions. (See, for example, Gold and Hudson 2003.)

Another key difference between DB and DC plans is funding flexibility. DB plans generally are funded over 30 years, with great flexibility in funding assumptions and ability to smooth required contributions. DC accrued benefits must be fully funded annually, and even quarterly for participant directed plans. The newly enacted Pension Protection Act (discussed below) generally reduces DB funding to 7 years and reduces assumption and contribution flexibility beginning in 2008, taking away another DB incentive.

Employee retention and demand also have been in flux for many years. Globalization and market pressures call into question the need to encourage long-service employees. Older employees require higher salaries and higher benefit costs, and often they may not be more productive than younger, cheaper employees. The employer effort to discourage unions reduces the ability of employees to effectively make demands in the workplace. When a union is present, 68% of union contracts provide a DB pension plan to the employees (*Employee Benefits in Private Industry in the United States* 2006).

DB plans retain an advantage over DC plans in their ability to be used for more than retirement purposes. DB plans may be used to provide disability and early-retirement benefits. They also may be used to pay out severance-type benefits. DC assets do not permit these additional uses.

The reasons usually propounded for the death of DB plans are overregulation, both statutory and regulatory; contribution limits that drove executives to nonqualified compensation; and restricted use of excess assets. It is probably impossible for empirical studies to determine the exact causes, but Congress can try to undo some of the perceived impediments and see if reversing course works. Of course, there are obstacles to undoing history. Every provision in law has a stakeholder who advocated it, and it is unusual for individuals to agree to undo their handiwork.

Other issues continue to generate strong emotion, and it is not easy to find a middle ground. The majority of stakeholders would likely agree that it may be desirable or necessary to permit corporate officers and senior management to enjoy greater benefits from a DB plan to encourage their interest in them. However, determining how much they can earn under a plan is not so simple. The federal deficit makes such a decision even more difficult if offsetting revenues cannot be found.

Permitting broader employer use of DB pension assets causes similar angst. Participant advocates understand that employers may be more interested in DB plans if they can use the contributions for multiple purposes and do not risk losing any of the funds. But how much can be used and for what purposes is not an easy determination for those who believe contributions represent deferred employee wages.

Another Step Backward for DB Plans— The Pension Protection Act

Just as pension stakeholders were beginning to discuss how to save the DB system, along came another setback. The stock market downturn in 2001 was an unexpected blow for most employers (as well as for millions of other investors). During the 1990s, employers grew dependent on strong stock market returns to fund their pension plans. During this period most DB plans were considered overfunded, and employers were not required to make any annual contributions at all. The 2001 downturn, along with falling interest rates, boosted the present value of DB pension liabilities and thus required a substantial increase in employer pension contributions.

After a funding holiday of multiple years, and with dwindling plan commitment, employers were reluctant and sometimes financially unable to make increased contributions. The employer community realized that one way to reduce the increase would be to change the assumptions to reduce the present-day value of liabilities.

An easy target was the interest rate required to value plan liabilities. The rate had always been based upon 30-year Treasury bond rates, but during the brief period when the U.S. federal government was running a budget surplus, the Clinton administration stopped issuing the long-term bonds. Employer consultants had long wanted to switch to higher yield corporate bonds, and the end of the 30-year note combined with impending higher contributions (and a Republican president and Congress) made this a good time to seek a change in rates. The employer lobbyists made their case to Congress. Some members readily agreed to the employer request, but because of the complexity of the issue (what exact rate or rates to use), others asked the Bush Department of the Treasury for comments.

Also during this time, the fortunes of the Pension Benefit Guaranty Corporation (PBGC) began to change rapidly. In 2001, the PBGC had a $10-billion surplus. Over one year, the surplus became a $10-billion deficit. The following year the deficit exceeded $20 billion ("PBGC Releases Fiscal Year 2004 Financial Results" 2004). Though the PBGC claimed to have sufficient assets to pay retirees pension benefits for many years into the future, it estimated that it faced up to $100 billion in possible additional liabilities, based on $450 billion in employer underfunding. Fears that the federal government could be called on to bail out the PBGC just like it had the savings and loan industry decades before created public fears of a pension crisis.

The Department of the Treasury delayed a response until being formally called to hearings before the House Committee on Ways and Means. Peter Fisher, undersecretary for domestic finance of the Department of the Treasury, argued that a significantly different interest measure was needed. Fisher agreed that corporate bonds were a more accurate measure than Treasury bills, but he argued that there needed to be a series of rates tied to the duration of pension plan liabilities (known as a yield curve; "Challenges Facing Pension Plan Funding" 2003).

Employers strongly opposed imposition of a yield curve, which would require employers with older workers—and thus liabilities that soon would be due—to use the lowest interest rates and highest funding. Time was running out, as corporate pension contributions were due on April 15th. Over a few months, the Congress agreed to switch to a corporate bond rate for two years with the expectation that the administration would submit a comprehensive proposal to the Congress (Pension Funding Equity Act of 2004, P.L. 108-218).

The administration worked intensively throughout 2004 to review the DB funding rules. Upon President Bush's reelection in 2004, the administration presented its pension funding reform proposal to the Congress as part of the FY2006 budget request. The proposal was harsh. It proposed reducing pension plan funding from 30 to 7 years. It proposed eliminating the ability to smooth assets and liabilities over time. And it proposed adopting a full corporate bond yield curve to value liabilities.

John Boehner, chairman of the U.S. House Committee on Education and the Workforce, and Charles Grassley, chairman of the U.S. Senate Committee on Finance, promised swift consideration of the administration proposal. Representative Boehner had been proposing other non-funding pension reforms that primarily benefited the financial services industry, and the funding bill was an opportunity to pass these reforms as well. (The Bush proposal conveniently included support for them.) Senator Grassley was more concerned for the financial health of the PBGC and possible taxpayer liability. Hearings were held throughout 2005, and the respective committees of jurisdiction began drafting legislation ("Financial Status of the Pension Benefit Guaranty Corporation and the Administration's Defined Benefit Plan Funding Proposal" 2005; "Retirement Security Crisis" 2005; "President's Proposal for Single-Employer Pension Funding Reform" 2005; "PBGC Reform: Mending the Pension Safety Net" 2005; "Defined-Benefit Pension Plans and Lessons Learned from the United Airlines Case" 2005; "Pension Double Header" 2005; "H.R. 2830" 2005; "The Pension Benefit Guaranty Corporation" 2005; "Funding Rules for Multiemployer Defined Benefit Plans in H.R. 2830, the 'Pension Protection Act of 2005'" 2005).

The chairmen of the House Committee on Education and the Workforce and the Senate Committee on Health, Education, Labor and Pensions were caught in the middle. Both Representative Boehner and Senator Enzi, chairman of the Senate committee, wanted to support the administration and the employer community. Employers did not like the administration proposal, though they had to be careful in their criticism. The two chairmen tried to draft legislation that threaded the needle between the two sides. Boehner's bill, which largely followed the administration proposal with a few key modifications, was introduced on June 9 and passed by committee on June 30, 2005 (H.R. 2830, 2005). The most notable change was deletion of the yield curve. The Boehner bill proposed three interest rates as a compromise. All Republicans voted for the bill; the Democrats voted neither for nor against but simply present. Democrats on the House committee supported strengthening the funding rules, but they were concerned that the combined effect of the changes in funding rules would be to push employers out of the DB system. Analyses by both the Congressional Budget Office and PBGC concluded that the bill was worse than continuing current law, as neither employer contributions nor the PBGC deficit would be improved ("Cost Estimate for H.R. 2830, Pension Protection Act of 2005" 2005; "Analysis of the Pension Benefit Guaranty Corporation on H.R. 2830" 2005).

Consideration by the Senate was propelled by outside events. On September 14, 2005, both Delta and Northwest Airlines filed for bankruptcy and threatened to terminate their DB plans. Both airlines said that they would not terminate if Congress provided them additional time to fund their pension plans. The administration opposed such specialized relief, but Senate support was swift and strong. The pension funding reform bill was the best legislative vehicle to help the airline industry.

Senators Baucus and Grassley, the ranking member and chair, respectively, of the Senate Committee on Finance, were strongly supportive of the administration's proposal. Marrying it with airline relief would guarantee Senate approval. Senators Enzi and Kennedy, chair and ranking member, respectively, of the Committee on Health, Education, Labor and Pensions also moved quickly to report their part of the funding bill. Senate passage occurred on November 16, 2005, and House passage on December 15, 2005. Though the conference on the bill was slow, pressure came again from Northwest, calling for a decision by end of July 2006 or the company would terminate, propelling the House and Senate to finalize a bill. The final politics took an odd twist. The Senate wanted some unrelated tax provisions added to the bill, but the House decided to keep the provisions off the conference for use with another bill. Because time was short, the House passed a new freestanding bill that reflected the agreement of the key conferees (H.R. 4). The Senate reluctantly took up the bill without amendment so it could be sent to the president.

On August 17, 2006, President Bush signed into law the Pension Protection Act. Weighing in at over 900 pages, the new law contains hundreds of new ERISA provisions and likely will be the source of regulatory and plan activity for years to come. It is also suspected that the new law will require additional and possibly multiple congressional amendments over the coming years.

The Need for a National Retirement Policy

Irrespective of the Pension Protection Act, U.S. retirement policy remains at a crossroads. The decline of DB plans has only increased the pressure on and importance of Social Security. If employer-based DB plans do not stabilize or revitalize, then Social Security will be the sole DB plan for almost all Americans.

Designing an adequate retirement security need not be difficult for the United States. Our demographics and our economic resources can support a sustainable system in which individuals work until a societally agreed-upon minimum retirement age, at which time individuals will receive sufficient income to live out their remaining years. All key stakeholders, including employees and employers, have an interest in an employment system in which individuals do not work until death, but rather are able to "retire" after having completed a reasonable career of employment. If an individual works for at least 30 years and sets aside an adequate level of income during that time, sufficient funds can be accumulated to provide income for an additional 20 or so years. Such funds can be set aside through a government-based, employer-based, individual, or combination pool. The main challenge is to set aside an adequate level of funds (and not to borrow against such funds before retirement). Regrettably, the United States has not been able to comprehensively decide the structural makeup (government, employer, etc.) or adequacy levels for the U.S. retirement system.

The strongest and most central retirement income component, Social Security, will have to be decided in the coming decades. According to the Social Security Trustees Report (*Annual Report of the Board of Trustees of the Federal Old-Age and Survivors Insurance and Federal Disability Insurance Trust Funds* 2006), Social Security will begin in 2017 to pay out more than it takes in and will not be able to pay full benefits by 2040. Since Social Security covers over 97% of employed individuals and provides more than half of retirement income to one third of recipients and more than two thirds of retirement income to one third of recipients, Social Security likely will need a combination of amendments that will largely preserve benefits through a combination of payroll tax enhancements and benefit adjustments and delays. The political sacrifices that will be necessary to address Social Security's long-term viability may leave little room to improve Social Security's average replacement rate of 42% to 44% other than for the lowest-income workers or the most vulnerable groups.

The upcoming debate over restructuring Social Security for future generations could and should be an opportunity also to establish a comprehensive retirement system for all deferred income, including employer pensions and personal savings. The main obstacle to a comprehensive solution, regrettably, is the fragmented nature of the existing retirement system and its stakeholders. Social Security experts typically focus on Social Security alone; private pension experts tend to focus on private pensions alone; and so on. In recent years when Social Security has been under review (1999 and 2005), Social Security aficionados were loathe to add private pension and savings issues to the debate. Their reasons appear to be several. Some fear that discussion of "private" pensions will lead to pressure to "privatize" Social Security. Some feel that Social Security's issues are of such complexity that policy makers cannot handle bigger problems. Others plead ignorance of the private pension system. There also appear to be some turf and jurisdictional conflicts that create some reluctance to broaden the policy debate. The result, however, is to the detriment of the United States's ability to conceptualize a national retirement policy or system.

The challenge remains: what income sources will supplement Social Security? Ignoring our other looming crisis—health care—retirement policy experts believe that typical individuals need a retirement income replacement rate of at least 75% of preretirement salary to live adequately in retirement. Subtracting Social Security (42% to 44%), the United States needs a system by which individuals are able to accumulate—through government, employment, personal savings, or some combination of them—at least 30% to 35% of preretirement salary for retirement.

Surveys and studies consistently show that Americans are not on track for this level of retirement income. Notably, the Center for Retirement Research found that almost half of Americans will not accumulate an adequate retirement income (*Retirements At Risk: A New National Retirement Risk Index* 2006).

Once again, as with ERISA and many other statutes, the question will become this: Who will resolve this challenge—the affected employer groups and consumer advocates or national policy makers?

And who leads whom? Congress has often been criticized for acting too cautiously and too slowly, but it is hard for legislation to proceed any other way. Members of Congress and their staffs really do not have the expertise to independently propose policy reforms. Most Congressional actions arise from a problem that is brought to someone's attention. Members or their staff may perceive that a problem exists, but they need expert advice to understand its dimensions and consider alternative solutions. The legislative process generally takes time—time to weigh the pros and cons of a proposal and to garner majority support.

The real challenge is for members of Congress, having undergone that policy development process, to propose the best reform and hold to it. However, in fairness, national policy cannot be just the whim or dream of a small handful but should reflect societal consensus.

At present, there largely has been silence, with a few flickering calls from the corners, regarding this policy debate. One of the most thoughtful attempts to solve the puzzle was put forth by Gene Sperling, national economic policy adviser to President Clinton, when the Democrats, under President Clinton, were being pressed on Social Security privatization by the Republican-controlled Congress. Sperling proposed to create a universal 401(k) that would provide all Americans a private retirement account in addition to Social Security, with matching government contributions for middle- and lower-income earners (Sperling 2005). A number of academics and think tanks have subsequently put forth similar proposals (see retirement security proposals put forth by the Aspen Institute, the New America Foundation, the Pension Rights Center Conversation on Coverage, and the Retirement Security Project).

The participant groups are the most committed and the most flexible on issues of retirement security. Most are willing to support a range of retirement security systems. The system can be constructed along government, employer, or individual lines. The main criteria are that it be universal and that it provide fair and adequate benefits to the lowest-income-earning quintiles.

The major obstacle, beyond stakeholder fragmentation, comes from the employer community. Employers are not unified or always forthcoming about what is wanted. Some employers oppose a governmentally organized system because it is contrary to their capitalist beliefs. Some, particularly the consulting and financial services community, oppose a government system because it threatens their own business interests. At the same time that employers tend to fear a government system, they are also not clear about their employer commitment.

What is the future for DB plans? According to the PBGC, over 40,000 employers still maintain such plans for 20 million active workers. And most of the public sector feels strongly that DB plans are a better model for that workforce. Unlike current trends in the private sector, state and local governments still have reasons to want to retain a stable and long-term workforce of firefighters, police, teachers, and other public servants. DB plans can retain a niche among employers that want to retain long-service workers, want funding flexibility (for tax, contribution, or nonpension purposes), or have employees who demand it.

What is the future for DC plans? Despite their popularity, 401(k) plans have fallen short so far as equals to DB plans. Median account balances were under $30,000 in 2004, according to the Congressional Research Service (*Retirement Savings and Household Wealth* 2006). According to the Employee Benefit Research Institute, 40% of participants use their 401(k) funds prior to retirement. While efforts to encourage automatic enrollment of workers in plans with simple balanced investment options are considerable and growing, they are not enough. Congress and employers must limit preretirement access to the funds. Unfortunately, both parties fear the wrath of employees who want their money now or who may not contribute at all if they are not guaranteed easy access.

So what are some simple and not-so-simple reforms that can be undertaken to ensure retirement income beyond Social Security? Policy makers of all stripes—Democrat and Republican, liberal and conservative—are starting to recognize that the next steps are automatic payroll deduction for all employees: if not to an employer pension plan, then to an Individual Retirement Account or supplemental Social Security–type account. The proposals are still being developed and key questions are not yet fully answered, but most proposals contain many similar elements. Most Democrats and Republicans accept that individuals must save, in addition to Social Security, in order to assure individual retirement security and for adequate retirement income. The differences lie in how much individuals must save, whether employers must also contribute, whether low-income earners would receive tax credits to encourage or offset their savings, and whether government would assist and oversee how these savings are invested.

The Social Security privatization and pension funding reform debates have filled the public arena with numerous employee and employer advocates who are considering each of these issues and how best to resolve them. They await the next opportunity in which Congress and the public consider fulfilling the promise of retirement security for the American people. Can Congress enact a second ERISA—a triumph of policy over the interest groups?

References

Annual Report of the Board of Trustees of the Federal Old-Age and Survivors Insurance and Federal Disability Insurance Trust Funds. 2006, May 1.

"Analysis of the Pension Benefit Guaranty Corporation on H.R. 2830," PBGC, June 30, 2005.

"Challenges Facing Pension Plan Funding." 2003. Hearing before the Subcommittee on Select Revenue Measures, House Committee on Ways and Means, Print 108-10. April 30.

"Cost Estimate for H.R. 2830, Pension Protection Act of 2005." 2005. As ordered reported by the House Committee on Education and the Workforce. June 30.

"Defined-Benefit Pension Plans and Lessons Learned from the United Airlines Case." 2005. Hearing before the Senate Committee on Finance. June 7.

Employee Benefits in Private Industry in the United States. 2006. National Compensation Survey, Summary 06-05. August.

"Financial Status of the Pension Benefit Guaranty Corporation and the Administration's Defined Benefit Plan Funding Proposal." 2005. Hearing before the Senate Committee on Finance. March 1.

"Funding Rules for Multiemployer Defined Benefit Plans in H.R. 2830, the 'Pension Protection Act of 2005.'" 2005. Hearing before the House Subcommittee on Select Revenue Measures, Committee on Ways and Means. June 28.

Gold, Jeremy, and Nick Hudson. 2003. "Creating Value in Pension Plans (Or Gentlemen Prefer Bonds)." *Journal of Applied Corporate Finance*, Vol. 15, No. 4 (Fall), pp. 51–7.

Government Accountability Office. 2005. *Information on Cash Balance Pension Plans.* GAO-06-42. October. Washington, DC: GAO.

H.R. 1102. 1999. "The Comprehensive Retirement Security and Pension Reform Act of 1999." Hearing before the House Subcommittee on Employer-Employee Relations, Committee on Education and the Workforce. June 29.

H.R. 2830. 2005. "The Pension Protection Act of 2005." Hearing before the House Committee on Education and the Workforce. June 15.

"Hybrid Pension Plans." 1999. Senate Committee on Health, Education, Labor, and Pensions. September 21.

National Compensation Survey: Employee Benefits in Private Industry in the United States. 2000. Bureau of Labor Statistics, U.S. Department of Labor.

"PBGC Reform: Mending the Pension Safety Net." 2005. Hearing before the Senate Subcommittee on Retirement Security and Aging, Committee on Health, Education, Labor, and Pensions. April 26.

"PBGC Releases Fiscal Year 2004 Financial Results." 2004. PBGC Public Affairs, November 15.

"Pension Double Header: Reforming Hybrid and Multi-Employer Pension Plans." 2005. Hearing before the Senate Subcommittee on Retirement Security and Aging, Committee on Health, Education, Labor, and Pensions. June 7.

"Pension Reform." 1999. Senate Committee on Finance. June 30.

"President's Proposal for Single-Employer Pension Funding Reform." 2005. Hearing before the Subcommittee on Select Revenue Measures, House Committee on Ways and Means, March 8.

Retirement Income Security in the U.S. 1985. Hearings before the Subcommittee on Social Security and the Subcommittee on Oversight, House Committee on Ways and Means. July 18, September 5–6.

Retirement Income Policy Act. 1986. Hearing before the Subcommittee on Savings, Pensions, and Investment Policy, Senate Committee on Finance. January 28.

Retirement Savings and Household Wealth: Trends from 2001 to 2004. 2006. Congressional Research Service, Library of Congress. May 22.

"Retirement Security Crisis: The Administration's Proposal for Pension Reform and Its Implications for Workers and Taxpayers." 2005. Hearing before the House Committee on Education and the Workforce, March 2.

Retirements At Risk: A New National Retirement Risk Index. 2006. Chestnut Hill, MA: Center for Retirement Research at Boston College. June.

Sperling, Gene. 2005. *The Pro-Growth Progressive: An Economic Strategy for Shared Prosperity*. New York: Simon and Schuster.

"The Pension Benefit Guaranty Corporation." 2005. Hearing before the Senate Committee on Budget. June 15.

US/UK Dialogue on Pensions. 2005. Conference Proceedings. AARP Global Aging Program. July 19.

Wooten, James A. 2004. *The Employee Retirement Income Security Act of 1974: A Political History*. Berkeley: University of California Press.

CHAPTER 10

The Politics of Pension Cuts

DAVID MADLAND
Georgetown University

Over the past five years, more than 10 million workers and retirees have had their company pensions or retiree health benefits cut, with many people losing tens or even hundreds of thousands of dollars in benefits.[1] Pensions and retiree health benefits are earned over a lifetime of work, and cutting them breaks a commitment between employer and employee. People often stayed with a company, forgoing other opportunities, for the security of these retirement benefits.

But only in certain cases have these monetary losses and broken promises provoked significant protests. In general, as companies have shed their legacy costs, workers and retirees have not taken political action.

Employees and retirees at IBM, Verizon, Duke Energy, AT&T, General Electric, Quest Communications, Bell Atlantic, Sears, Prudential Insurance, United Airlines, and others have protested a variety of changes to their retirement benefits by holding rallies, staging strikes, writing letters to their elected representatives, and calling press conferences as well as filing class action lawsuits and shareholder resolutions. Yet at many more companies, workers and retirees have taken no political action when their retirement benefits have been reduced. And perhaps more puzzling, even at companies such as Verizon and IBM, where workers have had significant success protesting certain kinds of pension changes, these same workers have done little to protest subsequent benefit cuts.

Overview

This chapter explores why only some retirement benefit cuts have produced a strong political reaction and why the overall level of reaction has been relatively muted. I explain how retirement benefits have been cut and how many people have been affected, and compare the relatively low level of protest about pension cuts to the more widespread reaction to proposed cuts to Social Security. I also discuss the general elements necessary for political action and how they relate to retirement benefit protests.

The size of the cuts, the number of people impacted, and the kind of people who are harmed would seem to indicate that significant protest is possible, or even likely. But many of the people who have lost are not organized, and they have lost benefits in ways that make remedying the cuts difficult. People who have lost retirement benefits tend to have the skills and financial resources that lead to action, but most are not unionized, which significantly hampers their ability to protest. In addition, addressing some types of cuts would require a significant new role for government, something these workers and retirees, who tend to believe in the American ethic of self-reliance, have been reluctant to support.

Who Has Pensions and Retiree Health Benefits

Understanding some of the basic facts of retirement benefit cuts—such as how many people have benefits, how many have lost benefits, and the different ways they can lose—is key to understanding the participation puzzle. More than 10 million Americans have lost retirement benefits over the past five years, and millions more could lose them in the future. The typical loss is in the tens of thousands, and a considerable number of people lose more than a hundred thousand dollars. Benefits can be cut in numerous ways.

Though pensions are not a universal program like Social Security, a significant number of the country's workers depend on pensions for retirement security. About a third of all workers and retirees have pensions or earn pension benefits. Of all currently employed people, 23%, or over 28 million workers, earn benefits in a traditional defined benefit (DB) pension plan, while 60% of current retirees, or over 18 million people, receive a pension (Copeland 2006).[2] (Retirees are more likely to have pensions than current workers because fewer firms today provide pensions and because figures for retirees represent a lifetime of work rather than just a snapshot in time about whether their current employer offers a pension.)

Figures on employer-provided health care are similar in scale to those for pensions. About a third of all retirees receive health benefits from their former employers; if spousal benefits are included the figure edges closer to half of all retirees (Fronstin 2001, Government Accountability Office 2005, Merlis 2006). Combined, nearly 18 million retirees have some form of employer-sponsored health coverage (Merlis 2006). Probably around a third of current employees work for a company that offers retiree health benefits (Kaiser Family Foundation and Health Research and Educational Trust 2005, Fronstin 2005).

Context of the Cuts

Though analyzing why employers have increasingly been cutting retirement benefits is beyond the scope of this chapter, the context of the cuts is worth mentioning. The most common explanation companies give is that they have been compelled to trim expenses in the face of increased global competition. A few employers even argue that they have been pushed to the edge of financial collapse by legacy costs.

These explanations are undoubtedly true for certain employers. But some companies that initially appear unable to manage retirement burdens may actually be in better shape than they claim. And many healthy companies are also cutting retirement benefits. For example, one study found that the typical company that has frozen its pension plan had a slightly better credit rating than the average firm sponsoring a plan (Mercer Human Resources Consulting 2006). Indeed, there is considerable evidence that many companies are reducing retirement benefits not because they have to, but because they can—because the law allows them to and because opposing political forces, such as unions, have been in decline.

Executives sometimes shield their own retirement benefits while cutting those for rank-and-file workers. According to a *Wall Street Journal* report, some companies that cut pensions for rank-and-file workers have maintained and even increased pension benefits for top executives in separate pension plans (Schultz and Francis 2006). McKesson established a pension plan for executives in 1995 but froze pensions of other workers two years later. Allied Waste Industries froze its pension plan for salaried workers in 1999, but four years later adopted a pension plan covering 10 executives. At BellSouth, pension obligations for ordinary workers have edged down 3% since 2000 but have increased 89% over the same period for executives.

Companies are not required to separately report the costs of executive pensions, but instead they often combine the liabilities of the two plans. This typically makes pension finances appear worse than they are. Standard pensions must be funded years into the future, while executive pensions typically have no assets set aside to pay for them.

Time Warner reported in financial disclosures that its pension plans are underfunded by 7% (Schultz and Francis 2006). But its pension for regular employees actually had a surplus and could pay benefits well into the future. Time Warner's executive pension plan was short $305 million. Combining the two plans gave an inaccurate picture of finances. Similarly at GM, the pension plans for most workers have enough assets to pay benefits and contain $9 billion more than is needed to meet obligations (Schultz and Francis 2006). But GM's executive pension plan has a liability of $1.4 billion.

Even during bankruptcy, executives are often able to protect themselves and their retirement benefits while passing on costs to regular workers. An examination of prominent bankruptcy filings by the *New York Times* found that executive benefits were preserved in every case reviewed, though benefits for workers were cut nearly every time (Henriques and Johnston 1996).

How Benefits Can Be Cut

Retirement benefits are largely based on an implicit contract between employer and employee: workers will earn benefits over their tenure with a company, and the company will pay out those benefits when the worker retires. In general, pension benefits that have already been earned cannot be reduced. However, benefits that workers expect to be able to earn in the future can be reduced, such as by terminating the plan or by changing the way benefits are calculated. Workers receive what they have earned up to the point of change, but not what they would have earned had the employer continued the old pension plan.

Because pensions are typically designed so that most benefits are earned toward the end of the worker's career, "expected" benefits are quite significant. Middle-aged workers with significant tenure in the company but years to go before retirement—workers midstream in the implicit pension contract—have the most to lose. Those with little service have not earned much. Workers nearing retirement have already earned most of the benefits they expect to earn.

Union contracts can protect against changes to retirement benefits to ensure that workers can continue earning future benefits and thus provide greater protections for the implicit contract. However, union contracts can be undone by bankruptcy courts.

Even benefits that have already been vested are at risk if a company files for bankruptcy. Pension plans are supposed to be fully funded, but many plans avoid this requirement and as a result are underfunded—meaning that the plan doesn't have enough assets to pay all claims. If a company with an underfunded plan goes bankrupt, the Pension Benefit Guarantee Corporation (PBGC) is responsible for paying benefits.

The PBGC covers only "basic" pension benefits earned before a plan ends. Retiree health benefits are not guaranteed, nor are many forms of early retirement pension benefits, disability benefits, death benefits, and additional pension benefits granted within the last five years. In addition, the PBGC sets a dollar cap on how much it will pay in annual benefits. For pension plans ending in 2006, the maximum guaranteed amount is about $4,000 per month for workers who retire at age 65. The guaranteed amount is lower for people under age 65 or whose pension includes benefits for a survivor or other beneficiary.

For workers without a union contract, retiree health benefits can be cut, changed, or eliminated at any point. Companies can change the rules midstream for how workers earn retiree health benefits, or they can reduce or completely do away with such benefits, even for current retirees. With retiree health care, there are virtually no legal protections for the implicit contract between employer and employee.

How Many People Have Lost and What They Have Lost

The number of people whose retirement benefits have been cut and the amount they have lost can only be roughly estimated. Plans vary across companies, can be cut in numerous ways, and don't affect everyone equally. Furthermore, government and private data are often incomplete and years out of date.

However, a reasonable estimate is that over the past five years, more than 10 million workers and retirees have seen their pension or retiree health benefits significantly cut. The 10-million figure counts only people who have had substantial retirement benefit losses and ignores potentially important but relatively minor cuts, such as the elimination of cost-of-living adjustments on pensions or increased deductibles on retiree health plans. It also ignores workers who start at a company receiving a less generous 401(k) plan instead of a traditional pension. The figure was arrived at by adding up the most common types of benefit cuts, as described below. Analysis of survey data confirms that 10 million is a reasonable estimate.[3]

As a simple rule of thumb, retirement losses are greatest in bankruptcy, where pensions and health benefits can be cut or eliminated. In bankruptcy, workers typically stop earning additional benefits, and even vested benefits are at risk. Losses are at a middle level for pension freezes and terminations, which have a similar effect on pension benefits. Both prevent workers from earning additional benefits, but when a pension is frozen it technically still exists and thus could potentially be restored at a later date. Losses are typically smallest for changes to retiree health benefits and for adjustments to pension formulas, such as cash balance conversions. As a general rule, workers lose more than retirees.

Seven hundred thousand people had their fully funded pension plans terminated in the period between 2000 and 2005, according to PBGC data. A safe estimate is that the pension plans of 3 million workers, or 10% of workers with a pension, are currently frozen. However, figures are rough: freezes are a relatively new trend that is rapidly increasing, and even the Government Accountability Office, the investigative arm of

Congress, could not find out how many companies have frozen their pension plans (Government Accountability Office 2003). Estimates generally indicate that between 9% and 17% of companies have frozen their pension plans, though these figures do not include recent announcements of freezes by very large companies, including IBM, Alcoa, Sprint Nextel, and Northwest Airlines, to name a few (Aon 2003, Pension Benefit Guaranty Corporation 2005b, Watson Wyatt 2005).

One academic study estimated that an average middle-aged worker loses an amount in excess of two years of wages when a pension is terminated (Ippolito 2004). These estimated losses are for typical cases; they can be much greater for employees who earn higher salaries and have long tenures with their company. VanDerhei and Copeland (2004) estimate that when a pension plan is frozen, a typical married 40-year-old male employee loses nearly $5,000 of benefits in each year of retirement, or a total of over $95,000 if he has an average life span in retirement.[4]

Cash balance conversions—so called because the value of the benefit is expressed as a lump-sum total cash figure rather than a yearly payout, as is typical of pensions—are a common type of pension formula change. Under a cash balance formula, each year of service is rewarded equally, instead of the later years being worth more. Though such a change does not necessarily need to reduce pension benefits, a comprehensive government review found that most people, including younger workers, were made worse off because cash balance formulas are typically less generous than previous formulas (Government Accountability Office 2005). Sometimes cash balance conversions actually prevent older workers from earning any additional benefits for several years, further reducing their pensions.

During a cash balance conversion, a typical married 40-year-old male employee loses nearly $1,500 per year in retirement, or approximately $28,000 in lifetime losses (VanDerhei and Copeland 2004).

The number of people whose pensions have been converted to a cash balance plan increased from 7 million in 2001 to 10 million in 2004, meaning that three million people were affected by a transition to a cash balance plan in just three years (Pension Benefit Guarantee Corporation 2005a). Because most people lose during a cash balance conversion, it is safe to assume that over the past five years more than 3 million people have been hurt by the transition to a cash balance plan.

According to PBGC data, between 2000 and 2005, about 1 million people had their underfunded pensions terminated in bankruptcy. When the PBGC recently took over four large pension plans, workers and retirees lost $6 billion of earned, vested pension benefits, or around

$20,000 per person (Pension Benefit Guaranty Corporation 2005a).[5] However, these losses do not include the value of retiree health benefits nor the value of what workers lost because they were no longer able to continue earning benefits in the terminated plan. If these losses are included, people lose much, much more. When one adds the value of losses workers face because they can no longer earn additional pension benefits, a typical midcareer male worker in a terminated plan probably loses around $100,000 in benefits.

Estimating how many people's retiree health benefits have been reduced and how much they have lost is an imprecise endeavor. Of the 18 million Americans currently receiving retiree health benefits, a reasonable guesstimate is that about half, or 9 million retirees, have lost all of their benefits or faced significant reductions of at least a thousand dollars or more per year.[6]

Adding all of these changes to pensions and retiree health benefits— 3 million people affected by pension freezes, nearly 2 million hurt by pension terminations, 3 million who lost during cash balance conversions, and 9 million harmed by retiree health cuts—means a reasonable estimate, one that avoids double-counting people who have been hurt by more than one type of change, is that at least 10 million people have faced significant cuts to their retirement benefits over the past five years. These cuts have cost workers and retirees, in total, hundreds of billions of dollars in lost benefits (see Table 1).

The Elements of Protest

By itself, anger about losing retirement benefits is not enough to lead to protest. In order to participate in politics, people need three things: the

TABLE 1
Estimated Pension Losses, 2000–2005

Type of reduction	Pension freeze	Pension termination: in bankruptcy	Pension termination: standard	Cash balance conversion
Estimated number of people affected	3,000,000	1,000,000	700,000	3,000,000
Estimated loss per midcareer worker	$74,000	$94,000	$74,000	$21,000

Note: Estimated dollar losses are based on current dollars using the following assumptions: 60% of people with pensions are married, 20% are single men, and 20% are single women. Life expectancy for a 65-year-old is an additional 17 years for a man and 19.7 years for a woman. These figures likely underestimate the dollar loss because singles are counted as never having been married, and thus benefits for divorced or widowed spouses are ignored.
Source: My estimate, based on government and private studies.

means to be able to protest, such as skills, resources, and organization; a motive to be involved; and opportunities to take action (McAdam, McCarthy, and Zald 1996). Though people who have lost retirement benefits would seem to have all three, a closer look shows that each element is limited in ways that are likely to reduce political activity.

Despite having the individual skills and financial resources that lead to action, most people who have lost benefits do not have the support of an organization, such as a union, to help them protest. In addition, restoring some types of cuts would require a significant new role for government, something these workers and retirees would seem reluctant to support.

Means

Resources, such as time, money, and skills, often learned in school, give people the ability to be able to get involved in politics (Verba, Schlozman, and Brady 1995). As a result, people who are wealthier, more highly educated, and older are much more likely to take part in political activities. Employer-based retirement benefits are overwhelmingly directed to these kinds of people, meaning workers and retirees who have lost retirement benefits have the personal resources that make participation in politics more likely.

But typically people need an organization, such as a union or an interest group like AARP, to help lead them into action (Zald and McCarthy 1987). Organizations mobilize people by reducing the costs of participation and increasing the benefits—for example, by organizing and coordinating activity, providing information and assistance, and making success seem more likely. Few people participate spontaneously in politics; instead they get involved when groups, political parties, and activists persuade them to take part (Rosenstone and Hansen 2003).

Mobilization thus works directly to encourage people to participate, but it also works indirectly by shaping people's perception of an issue and thus their motive for taking action. Mobilization helps people understand their alternatives and increases the likelihood that they believe their efforts will have some impact. People are more likely to recognize their own self-interest and act on it when they have been primed to think about the personal costs and benefits of a policy (Chong, Citrin, and Conley 2001).

People face a steep hurdle trying to figure out what can be done about a political problem, especially one as complex as retirement benefits. The laws regulating retirement plans are astoundingly confusing. In fact, ERISA, the main law regulating pensions has been called "the most complex piece of legislation ever passed by Congress" (Tepper 1977). In addition, companies have different retirement benefits and have changed them in varying ways. The difficulty deciding what alternatives can solve the problem is one of the reasons that mobilization by political elites is so important. Mobilization can help provide people with viable alternatives to support and thus increases the likelihood that people will participate.

As a result, unions—as virtually the only workplace organization that represents employees—have been especially important in generating protest activity about retirement benefit cuts. But unions represent just some of people who have lost retirement benefits. Even though unionized employees receive retirement benefits at nearly twice the rate of nonunion employees, unionized employees make up only a small percentage of the workforce and thus a small percentage of those with pensions. In 2003, over 20 million nonunion workers earned pensions, compared to just over 7 million unionized workers (Copeland 2006).

AARP, which could help coordinate activity for nonunionized workers, has only occasionally become involved in employer-based retirement issues; it has instead chosen to make Social Security and Medicare its top priorities.[7] The limited mobilization of groups like AARP and the unions is a significant reason for the low levels of protest by the public.

Opportunity

People need opportunities in order to participate in politics. While it is hard to say precisely what constitutes a political opportunity, it is clear that certain situations, such as elections and demographic shifts, facilitate new opportunities for activity while others hamper it (McAdam 1982). Opportunities help give people a task—some tangible activity to participate in—making political activity easier and success seem possible.

The recent retirement benefit cuts seemingly have presented numerous opportunities for people to take action. A potential political opportunity is created every time a company cuts its retirement benefits. Additional potential political opportunities include several closely contested national elections and the introduction of numerous bills addressing retirement benefits and the passage of a new pension law.

In order to have a real opportunity to protest, people need a tangible action to take. Organizations can help let people know about opportunities to protest and even create new ones, such as rallies. But powerful existing organizations have either been unable to or chosen not to take full advantage of opportunities for protest. As a result of the limited role of AARP and the limited coverage of the workforce by unions, the opportunities for protest have been likewise limited.

Motives

It seems obvious that retirement benefit cuts would provide a strong motive for action. However, self-interest is not the only factor that influences people's attitudes and their willingness to take action. A combination of many factors, such as ideology or values and what someone thinks is possible, shape the perception of an inequity and the willingness to take action. People may not have a complete motive for action if they don't know what to do or don't think anything can be done (Gaventa 1980). They need to think there are possible alternatives and that the alternatives will work; when government intervention is required, they need to think that the government can and should be involved in addressing their grievance.

But in any situation, figuring out what to do is difficult. In the case of retirement benefit cuts, this is especially true. Not only is the issue particularly complicated and confusing, but most reductions to retirement benefits are legal. Employees who take a company to court about retirement benefits commonly lose. This legal fact has two effects. First, repeated losses reinforce positions of power and powerlessness and tend to leave those without power feeling that little can be done to change their situation and that alternatives are not practical (Lukes 1974, Gaventa 1980). These low expectations lead people to stay at home rather than participate in politics.

Second, because many reductions are legal, the law must be changed in order to restore benefits. This means that for people to act, in many cases they must support new laws, not just better enforcement. However, the nature of public opinion in America indicates that people are conflicted in their support for new roles for government. Americans, especially those with retirement benefits, are likely to believe that they should be responsible for their retirement and are reluctant to have the government play a large role.

Self-Reliance

In order to take political action, people need to want the government to be involved. And as much as workers and retirees may think retirement benefit cuts are unjust and should be remedied, most also believe in an individualistic ideology that rejects an expanded role for government. As a result, they are internally divided, or ambivalent, about whether to protest.

There is a long tradition of scholarship that argues Americans have a unique belief in the power of an individual to triumph over economic adversity and, as a result, are relatively unwilling to call for political solutions to economic hardship and inequality (Hartz 1955, Schlozman and

Verba 1979). As these arguments go, Americans don't make political demands about many economic issues because they believe that economic inequality is either fair or not appropriate for government action. The American dream is to work hard and make it on your own, not to seek government assistance.

Polls consistently find that people of other nationalities are likely to believe the government is responsible for providing a secure retirement, while Americans are much more likely to believe they are personally responsible. A recent AARP poll found that half of all Americans believe individuals are primarily responsible for themselves in retirement, compared to less than 40% of the British and Germans and less than 20% of the French and Italians (AARP 2005).

However, Americans aren't so dogmatically individualistic as these statistics might seem to indicate. Rather, they support a shared division of responsibility among individuals, government, and employers. For example, when a recent poll asked who "should be primarily responsible" for helping workers prepare for retirement, 39% selected workers, 25% chose employers, and 18% selected the government (Reynolds, Ridley, and Van Horn 2005). Significantly, 17% volunteered "all three," a choice that wasn't even offered by pollsters.

Further, American individualism doesn't mean people are willing to let others out of their obligations. Pensions are not welfare checks handed out for not working, but rather benefits earned over a lifetime—a commitment between employer and employee that people have been counting on.

In addition, individualism and self-sufficiency are not the only values that Americans hold. Americans also value freedom, equality, and humanitarianism, among many others. American's may cherish individual initiative, perhaps even more strongly than other values, but they also recognize that some problems are beyond individual control and require government intervention.

A more accurate view of public opinion is suggested by Free and Cantril (1968). Most Americans, they argue, are conflicted in their views about government; they are predisposed to oppose government but at the same time very supportive of specific programs. When Americans discuss the general role of government, they believe in individualism, self-reliance, and private enterprise and prefer limited powers for the federal government. Hence, most of the public can be considered ideological conservatives. But when Americans discuss specific issues, they support government programs, and could thus be considered operational liberals. People want the government to, for example, reduce poverty and provide retirement security. Americans may not like government, but they do appreciate their Social Security checks.

This kind of ambivalence is especially likely in people with employer-based retirement benefits. Because of their self-interest, people with retirement benefits have an incentive to support greater government protections for such benefits. But people who are wealthier, more educated, and older—characteristics of people with retirement benefits—are more inclined to believe in individualism and private enterprise and to prefer limited powers for the federal government (Free and Cantril 1968). The system has worked for these people, and they are likely to attribute their success to individual efforts.

Finding a governmental solution that both solves the problem and doesn't impinge on individual freedoms is not easy, and sometimes is impossible. As a result, the range of policy options that people who have lost their retirement benefits are predisposed to support is limited.

Not only does ambivalence limit the range of policy options the public is willing to support, but it also reduces the likelihood that people will participate in politics. Political action is more likely when people believe there is a clear link between an injustice and a necessary corrective action, when they have a clear idea of what they want and believe that government can and should solve the problem. But when values are in conflict about the appropriateness of a policy, people tend to remain on the sidelines. For example, Cantril and Cantril (1999) examined the political activities of people with ambivalent views about government—people who were critical of government in general but still supported most specific programs—and found that they were less likely to participate in any kind of political protest than people with less value conflict. Summarizing their findings, the authors wrote that "the principal consequence of ambivalence is a decrease in both voting and other kinds of involvement" (p. 125).

The Level of Protest

In contrast to the reaction to reductions in employer-sponsored retirement benefits, the mere threat of reductions to Social Security almost invariably produces widespread political activity (Campbell 2003). Though there are some obvious differences between Social Security and employer-based retirement benefits—for example, one is a federal program while the other is run by private companies with some federal regulation—the two are in many ways quite comparable. Both are key components of our nation's retirement system and are relatively similar in scale. The median annual payments for Social Security and private pensions are nearly equal, at around $10,000 per year (Whitman and Purcell 2006). In 2000, pensions provided more than $450 billion in benefits, compared to $350 billion paid out by Social

Security (Hacker 2002). Throw in retiree health benefits, and the employer-based structure is much larger.

Even the potential cuts to both systems are similar. Recent reductions in employer-based retirement benefits are as large as those that would be caused by President Bush's proposal to create private Social Security accounts, according to estimates from the Center on Budget and Policy Priorities (Furman 2005). In addition, while the effects of proposed changes to Social Security are deferred years into the future, employer-based retirement reductions can have *both* delayed and immediate impacts—which would seemingly provoke more of a reaction, all else being equal.

Further, both Social Security and employer-based retirement benefits are of primary importance to a similar group of people—retirees and older workers—and are defended by a similar constellation of interest groups, including AARP and unions. Finally, both systems are heavily supported by taxpayers, with employer-based retirement benefits receiving one of the largest single tax breaks in the federal code, worth over $100 billion per year.

And yet, as can be seen in Figure 1, threats to Social Security, when they arose in 2005, generated far more protests than cuts to employer pensions.

FIGURE 1

A Comparison of Pension and Social Security Protest Activity, 1998–2006

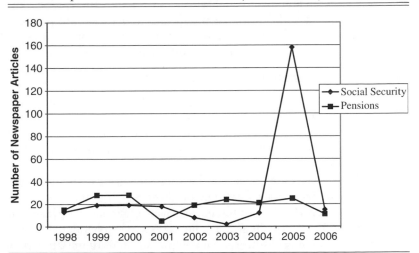

Source: My analysis of U.S. regional newspapers from Nexis database of Midwest, Northeast, Southeast, and Western sources, 1998 to November 15, 2006.

The data in Figure 1 refer to the number of newspaper articles from 1998 to 2006 about citizen efforts, such as rallies, strikes, and letter-writing campaigns, to protect Social Security and employer-based pensions. The figure is based on Nexis searches of over 250 U.S. papers for articles containing the word "pension" or "Social Security" within five words of any version of the words *protest*, *rally*, *complain*, or *object*. Articles were then read and coded. For an article to be counted, protest needed to be about the pension or Social Security benefits of a group or class of people, rather than an individual, and include activity by citizens, workers, or retirees, rather than just elected officials. Analysis of 2006 articles does not include any article written after November 15.

Newspaper coverage provides a good baseline for comparison, as there is no expectation that protest about pension cuts will take a different form than protest about Social Security. Although news coverage cannot capture all forms of political protest, the screen picked up a wide range of protest activity, including rallies, marches, press conferences, strikes, meetings with elected officials, class action lawsuits, and shareholder resolutions. In short, newspaper stories portray times when workers and retirees have chosen to make their grievances about benefit cuts public.

What is particularly striking about the results shown in Figure 1 is that a potential threat to Social Security benefits—President Bush's proposal in 2005 for personal accounts that never even materialized into a formal plan—produced far more of a reaction from workers and retirees than actual cuts to employer-based retirement benefits. In addition, during years when Social Security was not directly threatened but pensions were being cut for millions of people, the two types of retirement benefits led to similar levels of response by workers and retirees.

Who Has Lost Benefits

The low level of protest can largely be explained by looking at who has retirement benefits. Though many people who have lost benefits have individual attributes that lead to political action, most face an uphill battle without an organization, such as a union, to help facilitate their protest.

People who are more educated, have higher salaries, and are older are much more likely to have retirement benefits. For example, workers with salaries over $40,000 are three times as likely to have a pension as those earning less, according to a June 2005 survey conducted by the Heldrich Center for Workforce Development at Rutgers University (Reynolds, Ridley, and Van Horn 2005). People with a college degree are 1.5 times more likely to have a pension than those without a university education. In short, people with retirement benefits are middle and upper-middle class people with the skills and resources to make political demands.

Not surprisingly, pension cuts have disproportionately affected people fitting this profile. Of current workers whose pensions have been cut, 78% earn over $40,000 per year.[8] Similarly, more than 70% of workers whose pensions have been cut are between the ages of 45 and 64. Nearly 60% of workers who have lost pension benefits have attended one or more years of college.

Despite these individual resources, the vast majority of people who have lost benefits do not have ready access to a workplace organization, such as a union, that could help mobilize protests. Nearly two thirds of workers who have lost pension benefits are not unionized.

The Importance of Organizations

When people who have lost benefits have an opportunity to express their anger and an organization to coordinate their activities, they tend to respond. For example, when a member of Congress asked for United Airlines workers and retirees to submit testimony by email about the impact of the company's bankruptcy on their pension benefits, the unions that represent United workers, including the International Association of Machinists and Aerospace Workers, the Air Line Pilots Association, and the Association of Flight Attendants, mobilized their members to respond. In a short period, the unions helped generate more than 2,000 email messages from workers and retirees, which "overwhelmed" the office of Congressman George Miller, the ranking Democrat on the House Committee on Education and the Workforce, who had requested the testimony (Miller and Schakowsky 2005).

Similarly, when AARP asked its members to comment on a proposed Equal Employment Opportunity Commission rule about age discrimination in retiree health benefits, the EEOC received more than 30,000 comments, the vast majority postcards from AARP. A typical rule generates fewer than 200 comments (West 2004).

However, as earlier noted, AARP has not consistently attempted to mobilize people about employer-based retirement benefits. As a result, unions have been especially important in generating protest activity about retirement benefit cuts. Unionized employees accounted for 60% of pension protest activity from 1998 to 2006, according to my analysis of newspaper articles—despite the fact that most people who have lost pension benefits are not unionized.[9] The disproportionate role that unionized employees have played in protesting retirement benefit cuts can be seen in Figure 2.

FIGURE 2
A Comparison of Employee Protest Activity by Unionization

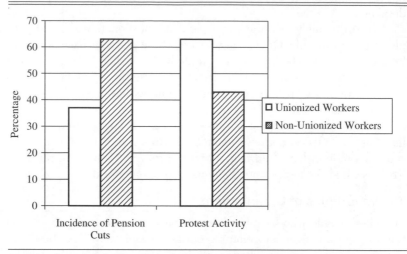

Some articles included activity by both union and non-union workers, and thus protest
activity by union and non-union workers adds to over 100%.
Source: My analysis of a June 2005 survey by the Heldrich Center for Workforce Development at Rutgers University and newspaper articles from 1998 to 2006.

The role of organizations' mobilizing people and helping create
opportunities to protest has likely been the most important factor in
protest about retirement benefit cuts. When unions or AARP have been
involved, protest is common. But unions only represent a small percentage of the workforce, and AARP has only on certain occasions attempted
significant mobilization. As a result, most people who have lost retirement benefits haven't been mobilized by an existing powerful organization such as a union or AARP.

Though the lack of organization has been very important in limiting
protest, workers and retirees have overcome this obstacle on numerous
occasions. In fact, at times the hurdle of organizing has been relatively
easy to surmount. For example, when a small group of retired United
Airlines pilots sent a letter to fellow retirees asking them to join a new
group fighting to preserve their pension benefits during the airline's
bankruptcy, more than 80% joined the group and contributed the $135
membership fee.[10] During bankruptcy, retired airline pilots were no
longer represented by the Air Line Pilots Association, their former union.
Only current employees are legally represented by unions, though some
unions try to represent the interests of both workers and retirees.

Probably the most well-known, forceful, and sustained protests to retirement benefit cuts came from nonunionized IBM workers opposing the cash balance conversion of their pensions. No existing organization represented the workers, and there were no existing political opportunities for them to tap into. Instead, IBM workers created new organizations and opportunities.

When IBM reduced the expected pension benefits for some of its workers in 1999 as part of a cash balance conversion, workers reacted strongly, creating several online organizations to fight the change. Workers strategized about how to respond and organized protests on several fronts, filing class action lawsuits and complaints with federal agencies and elected officials, introducing shareholder resolutions, and even commissioning planes to fly banners opposing the cuts. IBM workers generated tens of thousands of email messages, wrote many, many letters to Congress and numerous federal agencies, and jammed the phone lines of their elected officials. The employees won, at least partially, and succeeded in reversing the cuts for a significant percentage of employees.

Similarly, workers and retirees at numerous companies have formed groups such as the Association of BellTel Retirees, the AT&T Concerned Employee Retiree Council, the Duke Energy Employee Advocate, the National Association of Retired Sears Employees, the Bell Atlantic Employees Coalition for Retirement Security, the Association of US West Retirees, the United Retired Pilots Benefit Protection Association, and the Pension Preservation Network. Retirees have even created the National Retiree Legislative Network to coordinate the political activities of the more than two million members of company-based groups.

Some workers and retirees have thus been able to organize on their own and overcome an obstacle that has limited the protest activity of many people. However, organizing is not the only hurdle workers face, and even workers and retirees who have created groups to represent them have been relatively quiet about certain kinds of benefit cuts.

Other Obstacles

It is relatively easy for union and public sector workers to figure out what to do when their benefits are threatened. Such workers have significant advantages that help them find solutions to retirement benefit cuts, and they have greater opportunity to protest cuts within the existing legal framework.

Unions employ professional staff to help develop solutions, and they have well-established connections with elected officials who can introduce policy changes. In addition, the pensions of unionized workers cannot be changed except through the collective bargaining process or bankruptcy court. Although the outcomes in bankruptcy court often do not protect pensions, the bankruptcy process allows for workers and retirees to air their grievances. Similarly, any changes to the pensions of public sector workers must be negotiated in a public forum, providing workers a clear target for protest.

By comparison, nonunion private sector workers face greater barriers when looking for solutions and opportunities to protest. They don't have ready-made forums for protest, and they typically don't have professional staff to analyze policies or established connections with politicians. In addition, finding solutions to certain kinds of cuts that they are likely to face is especially difficult. Because companies may legally freeze or terminate their pensions at any time, addressing these changes within the existing legal framework is virtually impossible.

Not surprisingly, nonunion private sector workers have protested relatively infrequently, as can be seen in Figure 3. Even though nearly half of pension cuts have been imposed on these workers, they have protested only one third as frequently as have workers who are either unionized or work for the government.

The additional hurdles that nonunion private sector workers face trying to figure out what to do have been overcome on several occasions,

FIGURE 3
A Comparison of Employee Protest Activity by Unionization and Private vs. Public Sector

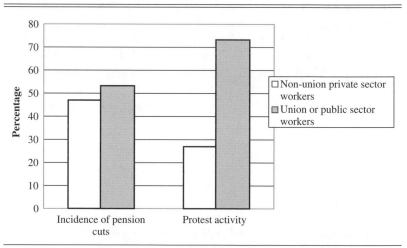

Source: My analysis of the June 2005 survey of the Heldrich Center for Workforce Development at Rutgers University and newspaper articles from 1998 to November 15, 2006. People who work for nonprofit organizations are counted as working for the private sector.

most notably during cash balance conversions at IBM, Verizon, and several other companies. Cash balance conversions led to significant protest activity, generating nearly half of the pension protest articles by nonunion private sector employees, according to my review.

Similarly, cuts to retiree health benefits have generated protest, despite numerous obstacles. For example, retirees of Bell Atlantic, Lucent, and several other companies have organized new groups to protect their retiree health benefits and have created new political opportunities. These retirees decided that to protect their retiree health benefits they needed to pressure Congress to extend the same type of regulations that govern pensions. They have succeeded in getting a bill introduced to do just that and have held rallies and written numerous letters to support the bill.[11]

In contrast to protests about these types of benefit cuts, there has been very little reaction to pension freezes. Even the previously raucous IBM employees have been relatively quiet since the company announced in January 2006 that it was freezing its pension plan—a change that produced greater losses than the cash balance conversion. Workers haven't filed class action lawsuits or overwhelmed congressional offices with calls or mail. In fact, far fewer have phoned or written letters, even to the elected officials who had previously championed their cause.

Senator (formerly Congressman) Bernie Sanders represents the state of Vermont, where many IBM employees live. He was a leader in Congress for the IBM workers and others affected by cash balance conversions, and he helped introduce and pass legislation to prevent the IRS from deciding that cash balance conversions were legal. Huge volumes of constituent calls, letters, and email messages motivated the representative to take action about the cash balance conversion.[12] But after IBM's pension freeze, few people got in touch with him.

Email traffic on IBM employee websites has also been significantly down compared to the levels experienced during most of the cash balance protests. For example, in 1999, when IBM announced its cash balance conversion, employees set up a Yahoo group about IBM's pensions and exchanged over 4,000 emails per month over the next four months.[13] During the first 16 months, they never sent fewer than 1,000 emails per month on the site.

But when IBM announced its pension freeze in January 2006, email traffic in the user group rose only for a very brief time and reached only a quarter of the level it did in 1999. The pension freeze caused email traffic to increase from 239 messages in December 2005 to 1,195 in January 2006, but by February the number of messages had fallen below 400 and remained at that level for the rest of the year. There is no evidence that email exchanges moved to a different venue.

The nonreaction by IBM workers to a pension freeze is not an isolated case. In my review of newspaper articles, I did not find one example of a protest about pension freeze or termination by nonunion private sector workers.

The Role of Government

Why little protest has occurred when companies freeze pensions can only be suggested here; further exploration of the topic is the subject of my ongoing research. Preliminary work suggests that retirement benefit changes that can be remedied, or at least potentially remedied, within the existing legal framework have often provoked strong responses from workers and retirees. But when addressing cuts requires a new, more involved role for government, there has been little protest.

Cash balance conversions, protesters argued, were already illegal under existing age-discrimination laws. To protect their health benefits, retirees argued that existing law should be extended beyond pensions. But to stop pension freezes, a new, more socialist role for government would likely be required.

Supporting a new role for government has been a high hurdle for workers and retirees to overcome, as can be seen in Table 2. The table notes, for different cases of retirement benefit cuts, the presence or absence of the factors—means, motives, and opportunity—that lead to political action. The information is based on the status of the cases at the time of the retirement benefit cut; some cases may have different characteristics at later stages.

As can be seen in Table 2, political action occurred in cases where all three factors were present, but it also occurred in cases with no existing political organization and no existing political opportunity. However, workers and retirees have strongly protested *only* when the type of action necessary to protect benefits requires enforcement of existing law or a slight expansion of the government's role. Protest has not happened when political action required a more fundamental change in the role of government.

Possible explanations for this lack of protest certainly include the limited mobilization by existing organizations and a political climate that makes new regulations difficult to impose. However, as has been discussed at length, people have overcome numerous obstacles to protest, including creating new organizations and new policies. Perhaps people—as much as they may want to fix the problem—are reluctant to have the government play a much more involved role in retirement.

As can be seen in Table 3 and was previously discussed, most Americans believe that individuals, not the government, should be primarily

TABLE 2
Types of Cases of Retirement Benefit Cuts, Arranged by Means,
Motive, and Opportunity

Case example	Means: existing organization?	Motive: fits existing government role?	Opportunity: existing political opportunity?	Protest?
Cash balance: IBM and Verizon	No	Yes	No	Yes
Pension freeze: IBM and Verizon	Yes	No	No	No
Cash balance: several companies	No	Yes	Yes	No
Retiree health age discrimination: Bell/Verizon/ Lucent	Yes	Yes	Yes	Yes
Retiree health cuts: Bell/Verizon/ Lucent	Yes	Extension	No	Yes
Pension termination in bankruptcy: United Airlines	Yes	Extension	Yes	Yes
California public employees	Yes	Yes	Yes	Yes
Oregon public employees	Yes	Yes	No	Some

responsible for their retirement. This is especially true for wealthier, more educated, and older people. Of people with a college degree, 50% believe that workers should be primarily responsible for their retirement, compared to 34% of those with a high school education or less. Only 11% of people with a college degree think that the government should have the primary role in retirement, while 24% of those with less education do. Comparisons between older workers and younger workers produce about the same disparities.

Not only do people with pensions tend to have an ideological opposition to government intervention, but the very people who are especially likely to need government help protecting their pensions—namely nonunion private sector workers—are even less inclined to support such policies. Nonunion private sector workers are more likely than other workers to believe individuals should be primarily responsible for retirement, by 45% to 33%. Most of this difference is due to views of public sector workers compared to private sector workers, rather than differences between union and non-union workers. Of private sector nonunion workers, 15% believe government should be primarily responsible for retirement, a level similarly low to all other workers.

TABLE 3

Belief in Self-Reliance, by Income, Education, and Age

	Income (%)		Education (%)			Age group (%)					
	< $40,000	$40,000 +	No college	Some college	College degree +	18–34	35–44	45–54	55–64	65+
Workers	26	47	34	38	50	33	37	46	49	48
Employers	31	24	27	32	17	34	23	20	20	20
Government	27	13	24	14	11	22	16	17	14	8
All three*	16	17	14	16	22	10	25	17	18	24

Those surveyed were asked this question: Who do you think should be primarily responsible for helping workers prepare for retirement?

* "All three" was not an answer offered by the surveyors, but it was an answer volunteered by a number of respondents.

Source: My analysis of a June 2005 survey by the Heldrich Center for Workforce Development at Rutgers University.

TABLE 4
Belief in Self-Reliance by Whether Retirement Benefits Have Been Cut

	Retirement benefits cut?	
	Yes	No
Workers	43%	44%
Employers	17%	27%
Government	26%	13%
All three°	13%	16%

Those surveyed were asked this question: Who do you think should be primarily responsible for helping workers prepare for retirement? °"All three" was not an answer offered by surveyors, but it was an answer volunteered by a number of respondents.
Source: Author's analysis of June 2005 Heldrich Center for Workforce Development at Rutgers University.

Though a person's general political orientation could be changed by a single event such as losing retirement benefits, studies of lottery winners have found that such sudden increases of wealth didn't change their basic orientation toward economic redistribution (Doherty, Gerber, and Green 2006). In keeping with these findings, people who have lost benefits tend to believe that workers should be primarily responsible for retirement, with 43% supporting that sentiment—the same rate as people who have not lost benefits. People who have lost benefits, however, are more likely to believe the government should play the primary role in retirement, but even then only 26% percent of them do, as can be seen in Table 4.

The figures in Table 4 indicate that people who have lost benefits would likely be conflicted about supporting a new role for government in retirement. Though it is possible that the right kind of policy that balances the roles of all parties could generate support, finding such a policy is a difficult task.

Conclusion

Though the overall level of protest about retirement benefit cuts has been relatively low, when there is something to do and someone to organize it, people who have lost benefits have protested loudly. Even when there has been no organization to mobilize action, some people who have lost benefits have taken action, creating their own groups and making new opportunities. People have expressed a strong desire to keep their retirement benefits, but certain types of cuts have not generated much protest, possibly because solving the situation would require a more involved role for government.

Because of retirement benefit cuts, many people have been forced to make significant changes that have economic and social costs. People are working until they are older, getting a job during retirement, cutting expenses by such actions as moving in with children, getting by on much less than they are used to, and using governmental and private safety nets.

So far, most retirement benefit cuts have been undertaken in the private sector, but there are signs that the large-scale cuts may also expand to the public sector. Several interest groups and a number of elected officials have argued that the public sector can no longer afford to pay existing levels of retirement benefits and that cuts will be necessary. Up to this point, only a few states have made such changes, but many are considering proposals to do so.

If retirement benefit cuts continue in private industry or expand to the public sector, the social impacts could become much more pronounced. If, on the other hand, there is reason to expect that people will make political demands to protect retirement benefits, the consequences will be equally significant. State budgets may become strained. Business may become less competitive or at least have to rethink major strategic decisions if forced to bear all of their legacy costs. Federal intervention could impose large costs upon taxpayers and mark a significant new role for government in providing economic security.

Either way, the stakes are high. The future of retirement in America is at stake. Who will be able to retire? Who will pay?

Endnotes

[1] My estimate, discussed at length later in this chapter. I refer to changes to retirement plans that reduce expected future benefits as "cuts," which is standard in debates about Social Security.

[2] The 28 million estimate comes from multiplying the number of total workers (125 million) by the overall participation rate (51%) by the percentage of participation in defined benefit plans (44.3%).

[3] Ten million is probably a low estimate, as evidenced by a June 2005 survey conducted by the Heldrich Center for Workforce Development at Rutgers University in which 13% of workers say they have had their retirement benefits cut. Thirteen percent of the current work force is approximately 16 million people, and this figure does not include retirees.

[4] It should be noted that these estimates do not include replacement with a 401(k).

[5] PBGC staff in e-mail exchange indicated that 300,000 workers and retirees participated in plans at these four companies.

[6] These rough estimates are based on studies indicating that half of all companies have imposed caps on their payments. Though caps have not caused significant

reductions in all cases, when combined with the number of companies that have eliminated coverage for spouses as well as initiated other costly changes, half is a defensible approximation. The estimate also includes roughly 700,000 who have had retiree health benefits eliminated in the past five years. Of the 1 million people whose pension plan was terminated in bankruptcy, a reasonable estimate is that 700,000 worked for companies with retiree health plans and also lost these benefits.

[7] Personal interviews with AARP officials, August 4 and August 28, 2006. I am not making a value judgment about AARP's political choices, but simply indicating that the organization has placed less emphasis on employer-based benefits.

[8] This question was asked: "Since the start of your employment, has your current company changed its retirement plans in such a way that it will result in a lower retirement payout than you had anticipated?" Only workers with pensions were selected for this analysis. The question was asked only of people currently in the work force; retirees were not asked a similar question.

[9] My methodology is likely to undercount the number of union protests because articles do not always mention whether workers are unionized.

[10] Personal conversation with Roger Hall, president, United Retired Pilots Benefit Protection Association, November 22, 2006.

[11] Personal interviews with leaders of the National Retiree Legislative Network and the Association of BellTel Retirees.

[12] Personal interviews December 5, 2005, and August 15, 2006.

[13] http://finance.groups.yahoo.com/group/ibmpension/.

References

AARP. 2005. "International Retirement Security Survey," October. <http://www.aarp.org/research/work/retirement/irss.html>. [December 20, 2006].

Aon. 2003. "More than 20% of Surveyed Plan Sponsors Froze Plan Benefits or Will Do So." Press release, October 29.

Campbell, Andrea. 2003. *How Policies Make Citizens: Senior Political Activism and the American Welfare State*. Princeton, NJ; Princeton University Press.

Cantril, Albert, and Susan Cantril. 1999. *Reading Mixed Signals: Ambivalence in American Public Opinion about Government*. Washington, DC: Woodrow Wilson Center Press.

Chong, Dennis, Jack Citrin, and Patricia Conley. 2001. "When Self-Interest Matters." *Political Psychology*, Vol. 22, no. 4 (September), p. 877.

Copeland, Craig. 2006. *Retirement Plan Participation and Retirees Perception of their Standard of Living*. EBRI Issue Brief #289. Washington, DC: Employee Benefit Research Institute.

Doherty, Daniel, Alan Gerber, and Donald Green. 2006. "Personal Income and Attitudes Toward Redistribution: A Study of Lottery Winners." *Political Psychology*, Vol. 27, no. 3 (June), pp. 441–58.

Free, Lloyd, and Hadley Cantril. 1968. *The Political Beliefs of Americans: A Study of Public Opinion*. New York: Simon and Schuster.

Fronstin, Paul. 2005. *The Impact of the Erosion of Retiree Health Benefits on Workers and Retirees*. EBRI Issue Brief #279. Washington, DC: Employee Benefit Research Institute.

Fronstin, Paul. 2001. *Retiree Health Benefits: Trends and Outlook* EBRI Issue Brief #236. Washington, DC: Employee Benefit Research Institute.

Furman, Jason. 2005. *How the Individual Accounts in The President's New Plan Would Work*. Washington, DC: Center on Budget and Policy Priorities. February 4.

Gaventa, John, 1980. *Power and Powerlessness, Quiescence and Rebellion in an Appalachian Valley*. Urbana, IL; University of Illinois Press.

Government Accountability Office. 2003. *Private Pensions: Timely and Accurate Information Is Needed to Identify and Track Frozen Defined Benefit Plans*. GAO-04-200R. December 17. Washington, DC: GAO.

Government Accountability Office. 2005. *Retiree Health Benefits: Options for Employment-Based Prescription Drug Benefits under the Medicare Modernization Act*. GAO-05-205. February 14. Washington, DC: GAO.

Hacker, Jacob S. 2002. *The Divided Welfare State: The Battle Over Public and Private Social Benefits in the United States*. New York: Cambridge University Press.

Hartz, Louis. 1955. *The Liberal Tradition in America: An Interpretation of American Political Thought Since the Revolution*. New York: Harcourt, Brace.

Henriques, Diana, and David Cay Johnston. 1996. "Managers Staying Dry as Corporations Sink," *New York Times*, October 14, p. A1.

Ippolito, Richard. 2004. "Bankruptcy and Workers: Risks, Compensation and Pension Contracts, *Washington University Law Quarterly*, Vol. 82, no. 4 (Winter), pp. 1251–1303.

Kaiser Family Foundation and Health Research and Educational Trust. 2005. *2005 Annual Employer Health Benefits Survey*. September 14. Menlo Park, CA: Henry J. Kaiser Family Foundation; Chicago: Health Research and Educational Trust.

Lukes, Steven, 1974. *Power: A Radical View*. New York: Macmillan Education.

McAdam, Doug. 1982. *Political Process and the Development of Black Insurgency 1930–1970*. Chicago: University of Chicago Press.

McAdam, Doug, John D. McCarthy, and Mayer N. Zald (eds.). 1996. *Comparative Perspectives on Social Movements*. New York: Cambridge University Press.

Mercer Human Resources Consulting. 2006. *A Closer Look at Recent High-Profile Pension Plan Freezes*. February 27.

Merlis, Mark. 2006. "Health Benefits in Retirement: Set for Extinction." *National Health Policy Forum*, February 8. <http://www.nhpf.org/pdfs_bp/BP_RetireeHealth_02-08-06.pdf >. [December 20, 2006].

Miller, George, and Jan Schakowsky. 2005. *Broken Promises: The United Airlines Pension Crisis*. U.S. House of Representatives, June 13.

Pension Benefit Guaranty Corporation. 2005a. *The Impact of Pension Reform Proposals on Claims against the Pension Insurance Program, Losses to Participants, and Contributions*. October 26. Washington, DC: Pension Benefit Guaranty Corporation.

Pension Benefit Guaranty Corporation, 2005b. *An Analysis of Frozen Defined Benefit Plans*. December 21. Washington, DC: Pension Benefit Guaranty Corporation.

Reynolds, Scott, Neil Ridley, and Carl E. Van Horn. 2005. *A Work-Filled Retirement*. Newark, NJ: Heldrich Center for Workforce Development, Rutgers University.

Rosenstone, Steven J., and John Mark Hansen, 2003. *Mobilization, Participation, and Democracy in America*. New York: Macmillan.

Schultz, Ellen, and Theo Francis. 2006. "Hidden Burden," *Wall Street Journal*, June 23, p. A8.

Schlozman, Kay Lehman, and Sidney Verba. 1979. *Injury to Insult: Unemployment, Class, and Political Response*. Cambridge, MA: Harvard University Press.

Tepper, Irwin. 1977. "Risk vs. Return in Pension Fund Investment." *Harvard Business Review*, March/April, pp. 100–07.

VanDerhei, Jack, and Craig Copeland. 2004. *ERISA at 30: The Decline of Private-Sector Defined Benefit Promises and Annuity Payments: What Will It Mean?* EBRI Issue Brief #269. Washington, DC: Employee Benefit Research Institute.

Verba, Sidney, Kay Lehman Schlozman, and Henry E. Brady. 1995. *Voice and Equality: Civic Volunteerism in American Politics*. Cambridge, MA: Harvard University Press.

Watson Wyatt. 2005. "Recent Funding and Sponsorship Trends Among the FORTUNE 1000." *Insider*, June. <http://www.watsonwyatt.com/us/pubs/Insider/showarticle.asp?ArticleID=14750>. [December 20, 2006].

West, William. 2004. "Formal Procedures, Informal Processes, Accountability, and Responsiveness in Bureaucratic Policy Making: An Institutional Policy Analysis," *Public Administration Review*, Vol. 64, no. 1 (February), pp. 66–80.

Whitman, Debra, and Patrick Purcell. 2005. *Topics in Aging: Income and Poverty Among Older Americans in 2004*. Washington, DC: Congressional Research Service.

Zald, Mayer N., and John D. McCarthy, eds. 1987. *Social Movements in an Organizational Society*. New Brunswick, NJ: Transaction Books.

CHAPTER 11

Pension Policy Options: Meeting in the Middle

CHRISTIAN E. WELLER
Center for American Progress

TERESA GHILARDUCCI
University of Notre Dame

Most chapters in this volume describe policy directions that do not call for a return to traditional defined benefit (DB) plans or for a wholesale condemnation of defined contribution (DC) plans. Nearly all of the authors recognize that both types of plans can serve valuable roles with respect to labor relations management as well as retirement income security.

This is especially true for DB pensions. Lazonick (chapter 3) and Schieber (chapter 5) focus particular attention on employers and caution that since short-term financial goals shape employers' pension policy, firms will not meet future labor relations challenges. As the workforce ages, issues of retention, not recruitment, will dominate employers' labor concerns. Cash balance plans may help employers if firms follow Schieber's sensible advice to not blindly adhere to fashionable trends in benefit design and freeze DB plans and embrace 401(k)'s.

What is apparent, though, is that both DB and DC retirement savings vehicles require an overhaul to appropriately meet the challenges of a changed and changing workplace. Good pension reform should strengthen employment relations—the loss of DB pensions has reduced the efficacy of existing management tools. Reform should also improve retirement income adequacy and security, particularly in reducing the costs and risks associated with the current system of commercial retirement accounts. Common to these proposals is a theme of "meeting in the middle." For DB plans, this implies the incorporation of DC plan features, as is already the case for cash balance and multi-employer plans. And for DC plans, this means the incorporation of DB plan features, such as more professionally managed assets and greater access to low-cost annuities.

Public policy shapes employers' and workers' perceptions and judgments. And, as is often the case in public policy formation, public perception, interest group politics, and institutional realities stand in the way of successfully improving the U.S. retirement system (see chapters 9 and 10). An ongoing dialogue among employers, employees, and policy makers is necessary to address large and consistent problems in the U.S. retirement landscape.

DB vs. DC Plan Features: The Basics

Traditionally, most pension plans were DB plans, in which the employee is guaranteed a benefit upon retirement, usually based on years of service, age, and final earnings. The benefit formula is designed such that employees accrue most of their benefits during their last years of service. An employee typically is not immediately vested in a DB plan, but the maximum vesting period under existing regulations is five years for cliff vesting or seven years for a gradual vesting schedule. Accrued benefits for private sector DB plans are insured by the Pension Benefit Guaranty Corporation (PBGC).

Another form of DB plans is a cash balance plan, in which the employee accrues benefits in direct proportion to current earnings. A worker's (hypothetical) pension account is credited with an amount equal to a fixed share of the worker's wage each year, and the account balance is assumed to increase at a predetermined interest rate. As a result, younger workers accrue higher pension wealth under a cash balance plan than under a traditional DB plan, and vice versa. The maximum vesting period for a cash balance plan is three years instead of five, thus benefiting workers with shorter tenures.

Though workers pay indirectly for their pensions through lower wages, the employer is responsible for funding a DB plan's liabilities (promised benefits). Should a plan become overfunded because its assets performed better than expected or received more contributions than needed to fund actual benefits, employers are not required to increase benefits, so they do not have to make further contributions to the plan as long as the plan remains technically "overfunded." Current regulations, in fact, limit the amount of overfunding a plan can have and still receive tax benefits, effectively discouraging the employer from contributing to an overfunded plan. Employers also decide what economic assumptions to use to evaluate future earnings and liabilities, and these assumptions have a great deal of influence on the measurement and reporting of overfunding and underfunding.

Significantly, some DB plans, especially collectively bargained multiemployer plans, differ from this relationship between funding and benefits in one important aspect. Here, the union and the employer negotiate employer contributions and guaranteed benefit levels. If a multi-employer plan becomes overfunded, benefits may increase, depending on the approval of the plan's trustees.

Since the early 1980s, though, a smaller share of workers is covered by traditional DB plans, and a rising share by DC plans. The main characteristic of DC plans is that the risks of losing money (due to falling financial returns, bad investment choices, and excessive fees, or because retirees can live and collect benefits way beyond an average expected mortality age) are all borne by the individual worker, yet the control over most aspects of a DC plan rests with the employer, not the employee.

In a 401(k)-type plan—the most common DC plan—private sector employees promise to contribute a share of earnings to individual accounts, whose investment choices, vendors, and fees are controlled by the employer. The employer also chooses to sponsor such a plan or not. Employers usually contribute (either on a matching or a direct contribution basis) to their employees' accounts, but they are not required to do so. Employees are generally responsible for their accounts' investments, within some limits that can vary by plan. Occasionally, plans are directed entirely by professional trustees and managers. Employee and employer contributions are generally pre–income tax contributions, although still subject to FICA taxes, but there is a contribution maximum.

The biggest distinguishing feature between DC and DB plans is that a DC plan provides no guarantee of future benefits because the employee assumes all investment risks, and there is no PBGC-type insurance to offset severe losses. For example, most Enron employees held company stock as the vast majority of their 401(k) accounts when the company filed for bankruptcy in 2002, and so ended up with an account with no value. Similar DC plans exist for public sector workers (457 plans), and for private sector employees in some nonprofit organizations (403[b] plans).

All workers can, if their earnings are below certain limits, contribute to an individual retirement account (IRA). The tax advantages of IRA contributions are greater for workers who are not participating in an employer-sponsored qualified plan. The contribution limits to IRAs, though, are substantially lower than those for employer-sponsored DC plans. Otherwise, IRAs operate very similarly, although employees generally have more investment options than in a 401(k) plan. The administrative fees are also based on individual accounts and are, like 401(k) fees, charged on a retail basis. DB investment fees are lower because the asset base is much larger.

DB vs. DC Plans: The False Dichotomy

Despite the existence of these two types of pension design, the common view of a dualistic pension world is cartoonish. Almost all reports on pension trends reproduce variations of the same graph. The graph shows DB plans falling and DC plans rising over time. The graph suggests that DBs are declining into oblivion and that DCs are replacing them because DB plans have outlived their purposes, with DC growth as a natural response to economic change. But if a DB world consisted of, say, union workers in dying industries that stood separate from a DC world full of diverse, dynamic nonunion workforces, then total pension participants would equal the sum of those covered by DBs and DCs. That is not the case; the growth of DC plans has not led to more pension coverage. Total pension coverage dropped from 50% in 1999 to 45.3% in 2005, while at the same time DC plan coverage has grown (Purcell 2005, 2006).

In recent years, though, DC and DB plan coverages seem to have leveled off (Bureau of Labor Statistics 2006). The growth in DC plans is not expanding pension coverage because increasing numbers of workers are covered by both kinds of plans, DB and DC plans; DC plans are generally not replacing DBs, but supplementing them. Among 724 firms that remained in existence between 1981 and 1998—and sponsored a pension in all years—the most popular plan structure in 1981 was a DB plan standing alone; 44% of firms offered this structure, 14% offered only DC plans, and 42% offered both DBs and DCs. By 1998, among the same firms, only 11% offered just a DB plan, and those offering only a DC plan rose to a mere 17%. Overwhelmingly, the most common pension design adopted was the combination of DB and DC plans: 72% of large firms that have been in existence since 1981 sponsored both types by 1998 (Ghilarducci 2006; Ghilarducci and Sun 2006). That more and more companies are offering DC plans as a supplement to DB plans reveals two salient facts in devising good pension reform: DB plan coverage has traditionally been the primary vehicle to improving pension coverage, because DBs serve important goals in a productive economic system at the employer level.

British economist David McCarthy (2006) observes that employers include DB pensions in employment contracts because pensions "complete" and "ameliorate" flaws in existing markets. Employers and workers need DB pensions for different reasons. Workers as individuals cannot find affordable insurance against the longevity risk, idiosyncratic risk, and market risk. Likewise, employers do not face perfect labor markets, so they cannot know which employees are going to fit the job well, learn appropriate skills, and be dedicated enough to the work and to the employer to maintain employment. Also, because employees are risk averse when it comes to the chance they could lose their jobs or lose incomes and employers are risk neutral, the employer can reduce wages to pay for pension promise at an advantageous exchange (McCarthy 2006).

With the decline in DB pensions, employers are losing an important human resource management tool. They can no longer directly influence the labor supply of their workers (i.e., they are no longer able to induce them to work longer by offering a larger reward later, or to retire earlier by subsidizing early retirement with prefunded assets) (Wenger and D'Arcy, chapter 2). At the same time, employers are looking for new institutional designs to offer partial employment and phased retirement to their employees, absent widespread DB coverage (Hermes, chapter 4). If employers are becoming more short term because of changes in finance markets, and long job tenures become less prevalent in the "new economy," especially in information and communications firms, the relevance of DB pensions for employment relations will fall (Lazonick, chapter 3).

The relationship between pension design and labor productivity implies that public policy should make the stabilization and even the expansion of DB plans one of its goals.

As a second, public policy needs to address the shortcomings of DC plans that have prevented DCs from expanding pension coverage. In order to improve both employment relations and retirement income security, public policy needs to focus on strengthening DB plan coverage as well as improving the way DC plans operate. Specifically, DC plans do not help expand pension coverage to people who do not work for employers without pension plans. DCs do not provide annuities; they have high administrative costs, too.

Rodriguez and Grilla-Chope (chapter 7) present evidence about the low retirement savings of many families and the disparity between white and nonwhite families in preparedness for retirement. Perun (chapter 8) further points out that more and more workers are becoming exposed to longevity risk, since annuitization of accumulated account balances in DC plans is a rarity. Employers often do not offer beneficiaries the opportunity to purchase annuities, and workers underappreciate how much they need them.

The two policy goals—strengthening DB plans and improving DC plans—are not mutually exclusive. Much work remains to be done in the area of retirement income security. Interestingly, both types of plans appear to have learned from each other. More and more DB plans are incorporating features from DC plans and vice versa.

Hybridization of DB Plans

One promising path forward for DB plans may be to incorporate features from DC plans into DB plans; two kinds of hybrid plans, cash balance plans (Schieber, chapter 5) and multi-employer plans (Almeida, chapter 6), are especially promising if done right.

Cash Balance Plans

Hybrid plans combine many of the more attractive features of DB and DC plans into one plan design. One such design is a cash balance plan. Here, employees accrue benefits in proportion to their current earnings. A worker's (notional) pension account is credited with an amount equal to a fixed share of a worker's wage or fixed dollar amount each year, and the account balance is assumed to increase at a predetermined interest rate, the interest credit. In comparison, under a traditional DB plan, benefits are related to final (and presumably above average) earnings. As a result, younger workers accrue higher pension wealth under a cash balance plan than under a traditional DB plan, while older workers accrue pension wealth faster under a traditional DB plan.

In important aspects, cash balance plans operate like traditional DB plans. Investments are made in one large investment pool, the investment risks are borne by the employer, accrued benefits are insured by the PBGC, participants are automatically enrolled, and employees have the option of low-cost guaranteed monthly benefits—so-called annuities—as the default form of benefit distribution. Thus, cash balance plans, like all DB plans, can reduce longevity risk (i.e., the chance of outliving one's savings). However, when employees are given the choice between an annuity and a lump sum upon retirement, they tend to choose the lump sum (Cahill and Soto 2003). Consequently, lump sum distributions are considered the typical withdrawal option under cash balance plans (Table 1).

In other aspects, cash balance plans behave like DC plans. Employees have notional account balances that can be rolled over into other qualified retirement plans when one job ends before retirement. Cash balance plans also accrue benefits in notional accounts relative to workers' current wages. Thus, with frequent job changes workers no longer lose out on larger future benefit increases that typically occur under traditional DB plans for more senior employees with higher wages.

This does not mean, though, that either type of DB plan is better. That determination depends on the characteristics of a particular workforce, especially turnover rates and mobility across industries. Where mobility is greater, workers may be better off with a cash balance plan. It also depends on the characteristics of the specific plan. Often early-retirement subsidies are eliminated in the conversion from a traditional DB plan to a

TABLE 1
Characteristics of Typical Pension Plans, by Plan Type

| Characteristic | DB plans | | 401(k) Plans |
	Traditional	Cash balance	
Participation	Automatic	Automatic	Voluntary
Contribution	Employer	Employer	Employer and employee
Investments	Determined by employer	Determined by employer	Determined by employee
Withdrawals	Annuity	Lump sum	Lump sum
Rollovers before age 65	Not permitted	Permitted	Permitted
Benefit guarantee	PBGC	PBGC	No guarantee

Source: Clark and Schieber (2002).

cash balance plan (Weller 2005a). While this may leave the full retirement benefits intact, it would mean a benefit cut for workers who had counted on retiring early. In industries with long tenures and physically demanding occupations, the reduction of early-retirement subsidies may be especially harmful (Weller 2005b).

The commonalities and differences between traditional DB plans, 401(k) plans, and cash balance plans are summarized in a stylized form in Table 1.

Among DB plans, there has been a shift toward hybrid plans, which made up less than 4% of all plans in 2001 but amounted to 6% in 2004 (Table 2). Among plans with 5,000 or more participants, the share of

TABLE 2
Share of PBGC-Insured Hybrid Plans, by Plan Size, 2001 and 2004

Beginning of year	2001 (%)	2004 (%)
Total hybrid plans as share of total plans	3.7	6.0
Hybrid plans as share of plans with 5,000 or more participants	22.0	30.5
Hybrid plans as share of plans with 1,000–4,999 participants	10.4	13.4
Hybrid plans as share of plans with fewer than 1,000 participants	2.3	4.2
Participants in hybrid plans as share of total participants	20.5	29.0
Participants in hybrid plans with more than 5,000 participants as share of plans of same size	25.0	34.7
Participants in hybrid plans with 1,000–4,999 participants as share of plans of same size	11.5	15.1
Participants in hybrid plans with fewer than 1,000 participants as share of plans of same size	4.4	5.8

Notes: Figures refer to single-employer programs only. "Hybrid plans" include all types, of which cash balance plans and pension equity plans are the most common.
Source: PBGC (2005).

hybrid plans rose from 22% in 2001 to 30.5% in 2004 (Table 2). Consequently, the share of participants covered under a cash balance plan
grew from 20.5% in 2001 to 29% in 2004 (Table 2).

Although the growth of cash balance plans has continued in recent
years, their attractiveness has been diminished by legal and economic
uncertainties associated with DB-plan funding, as Schieber argues in
chapter 5. The recent financial troubles of many private and public sector DB plans help to illustrate this point. DB plans encountered problems as the stock market dropped sharply in 2001 and 2002 and interest
rates declined to very low levels (and remained low for several years),
resulting in fewer assets and higher liabilities. Such declines are characteristic of most recessions, although the declines in 2001 and 2002 were
unusually large.

The old pension funding rules under ERISA and the new funding
rules under the Pension Protection Act of 2006 (PPA) certainly intended
to encourage employers to sensibly build up reserves in good times in
order to rely on them in bad times. The idea of smoothing was embedded in both approaches. For different reasons, mainly brought on by an
imprudent use of credit balances and a distortion of some tax regulations
limiting the size of the financial cushion, the swings in the market could
often cause unexpected swings in pension contributions. Consequently,
employers cite the unpredictability of contributions as their number one
concern related to DB plans (Hewitt Associates 2003), which may
explain the fact that increasingly healthy plan sponsors have abandoned
their DB plans (Munnell et al. 2006).

There are a number of technical changes to the funding rules,
including less smoothing of asset and liability values and the use of a
modified yield curve, which introduces the use of more volatile short-
term interest rates into the valuation of pension liabilities. The specific
ways the PPA could be reformed are articulated in Figure 1. These
accounting changes could provide some planning certainty for cash
balance and other DB plan sponsors, in addition to the legislative certainty created by the PPA. Until Congress passed the PPA, sponsors of
cash balance plans also faced a legal uncertainty, because cash balance
plans were universally judged age discriminatory by the ruling of the
Southern District Court of Illinois in *Cooper v. IBM Personal Pension
Plan* (Weller 2005a). The new law establishes cash balance plans as not
age discriminatory if they started on or after June 29, 2005, and if
under the terms of the plan a participant's accrued benefit is equal to
or greater than that of a similarly situated younger person. The law
does not apply to plans created prior to June 29, 2005 (Groom Law
Group 2006).

FIGURE 1
Reforming the PPA Funding Rules

Pension regulations could be revised so that 20-year smoothing mechanisms are applied for both assets and liabilities. If stock prices and interest rates could be based on an estimate of their average over a 20-year period, actuarial surpluses and shortfalls should become less prevalent (Weller and Baker 2005). This process assumes that stock prices will adjust toward a long-run average over a long enough period of time, which is lower than they are in bubbles. This approach would reduce the value of stocks on the books of a pension plan, when stock prices are high and when the effect that the funding ratio—assets to liabilities—would be lower, too. The result is that employers would have to make more contributions than they otherwise would when times are good and fewer contributions when times are bad.

In addition, employers could be required to make regular contributions that adequately reflect the cost increases associated with newly earned benefits during the current period. These contributions are called normal cost contributions.

To combat the fear that too much of the employer's money will be tied up in an overfunded pension plan, the rules could allow employers to reduce regular contributions if the funding ratio exceeds a previously specified threshold, such as 120% or 130% of accrued liabilities.

While the new law provided employers with legal certainty, it still left many uncertainties for participants in the case of a plan conversion to a cash balance plan. In particular, benefits for older workers can be, but don't have to be, eroded in the conversion (Groom Law Group 2006; Weller 2005a).

Multi-employer Plans

The other hybrid model of DB plans is a Taft-Hartley, or multi-employer, plan, which covers employees at several employers, often organized along occupational or industry lines. All or at least the vast majority of employees in multi-employer plans are covered by a collective bargaining agreement, and a plan's trustees are evenly split between union and management members. Under collective bargaining agreements, both benefits and employer contributions are typically negotiated. Should a plan become overfunded, the trustees can decide to increase benefits, reduce employer contributions, or both.

Multi-employer plans incorporate some DC plan features into DB plans. The regular contributions from employers make these plans appear, at least in theory, to employers more like DC plans than DB plans. Also, better-than-expected investment performance can result in

TABLE 3

Active Participants in Single-employer and Multi-employer DB Plans as Shares of
Private Sector Wage and Salary Workers

Years	Single-employer active participants (%)	Multi-employer active participants (%)
1980	27.3	7.7
1985	24.4	6.1
1990	22.7	5.3
1995	18.5	4.4
2000	15.8	4.2
2003	14.5	4.0
1980 to 2003	−46.7	−48.1

Source: Pension Benefit Guaranty Corporation 2005.

larger-than-expected benefits, adding a DC element for employees. In turn, though, the main features of DB plans remain: benefits are predetermined, generally paid out in the form of annuities, and insured by the PBGC.

The biggest challenge is that multi-employer DB plans in the private sector have declined along with single-employer plans (Table 3). While in 1980 7.7% of the private sector workforce was covered by multi-employer plans, the share had dropped to 4% in 2003, the last year for which data are available.

The policy question, therefore, is how at a minimum to stabilize the coverage of private sector workers under multi-employer plans. One of the first obstacles to stable or even increasing multi-employer plan coverage is a declining unionization rate in the private sector. As a general rule, workers can only participate in a multi-employer plan if they are covered by a collective bargaining agreement. As the private sector unionization rate has declined, so has coverage by collective bargaining agreements and the access to multi-employer plans. Hence, one way to improve multi-employer DB plan coverage is to raise the private sector unionization rate (e.g., through passage of the "Employee Free Choice Act.)"[1]

In addition, the recently enacted PPA has established a few steps toward recovery for severely underfunded multi-employer plans. In essence, when plans are severely underfunded the law requires them to address the situation through additional contributions or reduced benefit accruals. The new rules are more stringent than in the past.

In an effort to strengthen multi-employer plans, though, lawmakers may have gone too far. The PPA allows trustees to cut back accrued ancillary benefits, such as early-retirement subsidies. This is a departure from the anti-cutback rules established under ERISA. Because this is a departure from established pension funding principles, it may make multi-employer plans less attractive to plan sponsors and beneficiaries. One of the selling points of all DB plans is that accrued benefits cannot be taken away by the plan or the plan sponsor. Under the current law, this is no longer the case. With this added uncertainty, plan sponsors may shy away from multi-employer DB plans.

Given that other funding rules have been strengthened in the PPA, however, the new allowance for cutbacks in benefits may be redundant. Additional contributions and cuts in future benefits are already meant to improve the funding status of severely underfunded plans. And allowing cutbacks in accrued benefits may hurt this part of the U.S. retirement system overall.

The P.U.S.H. to Make DC Plans More Like DB Plans

The flip side to more hybridization in DB plans is a policy and legislative push to include more DB features in DC plans. The relevant proposals can be summarized by the acronym P.U.S.H.: They would allow for greater Pooling, promote Universal coverage, make savings more Secure, and increase the creation of Hybrid plans through incentives for annuitization. These proposals aim to address three aspects of DC pensions that do not serve public goals. First, high commercial fees for individual accounts reduce earnings and accumulations. Second, the structure of DC plans discourages universal coverage, and third, DC plans encourage lump sum distributions, leaving no secure income guaranteed for a retiree's lifetime.

A number of proposals have focused on the cost savings from pooling a large number of small accounts. Originally, Baker (1999) suggested that the government establish a default investment option modeled on the Thrift Savings Plan for federal workers. Investment options would be limited to a small number of index funds. Because such a plan could take advantage of simplicity and economies of scale, management fees would be substantially lower than rates prevailing in private sector plans (Congressional Budget Office 2004). This proposal was adopted at the state level—for instance, in Washington by the Economic Opportunity Institute under the Washington Voluntary Accounts proposal (Idemoto 2002) and in Pennsylvania under the Pennsylvania Voluntary Account proposal (Weller, Price, and Margolis 2006).

The idea of pooling small account balances has also been supported by conservatives. For instance, a similar proposal was included in President Bush's proposal to privatize Social Security (Commission to Strengthen Social Security 2001). The administration estimated that the combined costs for fund administration annuitization would amount to

30 basis points of assets annually. Also, in their proposal for "automatic IRAs," Mark Iwry from the Brookings Institution and David John of the Heritage Foundation (Iwry and John 2006) included a call for pooled, low-cost, government-administered accounts.

Another DB plan feature that is reflected in proposals to restructure DC plans is universal coverage, which would make saving for retirement easier. However, there is generally a qualitative difference to DB plans. Universal coverage under DB plans automatically includes benefit accruals for vested employees, while proposals for universal DC coverage generally include only universal access to a savings account (i.e., the possibility of wealth creation without any assurance of contributions).

Yet three examples of moving toward universal coverage in DC plans are "automatic 401(k)'s" (Gale, Iwry, and Orszag 2005), "automatic IRAs" (Iwry and John 2006), and "universal 401(k)'s" (Sperling 2005). Under the first plan, employees who work for an employer that offers a 401(k) plan would be automatically enrolled in that plan, but they could opt out if they so desired. This proposal takes advantage of employee inertia, which, among other factors, has kept take-up rates of existing DC plans low among, for instance, low-income workers. Other features could be automatic default investment options (replacing the current practice of allocating funds toward safe and low-return money market mutual funds), automatic escalation that would increase contribution rates every time a worker receives a raise, and automatic rollovers into an IRA upon a worker's termination of employment under a qualified plan.

The second proposal, automatic IRAs, would require each employer with 10 or more employees to offer the opportunity of automatic payroll deductions into designated IRAs. To increase participation, Iwry and John (2006) suggest coupling the program with automatic enrollment. To minimize costs, government-administered accounts could be offered as the default investment.

The universal 401(k) proposal, though, goes further and pays attention to the particular vulnerability faced by lower- and middle-class workers because of low amounts of savings. This proposal adds progressive saving incentives because it, like all of these plans, allows an employee to opt out of coverage even after being "automatically enrolled" (Sperling 2005). Although progressive incentives would not guarantee contributions, they would skew incentives toward low-income earners, where savings shortfalls are largest. The combination of universal access and progressive savings incentives could go a long way toward creating wealth for many middle-class families who currently do not save enough.

Rodriguez and Grillo-Chope (chapter 7) note several of the ideas that have been proposed and push the envelope on helping low-income workers far beyond automatic enrollment and tax credits. They argue that in light of all the problems with DC plans, automatic enrollment should be part of the overall approach. First, workers, especially minority and low-income workers with limited investment experience, will need more financial education to take full advantage of any proposals enacted to increase participation in DC plans. Workers should receive a refundable savings-advice tax credit, which may induce more low-income and minority workers to seek professional financial advice. Using the income limits for the low-income Savers' Credit, this refundable tax credit would give some tax benefits to low-income workers, who do not benefit from the current system of tax deduction for financial advice since they have low or no federal income tax liabilities. In addition, community groups should receive grants to establish tax preparation for low- and moderate-income families. Second, Rodriguez and Grillo-Chope propose a tax credit for employers who offer higher matches under DC plans to their low- and moderate-income workers. Third, asset tests for means-tested programs should be loosened to exclude retirement savings. This would give retirement income for low-income workers, many of whom are minority workers, an additional boost.

If the above-mentioned proposals were enacted, DC plan assets would often become more secure. Plan assets would be relatively well diversified since investment options would be limited to a small set of index funds. In addition, taking advantage of employees' inertia could mean more regular contributions, which in turn could mean that workers would take better advantage of dollar cost averaging. Idiosyncratic risk, and to a much smaller degree market risk, would be reduced. Furthermore, more widespread financial education would presumably allow more workers to take advantage of the full range of savings options and measures to secure their savings, such as diversification and dollar cost averaging.

Other proposals are aimed at lowering longevity risk under DC plans by tying tax deductions to incentives for converting savings into annuities. The Retirement Security for Life Act of 2005 (H.R. 819), sponsored by Rep. Nancy Johnson (R-CT), and the Lifetime Pension Annuity for You Act of 2005, sponsored by Rep. Earl Pomeroy (D-ND), include separate tax deductions for savers who annuitize their DC plan assets. Although ways have to be found to get workers to reduce longevity risk through annuities, these bills are flawed for two reasons (Weller 2005a). First, the biggest tax incentives would accrue to savers who already have the most wealth. Second, the tax incentives would give an advantage to DC plans over DB plans. This disadvantage could hasten the decline in DB plan coverage. Even though these particular proposals are ill-suited to effectively address longevity risk, they show that there is increasing bipartisan interest in raising retirement income security under DC plans.

Perun (chapter 8) introduces a regulatory approach to increase the take-up rates of annuities in DC plans. The idea is to create an optional federal charter for life insurance companies, who are typically covered by an array of state laws and regulations. Insurance companies could choose to opt into a newly created federal regulatory system. This, argues Perun, would have the effect of making annuities more attractive by achieving uniformity and standardization in the insurance market, and plan sponsors could no longer breach fiduciary responsibilities by choosing between different types of annuities. This should entice sponsors of DC plans to offer more annuities as pay-out and investment options. By coupling annuities in DC plans, the costs of a lifelong stream of income could be reduced, which again would help increase the take-up rate.

A few proposals have included mandatory employer contributions in an effort to increase DC plan coverage. For instance, Weller (2007) has developed a proposal called "Personal Universal Retirement" (PURE) accounts. The costs and risks of these accounts will be kept low by managing the funds through a government entity, such as the Federal Retirement Thrift Investment Board (FRTIB). Professional fund managers invest the funds of PURE accounts according to workers' instructions. The investment options are the same as those for the Thrift Savings Plan (TSP), to keep administrative costs to a minimum. Furthermore, universal employer contributions of at least 3% of earnings to a qualified pension plan or to a PURE account are required. These would be pre–income tax but subject to FICA. In addition, low-income workers would qualify for direct, non-elective contributions, while higher income earners could qualify, up to a limit, for government matching contributions.

Also, Ghilarducci (2007) has proposed "Guaranteed Retirement Accounts" (GRAs), which incorporate the low cost and effective risk management advantages of pooling assets, require coverage, and assure that assets are paid out in annuities. The GRAs are funded by a mandated 5% contribution on earnings up to the Social Security maximum, split evenly between the employer and employee, that goes into a national fund comprising individual accounts. Contributions are recorded in individual accounts and the account values represent individuals' claims on future benefits. Unlike a conventional DC plan, the rates of return are guaranteed; the U.S. government will guarantee a rate of return of 3%, with excess returns added, depending on the fund's earnings. Workers and retirees can add to the accounts at any time with pre- and posttax dollars. By reconfiguring the current tax subsidies for retirement plans—which give people earning over $100,000 per year more than $7,400 in tax subsidies while middle- and working-class workers receive practically nothing—each employee will receive a tax credit of $600. This tax rebate will go directly into employees' individual accounts and will add to national savings. The rebate will also soften the impact of a 5% mandated contribution for lower income workers—most workers will pay much less than 5%. The efficient and well-managed Social Security Administration will administer the accounts. Qualified DB plans will be able to opt out of the mandate. At retirement, the accounts will be annuitized, and employees may opt to withdraw a lump sum worth a maximum of 10% of the account value. The GRAs, combined with Social Security, are designed to guarantee the average worker 70% of preretirement earnings at retirement.

The policy discussion on retirement savings plans in general and the debate about DC plans in particular highlight the fact that experts and policy makers understand that the distinction between DB and DC plans is artificial and often overblown. Instead, public policy experts are attempting to introduce the most attractive features of the other system into the existing DB and DC platforms. The final result may be the widespread use of hybrid DB plans and P.U.S.H.-type DC plans.

Turning Ideas into Policy

The loss of traditional pensions and their incumbent features can have serious ramifications for employment relations and the economy at large. To counter these adverse implications, this volume leads with two broad policy goals: strengthen DB plans and vastly improve DC plans. Addressing these goals would mean to introduce DB plan features into DC plans and vice versa. Often this will require legislative changes to make it easier for employers and employee representatives to design retirement vehicles appropriate for the current and future labor markets.

While this volume sketches out a rather comprehensive policy agenda for private sector retirement savings vehicles, these proposals still need to be translated into legislative action. Varnhagen (chapter 9) provides a detailed legislative history of the current retirement savings framework that reveals that effective congressional action to improve the retirement saving system requires a stronger involvement of constituent groups, particularly non-employer groups. Constituent groups, such as women's groups, have tended to be more active than others, but have given over much of the public policy discussion to employer advocates in recent years.

Madland (chapter 10) argues similarly that effective public policy needs public support. In comparison to Varnhagen, who approaches the issue from a congressional perspective, Madland approaches the question of public engagement from the perspective of individuals affected by benefit cuts.

For people to participate in politics, three things are necessary: the means to protest, such as skills, resources, and organization; a motive; and opportunities for action. Congressional action needs to follow suit. This, however, will require an understanding of the inadequacy of retirement savings and, more importantly, a willingness of lawmakers to address remaining and new shortcomings in ERISA.

One of the bigger constraints for the public to get actively involved in policy discussion is the lack of resources. Most importantly, Madland argues, people need an organization to help mobilize and voice their concerns. In the retirement security arena, the two primary organizations that seem to have taken this role are unions and AARP. Yet, with private sector unionization rates declining, unions have fewer opportunities to advocate on behalf of those workers who do not have adequate retirement income. And, as Madland argues, AARP, which has been an effective voice in discussions over public sector retirement benefits, such as Social Security and Medicare, has been less involved in debates over private sector retirement benefits. In the gap left by unions and AARP, numerous associations have stepped up and taken on the challenge of advocating on behalf of workers and retirees, at least in the face of actual or threatened benefit cuts.

Yet, these organizations, which are often founded on an ad hoc basis, are likely less effective in advocating for positive changes. Most importantly, by definition these institutions, such as numerous retiree organizations at large U.S. corporations, have been created to protect existing benefits, not to argue for positive policy changes. Consequently, a change that could help provide workers and beneficiaries with a voice in the policy process would be the labor law changes already discussed, which would foster a revival in private sector unionization rates.

The last obstacle to getting the public more involved in finding solutions to retirement income challenges (i.e., that there are few clearly apparent solutions), could be overcome through stronger legislative action. In light of Varnhagen's argument that legislative action will require stronger public involvement, this creates a "chicken and egg" problem. To overcome this seeming stalemate, Varnhagen proposes to streamline the national dialogue by establishing a single government agency to forge national retirement policy and by creating an ongoing employer and employee national advisory board on retirement policy, which will serve Congress and the executive branch.

Conclusion

This volume highlights the importance of retirement savings for employment relations. Current economic trends, though, have diminished the role of DB pensions and have left newer DC plans inadequately equipped to address employer and employee needs. The proposed solutions imply the introduction of DC plan features into DB plans and vice versa. To accomplish this on a national scale will require an ongoing dialogue among employers, employees, and policy makers.

Endnote

[1] The Employee Free Choice Act, first introduced in Congress in 2004, would allow workers to form a union if a majority of eligible workers sign cards indicating that they want to be covered under a collective bargaining agreement. The National Labor Relations Board would certify that a majority of eligible workers did indeed sign union cards. In addition, the Employee Free Choice Act would triple penalties imposed on employers found in violation of the National Labor Relations Act, and binding arbitration would be available to facilitate the agreement of the first contract. This act would presumably lower the barriers to union organization and raise union membership rates.

References

Baker, D. 1999. *Pensions for the 21st Century*. New York: Century Foundation.
Bureau of Labor Statistics. 2006. *National Compensation Survey*. Washington, DC: Bureau of Labor Statistics.
Cahill, K., and Soto, M. 2003. *How Do Cash Balance Plans Affect the Pension Landscape?* An Issue in Brief No. 14. Chestnut Hill, MA: Center for Retirement Research at Boston College.
Clark, R., and Schieber, S. 2002. *The Emergence of Hybrid Pensions and Their Implications for Retirement Security in the 21st Century*. Paper presented at the Cash Balance Pension Plan Symposium, Society of Actuaries, Dallas, TX, May 31.
Commission to Strengthen Social Security. 2001. *Strengthening Social Security and Creating Personal Wealth for All Americans—Final Report of the President's Commission to Strengthen Social Security*. Washington, DC: Commission to Strengthen Social Security.
Congressional Budget Office. 2004. *Administrative Costs of Private Accounts in Social Security*. Washington, DC: Congressional Budget Office.
Gale, W., Iwry, M., and Orszag, P. 2005. "The Automatic 401(k): A Simple Way to Strengthen Retirement Saving." *Tax Notes*, March.
Ghilarducci, T. 2006. *Future Retirement Income Security Needs Defined Benefit Pensions*. CAP Economic Report. Washington, DC: Center for American Progress.
Ghilarducci, Teresa. 2007. *Guaranteed Retirement Accounts: Towards Retirement Income Security*. Working paper. Notre Dame, IN: University of Notre Dame. January.
Ghilarducci, T., and Sun, W. 2006. "How Defined Contribution Plans and 401(k)s Affect Employer Pension Costs: 1981–1998." *Journal of Pension Economics and Finance* Vol. 5, no. 2, pp. 175–96.

Groom Law Group. 2006. *Summary Comparison of Current Law and the Principal Provisions of the Pension Protection Act of 2006: Single-Employer Pension Funding Reforms and Cash Balance Provisions*. Washington, DC: Groom Law Group.

Hewitt Associates. 2003. *Survey Findings: Current Retirement Plan Challenges, Employer Perspectives 2003*. Lincolnshire, IL: Hewitt Associates.

Idemoto, S. 2002. *Washington Voluntary Accounts: A Proposal for Universal Pension Access*. Seattle: Economic Opportunity Institute.

Iwry, M., and John, D. 2006. *Pursuing Universal Retirement Security through Automatic IRAs*. Working paper draft. Washington, DC: Retirement Security Project.

McCarthy, David. 2006. "The Rationale for Occupational Pensions." *Oxford Review of Economic Policy*, Vol. 22, no. 1 (Spring), pp. 57–65.

Munnell, A., Golub-Sass, F., Soto, M., and Vitagliano, F. 2006. *Why Are Healthy Employers Freezing Their Pensions?* CRR Issue in Brief #44. Chestnut Hill, MA: Center for Retirement Research at Boston College.

Pension Benefit Guaranty Corporation. 2005. *Pension Insurance Data Book 2005*. Washington, DC: Pension Benefit Guaranty Corporation.

Purcell, P. 2005. *Pension Sponsorship and Pension Coverage: Summary of Recent Trends*. RL 30122. September 8. Washington, DC: Congressional Research Service.

Purcell, P. 2006. *Pension Sponsorship and Pension Coverage: Summary of Recent Trends*. RL 30122. August 31. Washington, DC: Congressional Research Service.

Sperling, G. 2005. *A Progressive Framework for Social Security Reform*. CAP Economic Policy Report. Washington, DC: Center for American Progress.

Weller, C. 2005a. *Ensuring Retirement Income Security With Cash Balance Plans*. CAP Economic Policy Report. Washington, DC: Center for American Progress.

Weller, C. 2005b. *Raising the Retirement Age for Social Security: Implications for Low Wage, Minority, and Female Workers*. CAP Economic Policy Report. Washington, DC: Center for American Progress.

Weller, C. 2007. "PURE: A Proposal for More Retirement Income Security." *Journal of Aging and Social Policy*, Vol. 19, no. 1 (Winter), pp. 21–38.

Weller, C., and Baker, D. 2005. "Smoothing the Waves of Pension Funding: Could Changes in Funding Rules Help Avoid Cyclical Under-funding?" *Journal of Policy Reform*, Vol. 8, no. 2, pp. 131–51.

Weller, C., Price, M., and Margolis, D. 2006. *Rewarding Hard Work: Give Pennsylvanians a Shot at Middle Class Retirement Benefits*. Washington, DC: Center for American Progress; Harrisburg, PA: Keystone Research Center.

ABOUT THE CONTRIBUTORS

Beth Almeida is the assistant director for strategic resources at the International Association of Machinists and Aerospace Workers. An economist by training, she has represented the IAM in negotiations with major U.S. air carriers and has been a leader in developing strategies to protect the retirement security of airline employees through industry-wide participation in multi-employer pension plans. Prior to joining the IAM, Almeida was a visiting researcher at the University of Bonn in Germany and at INSEAD in Fontainebleau, France. Almeida is a graduate of Lehigh University in Bethlehem, Pennsylvania, and the University of Massachusetts Amherst.

Laura P. D'Arcy is a Ph.D. student at the School of Public Health at the University of North Carolina at Chapel Hill, Department of Health Policy and Administration. Her research interests include a variety of issues related to aging and health and labor economics, such as long-term care insurance, nursing home staffing, and health insurance for early retirees.

Teresa Ghilarducci is professor of economics at the University of Notre Dame and director of the Higgins Labor Research Center. Her new book, *When I'm 64: The Plot Against Pensions and the Plan to Save Them*, forthcoming from Princeton University Press, investigates the effect of pension losses on older Americans. Her book *Labor's Capital: The Economics and Politics of Employer Pensions*, MIT Press, won an Association of American Publishers award in 1992. She co-authored *Portable Pension Plans for Casual Labor Markets*. She serves as a member of the State of California Public Employee Post-Employment Benefits Commission and as a public trustee on the GM Defined Contribution Health Fund for UAW Retirees.

Luisa Grillo-Chope is an economic security policy analyst at the National Council of La Raza, where she leads research and policy analysis in addition to legislative advocacy on broad wealth and financial security issues—specifically, policies related to Social Security, pensions, and tax. Her written work includes the first major report on Latinos and the Social Security system, *The Social Security Program and Reform: A Latino Perspective*. She also assisted in the production and release of *Retirement Security for Latinos: Bolstering Coverage,*

Savings and Adequacy, the first major report to analyze the disparities in Latino retirement savings and offer real solutions. She has a B.A. from Oberlin College and a J.D. from Boston College.

Sharon Hermes is an economist at the U.S. Government Accountability Office. Her research focuses on the labor force participation of older workers, the economics of pensions, and Social Security. In 2006 and 2007 she did the Atlantic Fellowship in Public Policy and worked on pension reform in the United Kingdom at the Department for Work and Pensions. She received her Ph.D. in economics from the University of Notre Dame in 2004.

William Lazonick is professor of regional economic and social development at University of Massachusetts Lowell and distinguished research professor at INSEAD (European Institute of Business Administration). Previously, he was assistant and associate professor of economics at Harvard University (1975–1984) and professor of economics at Barnard College of Columbia University (1985–1993). He has a B.Com from the University of Toronto, an M.Sc. in economics from London School of Economics, and a Ph.D. in economics from Harvard University. In 1991, Uppsala University awarded him an honorary doctorate for his work on the theory and history of economic development.

David Madland is the director of the work/life program at the Center for American Progress, and he is completing his Ph.D. in government at Georgetown University. He also is a political consultant, primarily advising labor unions and environmental organizations. Previously, he worked for Congressman George Miller (D-CA) on the House Committee on Education and the Workforce as well as the Committee on Resources. He was policy director for the taxpayer watchdog organization Taxpayers for Common Sense and research director for Michela Alioto for Congress. He received his B.S. from the University of California at Berkeley.

Pamela Perun is policy director of the Initiative on Financial Security of the Aspen Institute, which develops asset-building savings plans for low- and moderate-income and moderate-income Americans. She is also a senior policy fellow at the Federal Legislation Clinic of the Georgetown University Law School, serving as a consultant to its Workplace Flexibility 2010 Project, and an affiliated scholar at the Urban Institute. She received a J.D. from the University of California at Berkeley, a Ph.D. in human development from the University of Chicago, and a B.A. from Wellesley College. She is a member of the Massachusetts, District of Columbia, and California bar associations.

Eric Rodriguez is director of the Policy Analysis Center at the National Council of La Raza (NCLR), the leading national Hispanic research and advocacy organization in Washington, DC. He coordinates NCLR's core operations of the Office of Research, Advocacy, and Legislation; he is also responsible for planning and preparing policy analysis, legislative, and advocacy activities related to economic, employment, and financial security public policy issues. Rodriguez serves as a board member of the Coalition on Human Needs and is a member of the National Academy of Social Insurance. He has a master's degree in public administration from American University in Washington, DC.

Sylvester J. Schieber has a Ph.D. in economics from the University of Notre Dame. He has served on the U.S. Social Security Advisory Board since 1998 and as chairman since October 1, 2006. From 1983 until he retired in 2006, he was at Watson Wyatt Worldwide. Prior to joining Watson Wyatt, he was the first research director at the Employee Benefits Research Institute in Washington, DC. Schieber has authored or edited 12 books on changing demographics, retirement security, and health issues. He has also authored journal articles and policy analysis papers on retirement and health benefits issues and is a frequent speaker before business and professional groups and congressional committees.

Michele Varnhagen has long served as a counsel to the U.S. Congress. From 1985 to 1998, she was counsel to the House Subcommittee on Labor Management Relations, and from 1989 to 1994, to the Senate Subcommittee on Labor chaired by Senator Howard Metzenbaum of Ohio. Since 1999, she has been Democratic counsel to the House Committee on Education and Labor. Ms. Varnhagen has participated in considering many pension, health, and labor laws, including the Family and Medical Leave Act, Pension Asset Reversion Act, and Older Workers Benefit Protection Act. She is a graduate of New York University and the Catholic University School of Law.

Christian E. Weller is a professor of public policy at the University of Massachusetts, Boston, and senior fellow at the Center for American Progress. His expertise includes pensions, Social Security, macroeconomics, and international finance. In 2006, he was awarded LERA's Outstanding Scholar-Practitioner Award. He is also a research associate with the Economic Policy Institute and a research scholar with the Political Economy Research Institute at the University of Massachusetts, Amherst. He has published more than 100 academic and popular articles and is frequently cited in the press. He has a Ph.D. in economics from the University of Massachusetts, Amherst.

Jeffrey B. Wenger is assistant professor of public policy at the University of Georgia's School of Public and International Affairs, Department of Public Administration and Policy. From 2000 to 2003, he worked as a research economist at the Economic Policy Institute. His research interests span a number of areas: in particular, unemployment insurance, health insurance, and pensions coverage. His research has been published in the *Journal of Policy Analysis and Management, Journal of Aging and Social Policy*, the *American Journal of Economics and Sociology,* and the *Journal of Pension Economics and Finance.* He received his Ph.D. in public policy analysis from the University of North Carolina, Chapel Hill.